GIRL COMICS

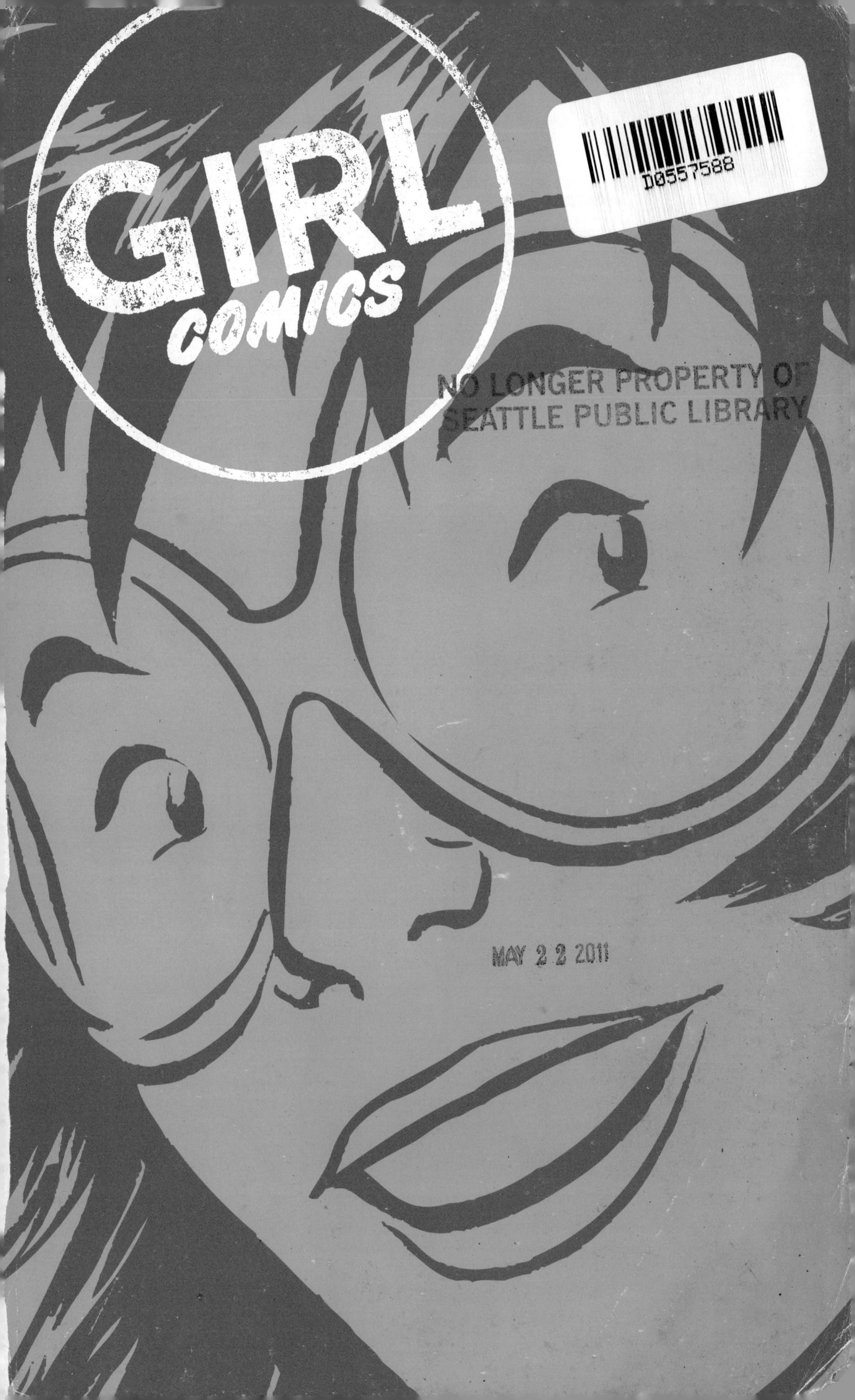

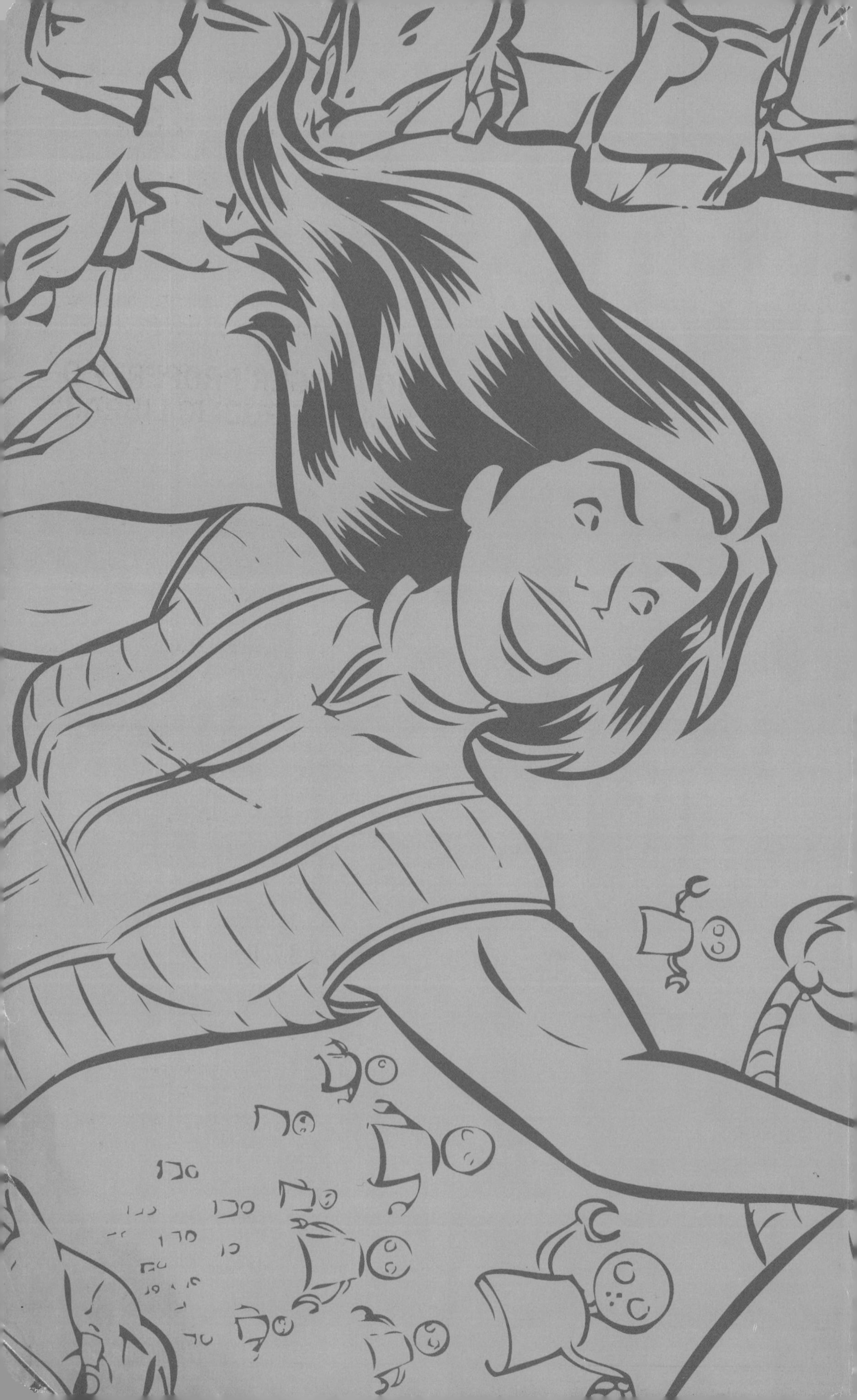

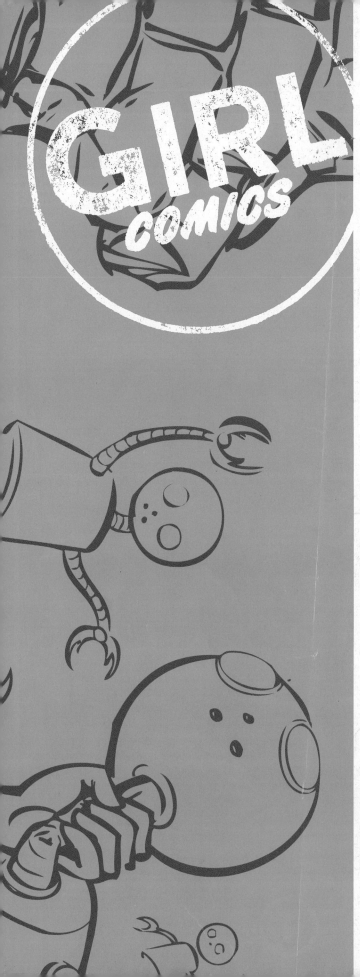

WRITERS
Colleen Coover, G. Willow Wilson, Trina Robbins, Valerie D'Orazio, Lucy Knisley, Robin Furth, Devin Grayson, Jill Thompson, Kathryn Immonen, Stephanie Buscema, Faith Erin Hicks, Abby Denson, Christine Boylan, Marjorie Liu, Louise Simonson, Lea Hernandez, Ann Nocenti, Kelly Sue DeConnick & Carla Speed McNeil

ARTISTS
Colleen Coover, Ming Doyle, Cris Peter, Stephanie Buscema, Nikki Cook, Elizabeth Breitweiser, Lucy Knisley, Agnes Garbowska, Emma Rios, Barabara Ciardo, Jill Thompson, Faith Erin Hicks, Emma Vieceli, Emily Warren, Cynthia Martin, June Chung, Sara Pichelli, Rachelle Rosenberg, June Brigman, Rebecca Buchman, Ronda Pattison, Lea Hernandez, Molly Crabapple, Adriana Melo, Mariah Benes & Carla Speed McNeil

LETTERERS
Colleen Coover, Kathleen Marinaccio, Kristyn Ferretti, Lucy Knisley, Faith Erin Hicks, Lea Hernandez, Star St. Germain & Carla Speed McNeil

PIN-UP ARTISTS
Sana Takeda; Colleen Doran; Ramona Fradon, Rebecca Buchman & June Chung; Stephanie Hans and Sho Murase

COVER ART
Amanda Conner & Laura Martin; Jill Thompson and Jo Chen

ASSISTANT EDITORS
Sana Amanat & Rachel Pinnelas

ASSOCIATE EDITOR
Lauren Sankovitch

EDITOR
Jeanine Schaefer

Special thanks to Irene Lee

COLLECTION EDITOR Jennifer Grünwald
EDITORIAL ASSISTANTS James Emmett & Joe Hochstein
ASSISTANT EDITORS Alex Starbuck & Nelson Ribeiro
EDITOR, SPECIAL PROJECTS Mark D. Beazley
SENIOR EDITOR, SPECIAL PROJECTS Jeff Youngquist
SENIOR VICE PRESIDENT OF SALES David Gabriel
BOOK DESIGN Jeff Powell

EDITOR IN CHIEF Axel Alonso
CHIEF CREATIVE OFFICER Joe Quesada
PUBLISHER Dan Buckley
EXECUTIVE PRODUCER Alan Fine

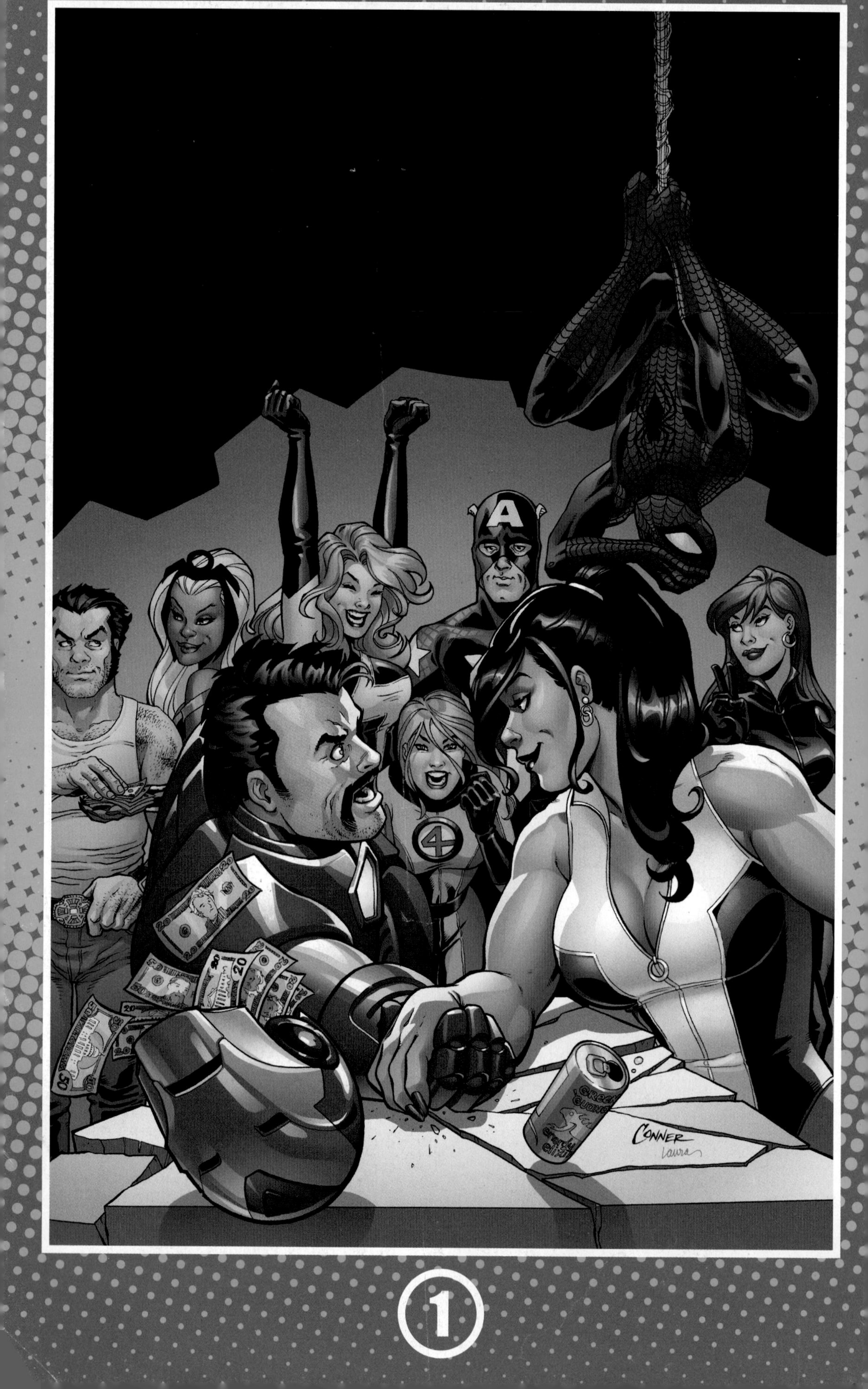

CONNER
Laura

1

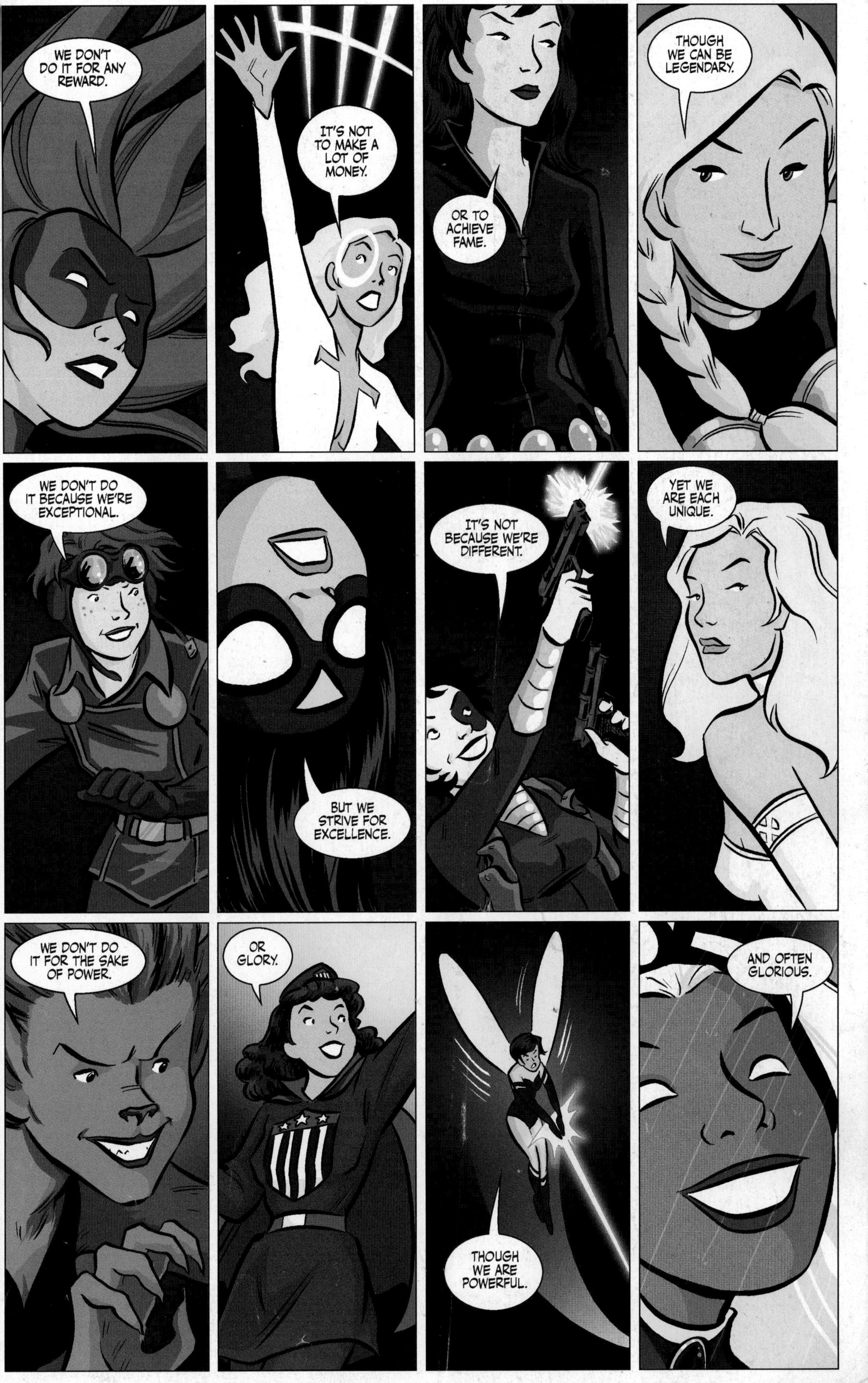
WE DON'T DO IT FOR ANY REWARD.
IT'S NOT TO MAKE A LOT OF MONEY.
OR TO ACHIEVE FAME.
THOUGH WE CAN BE LEGENDARY.
WE DON'T DO IT BECAUSE WE'RE EXCEPTIONAL.
BUT WE STRIVE FOR EXCELLENCE.
IT'S NOT BECAUSE WE'RE DIFFERENT.
YET WE ARE EACH UNIQUE.
WE DON'T DO IT FOR THE SAKE OF POWER.
OR GLORY.
THOUGH WE ARE POWERFUL.
AND OFTEN GLORIOUS.

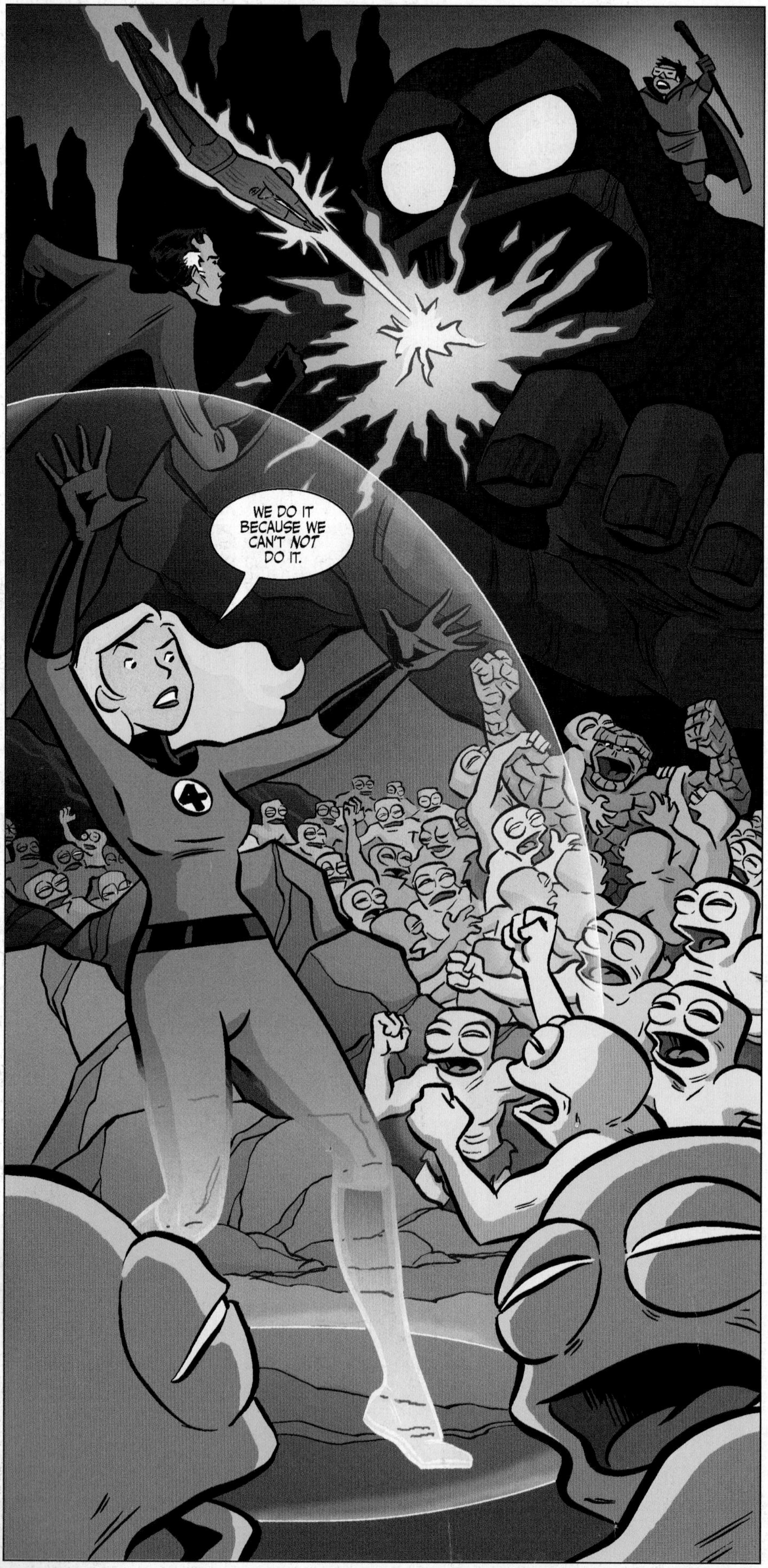
WE DO IT BECAUSE WE CAN'T *NOT* DO IT.

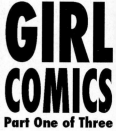

GIRL COMICS

Part One of Three

INTRODUCTION:
COLLEEN COOVER

COVER ART:
AMANDA CONNER & LAURA MARTIN

PRODUCTION:
IRENE LEE

ASSISTANT EDITORS:
SANA AMANAT & RACHEL PINNELAS

ASSOCIATE EDITOR:
LAUREN SANKOVITCH

EDITOR:
JEANINE SCHAEFER

EDITOR IN CHIEF:
JOE QUESADA

PUBLISHER:
DAN BUCKLEY

EXEC. PRODUCER:
ALAN FINE

SPECIAL THANKS:
SPRING HOTELING

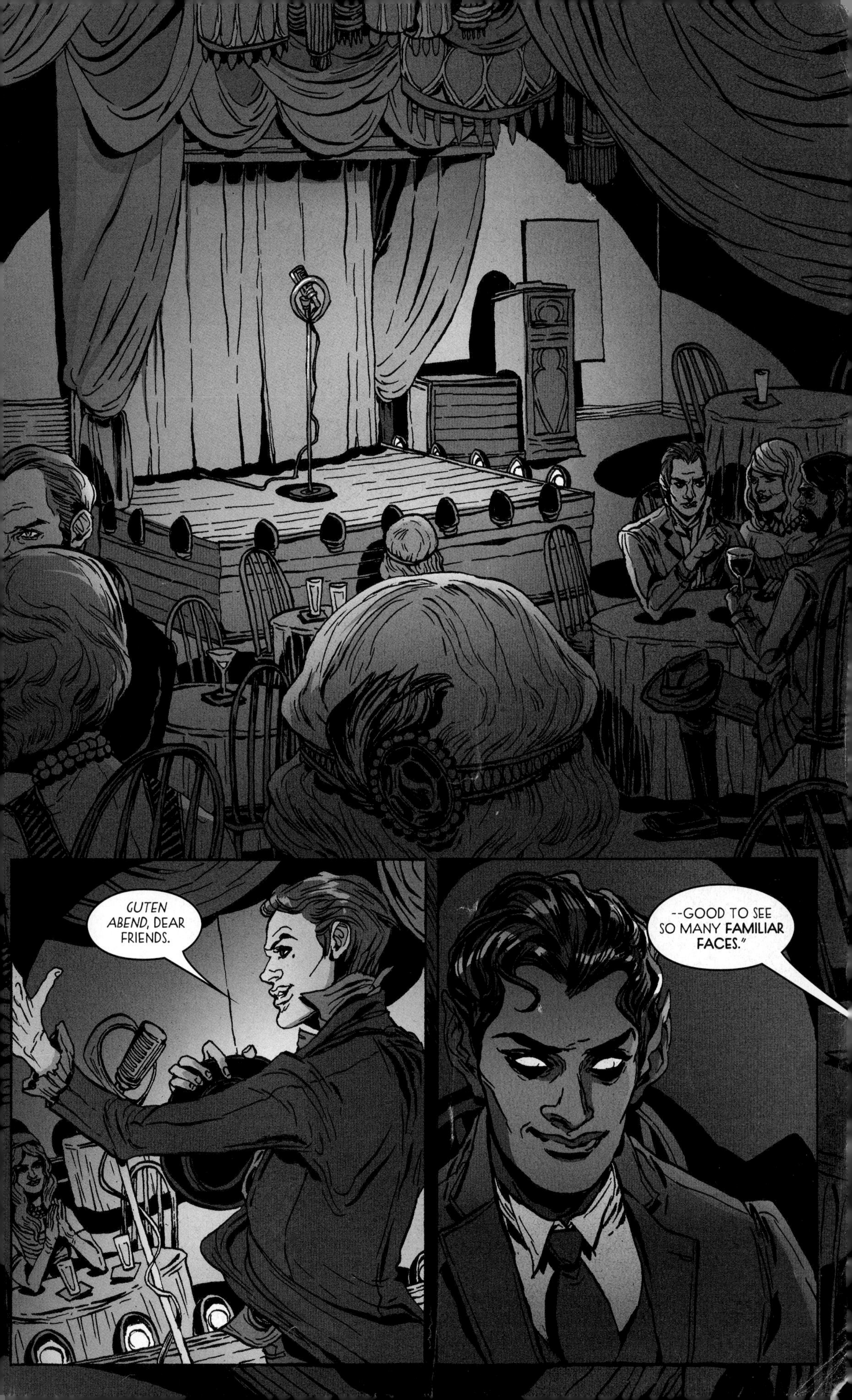
GUTEN ABEND, DEAR FRIENDS.
--GOOD TO SEE SO MANY FAMILIAR FACES."

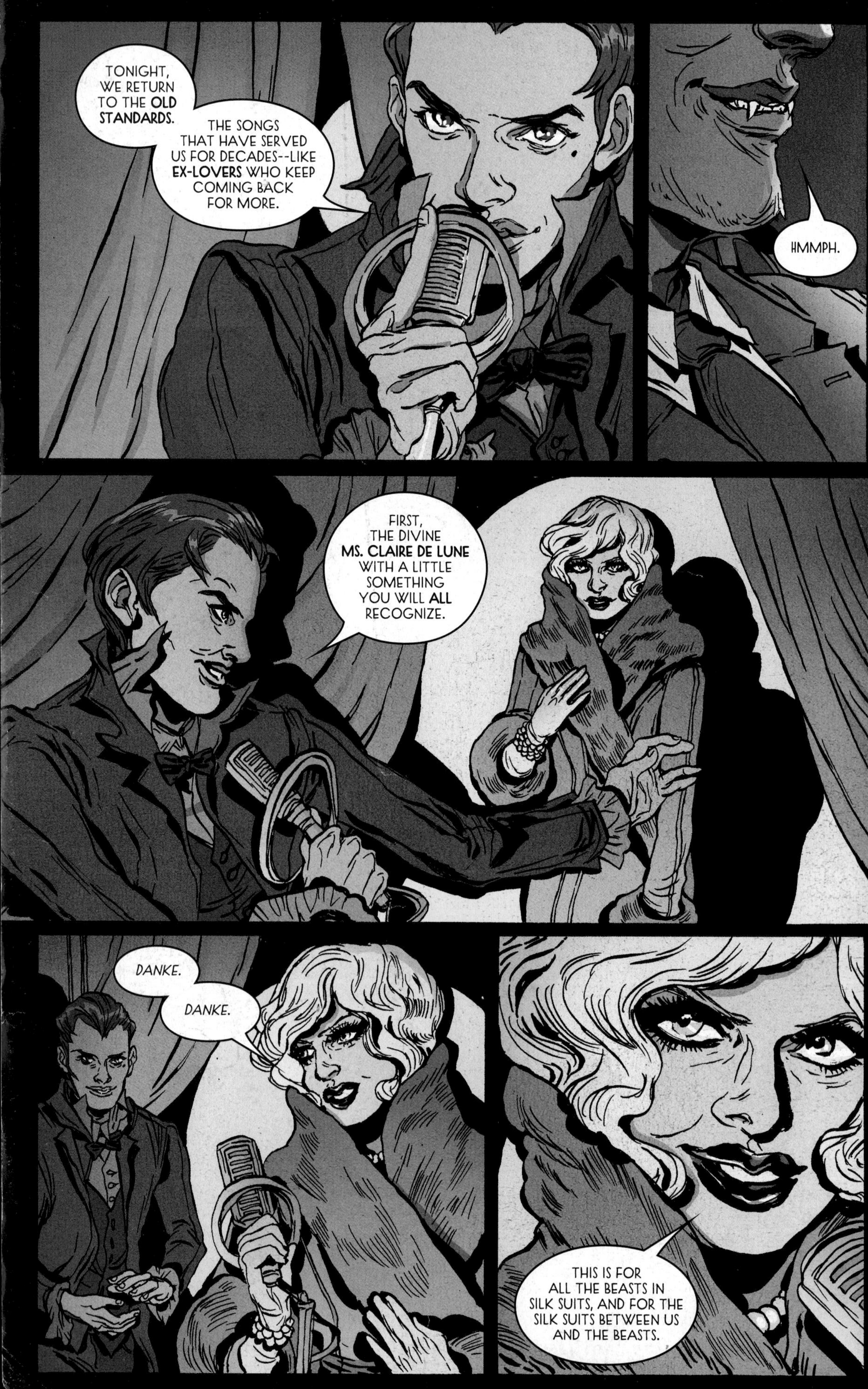
TONIGHT, WE RETURN TO THE OLD STANDARDS.
THE SONGS THAT HAVE SERVED US FOR DECADES--LIKE EX-LOVERS WHO KEEP COMING BACK FOR MORE.
HMMPH.
FIRST, THE DIVINE MS. CLAIRE DE LUNE WITH A LITTLE SOMETHING YOU WILL ALL RECOGNIZE.
DANKE.
DANKE.
THIS IS FOR ALL THE BEASTS IN SILK SUITS, AND FOR THE SILK SUITS BETWEEN US AND THE BEASTS.

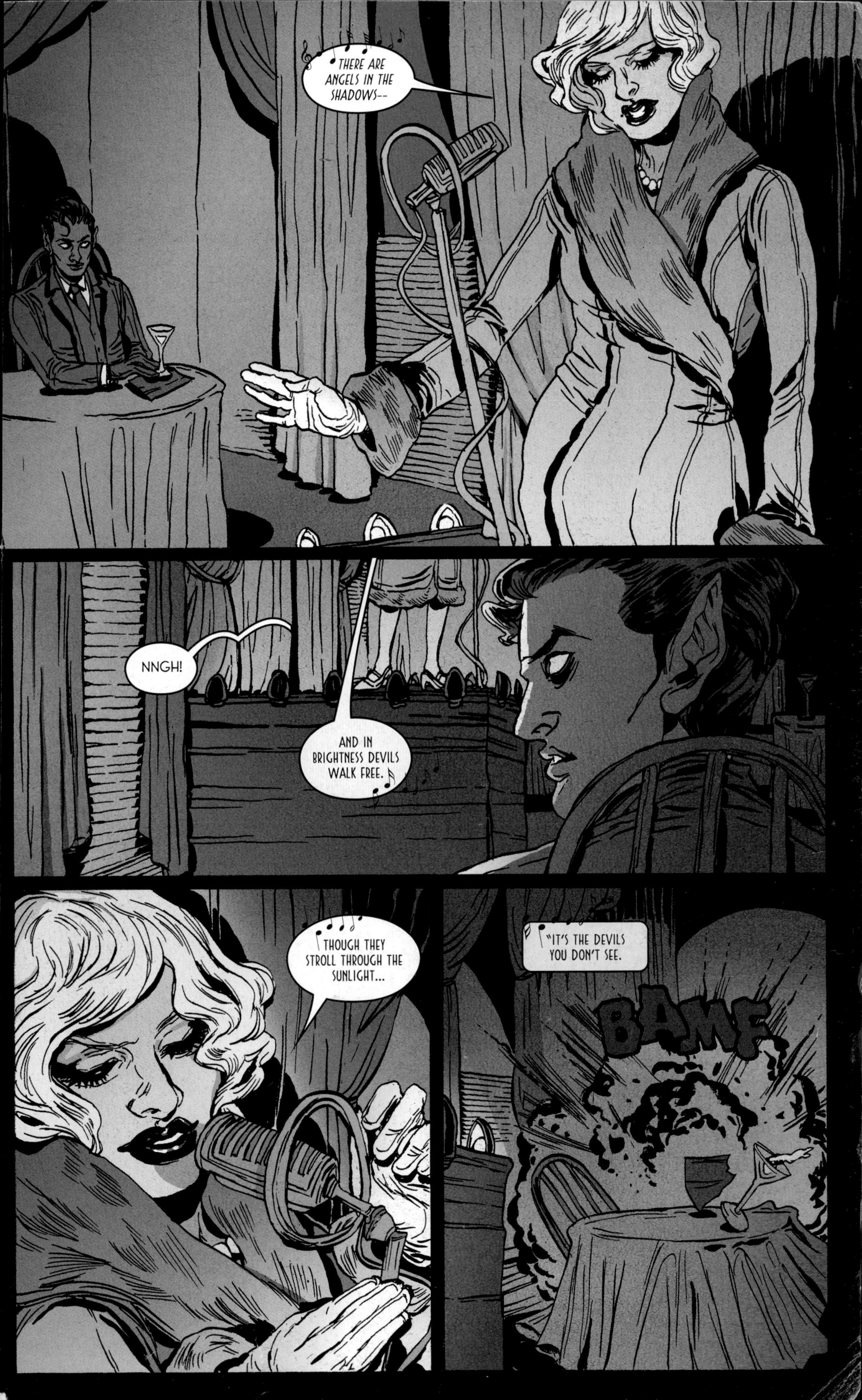
THERE ARE ANGELS IN THE SHADOWS--
NNGH!
AND IN BRIGHTNESS DEVILS WALK FREE.
THOUGH THEY STROLL THROUGH THE SUNLIGHT...
"IT'S THE DEVILS YOU DON'T SEE.
BAMF

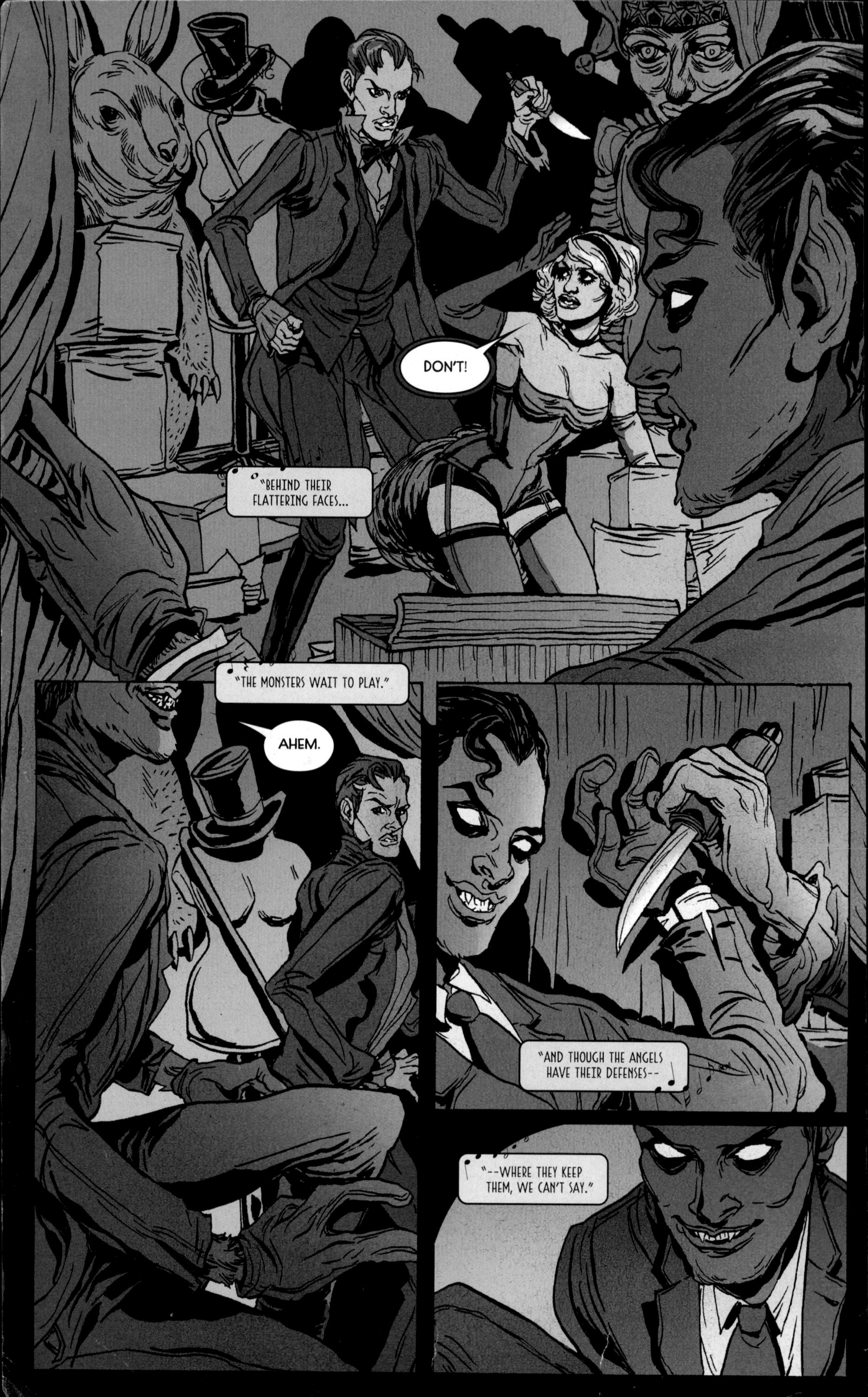
DON'T!
"BEHIND THEIR FLATTERING FACES...
"THE MONSTERS WAIT TO PLAY."
AHEM.
"AND THOUGH THE ANGELS HAVE THEIR DEFENSES--
"--WHERE THEY KEEP THEM, WE CAN'T SAY."

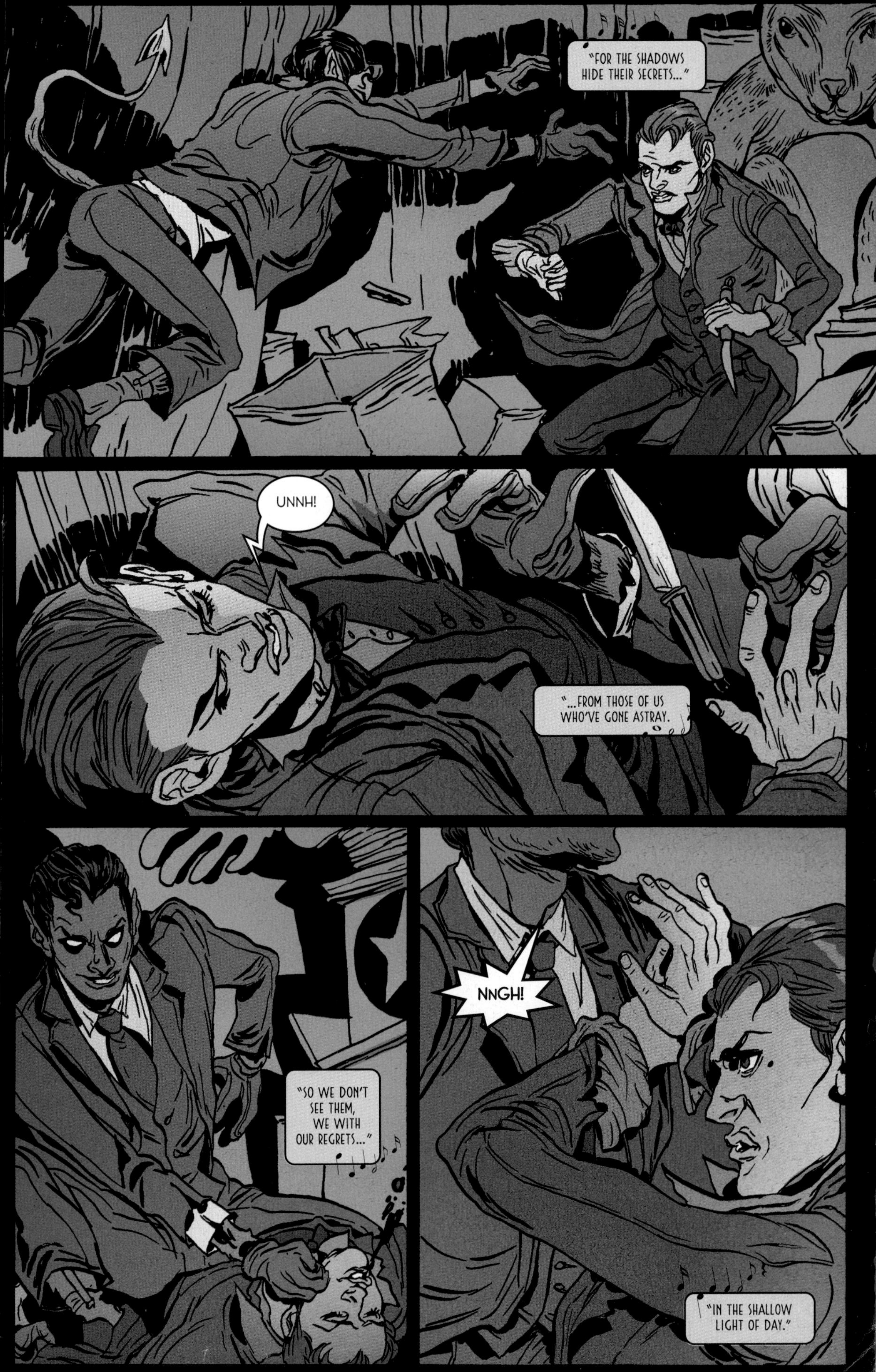
"FOR THE SHADOWS HIDE THEIR SECRETS..."
UNNH!
"...FROM THOSE OF US WHO'VE GONE ASTRAY.
"SO WE DON'T SEE THEM, WE WITH OUR REGRETS..."
NNGH!
"IN THE SHALLOW LIGHT OF DAY."

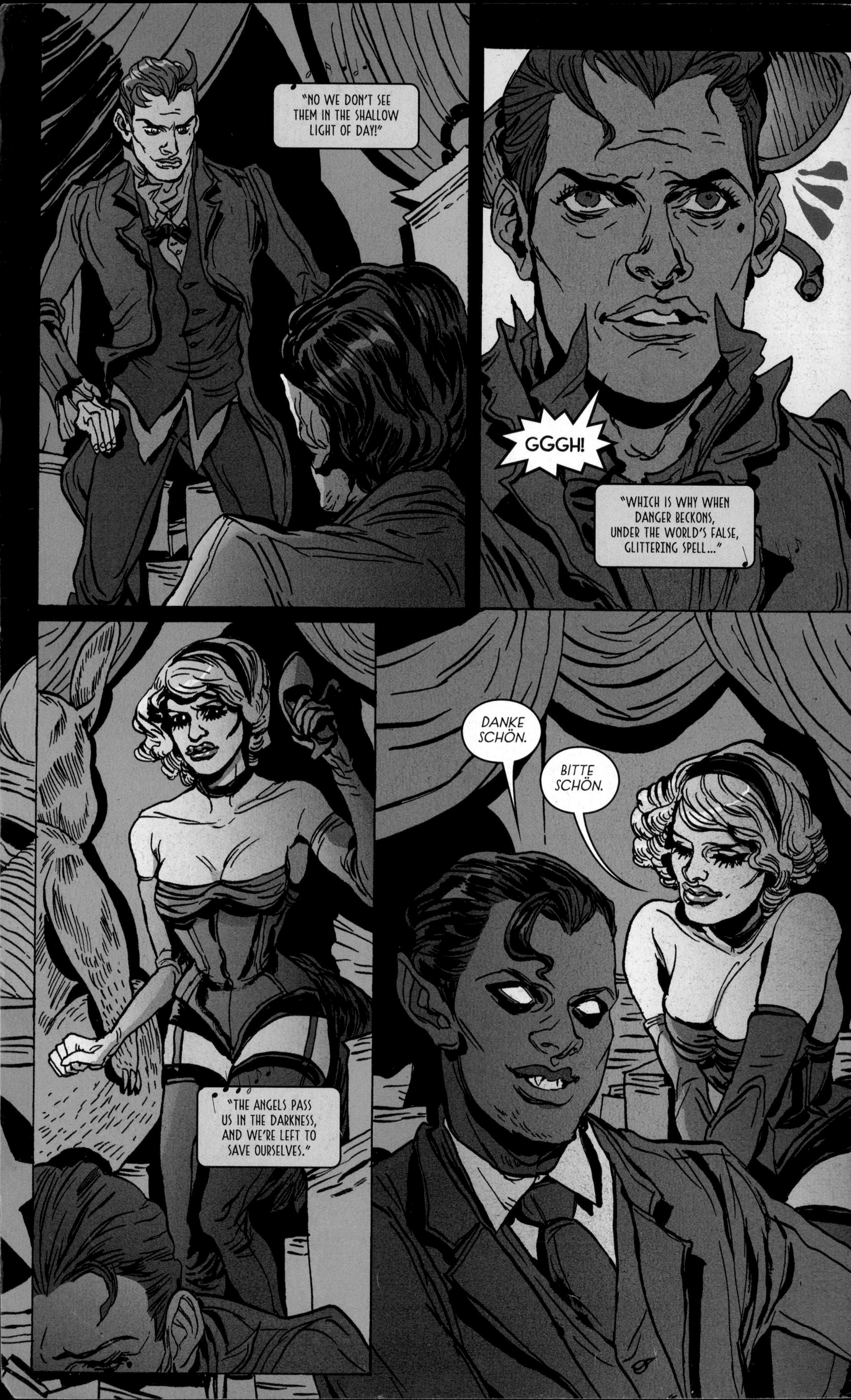
"NO WE DON'T SEE THEM IN THE SHALLOW LIGHT OF DAY!"
GGGH!
"WHICH IS WHY WHEN DANGER BECKONS, UNDER THE WORLD'S FALSE, GLITTERING SPELL..."
"THE ANGELS PASS US IN THE DARKNESS, AND WE'RE LEFT TO SAVE OURSELVES."
DANKE SCHÖN.
BITTE SCHÖN.

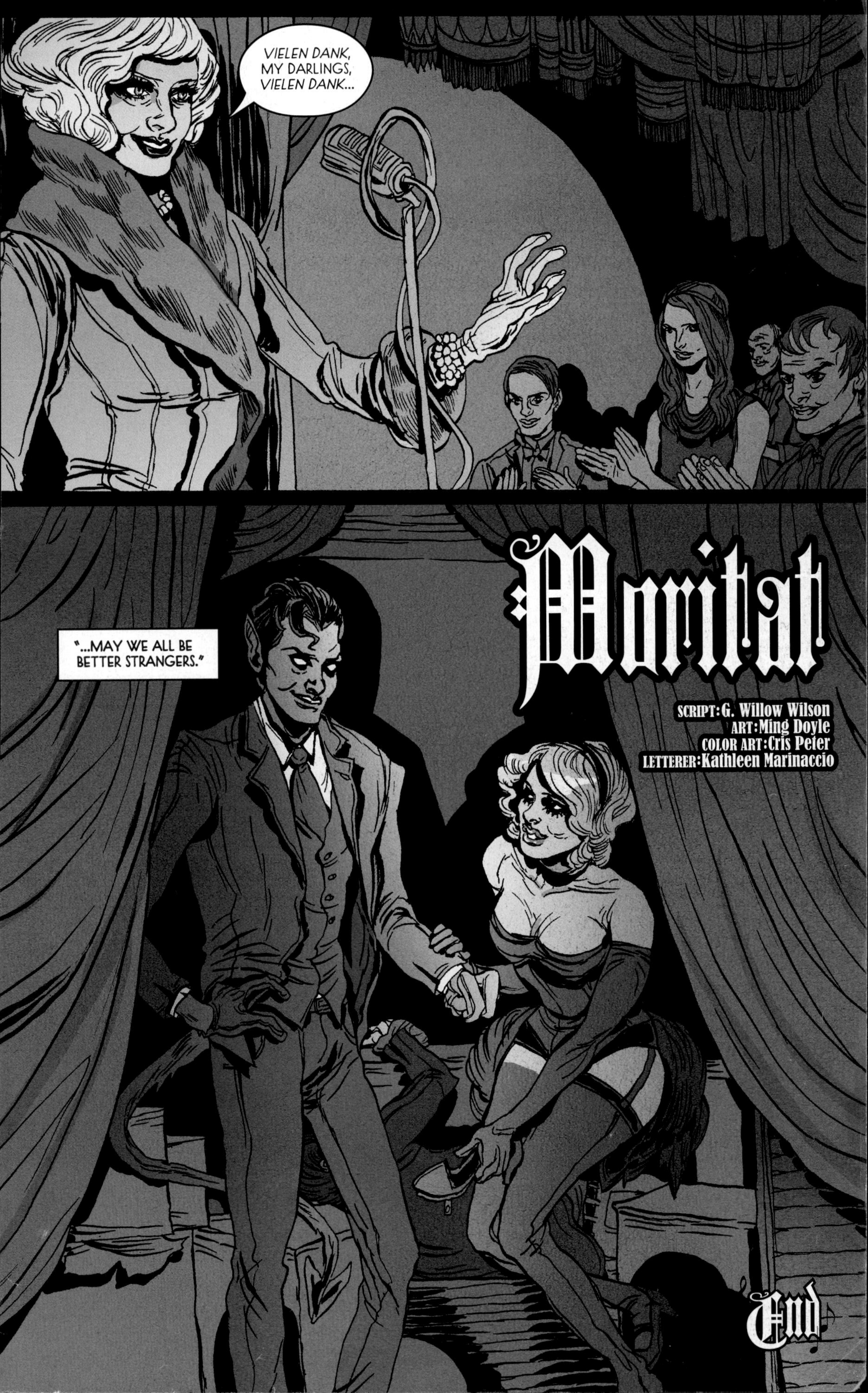
VIELEN DANK,
MY DARLINGS,
VIELEN DANK...
"...MAY WE ALL BE
BETTER STRANGERS."
Moritat
SCRIPT: G. Willow Wilson
ART: Ming Doyle
COLOR ART: Cris Peter
LETTERER: Kathleen Marinaccio
End

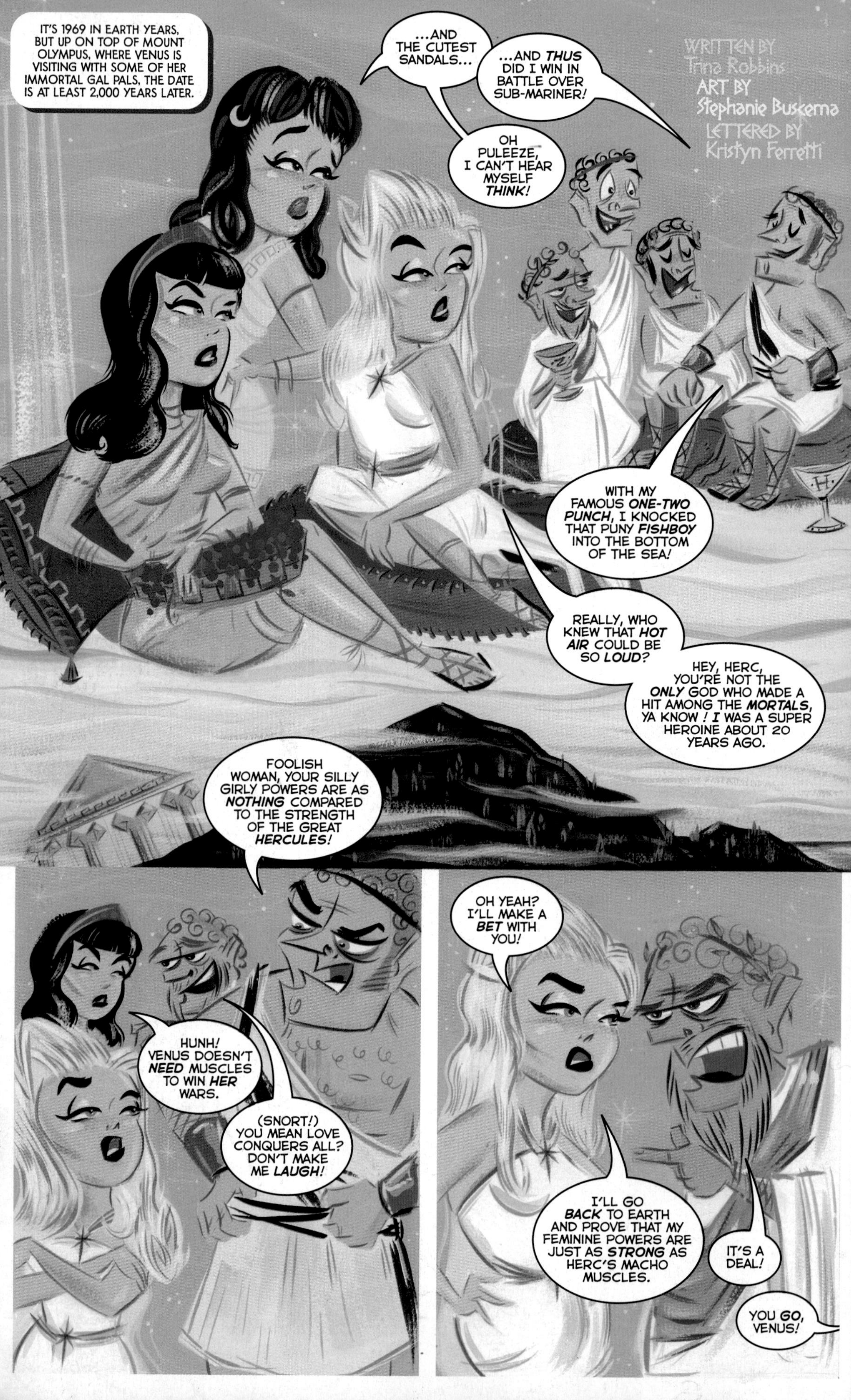
IT'S 1969 IN EARTH YEARS, BUT UP ON TOP OF MOUNT OLYMPUS, WHERE VENUS IS VISITING WITH SOME OF HER IMMORTAL GAL PALS, THE DATE IS AT LEAST 2,000 YEARS LATER.
...AND THE CUTEST SANDALS...
...AND *THUS* DID I WIN IN BATTLE OVER SUB-MARINER!
WRITTEN BY Trina Robbins
ART BY Stephanie Buscema
LETTERED BY Kristyn Ferretti
OH PULEEZE, I CAN'T HEAR MYSELF *THINK*!
WITH MY FAMOUS *ONE-TWO PUNCH*, I KNOCKED THAT PUNY *FISHBOY* INTO THE BOTTOM OF THE SEA!
REALLY, WHO KNEW THAT *HOT AIR* COULD BE SO *LOUD*?
HEY, HERC, YOU'RE NOT THE *ONLY* GOD WHO MADE A HIT AMONG THE *MORTALS*, YA KNOW ! *I* WAS A SUPER HEROINE ABOUT 20 YEARS AGO.
FOOLISH WOMAN, YOUR SILLY GIRLY POWERS ARE AS *NOTHING* COMPARED TO THE STRENGTH OF THE GREAT *HERCULES*!
HUNH! VENUS DOESN'T *NEED* MUSCLES TO WIN *HER* WARS.
(SNORT!) YOU MEAN LOVE CONQUERS ALL? DON'T MAKE ME *LAUGH*!
OH YEAH? I'LL MAKE A *BET* WITH YOU!
I'LL GO *BACK* TO EARTH AND PROVE THAT MY FEMININE POWERS ARE JUST AS *STRONG* AS HERC'S MACHO MUSCLES.
IT'S A DEAL!
YOU *GO*, VENUS!

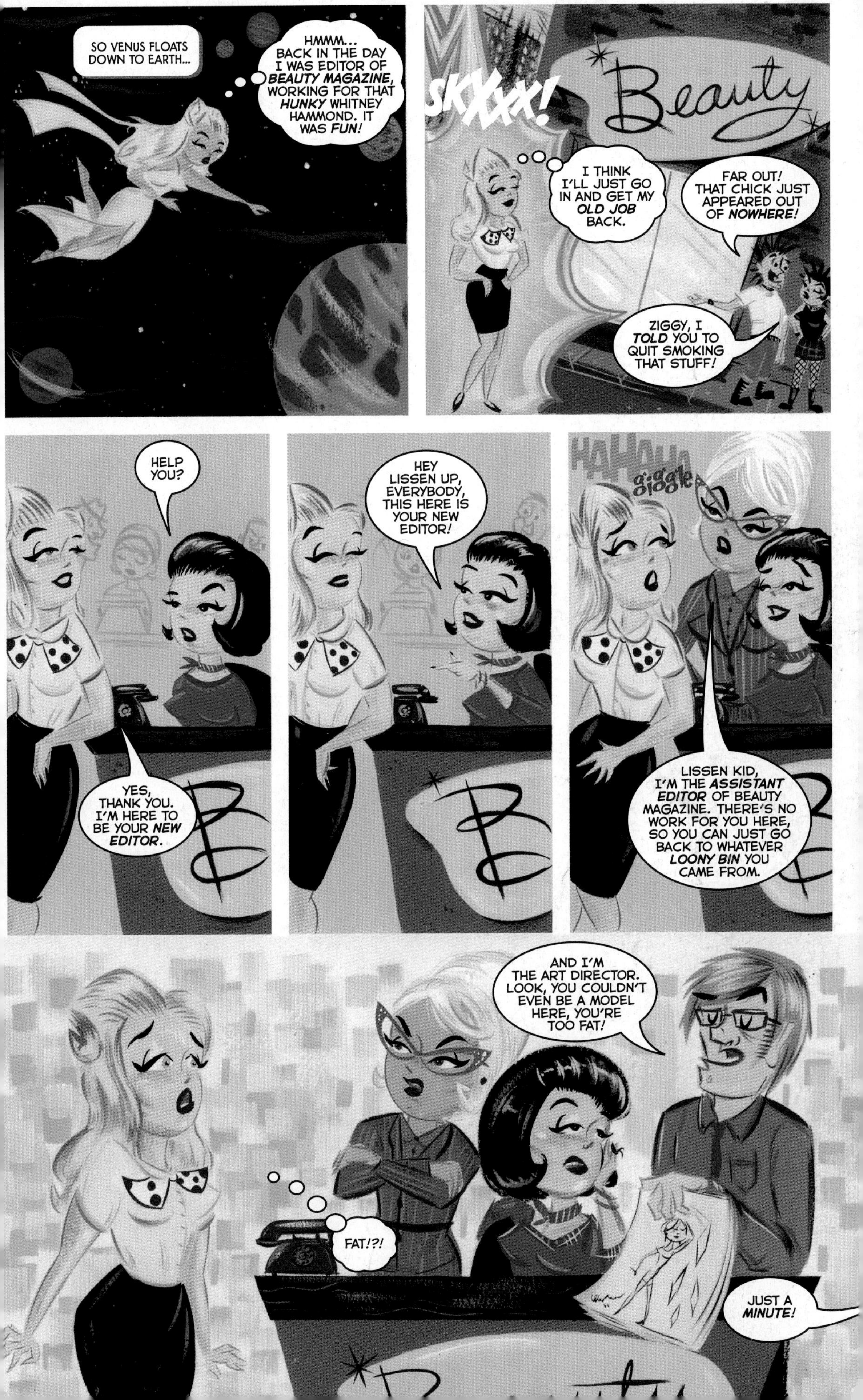

SO VENUS FLOATS DOWN TO EARTH...
HMMM... BACK IN THE DAY I WAS EDITOR OF BEAUTY MAGAZINE, WORKING FOR THAT HUNKY WHITNEY HAMMOND. IT WAS FUN!
SKXXX!
Beauty
I THINK I'LL JUST GO IN AND GET MY OLD JOB BACK.
FAR OUT! THAT CHICK JUST APPEARED OUT OF NOWHERE!
ZIGGY, I TOLD YOU TO QUIT SMOKING THAT STUFF!
HELP YOU?
YES, THANK YOU. I'M HERE TO BE YOUR NEW EDITOR.
HEY LISSEN UP, EVERYBODY, THIS HERE IS YOUR NEW EDITOR!
HAHAHA
giggle
LISSEN KID, I'M THE ASSISTANT EDITOR OF BEAUTY MAGAZINE. THERE'S NO WORK FOR YOU HERE, SO YOU CAN JUST GO BACK TO WHATEVER LOONY BIN YOU CAME FROM.
AND I'M THE ART DIRECTOR. LOOK, YOU COULDN'T EVEN BE A MODEL HERE, YOU'RE TOO FAT!
FAT!?!
JUST A MINUTE!

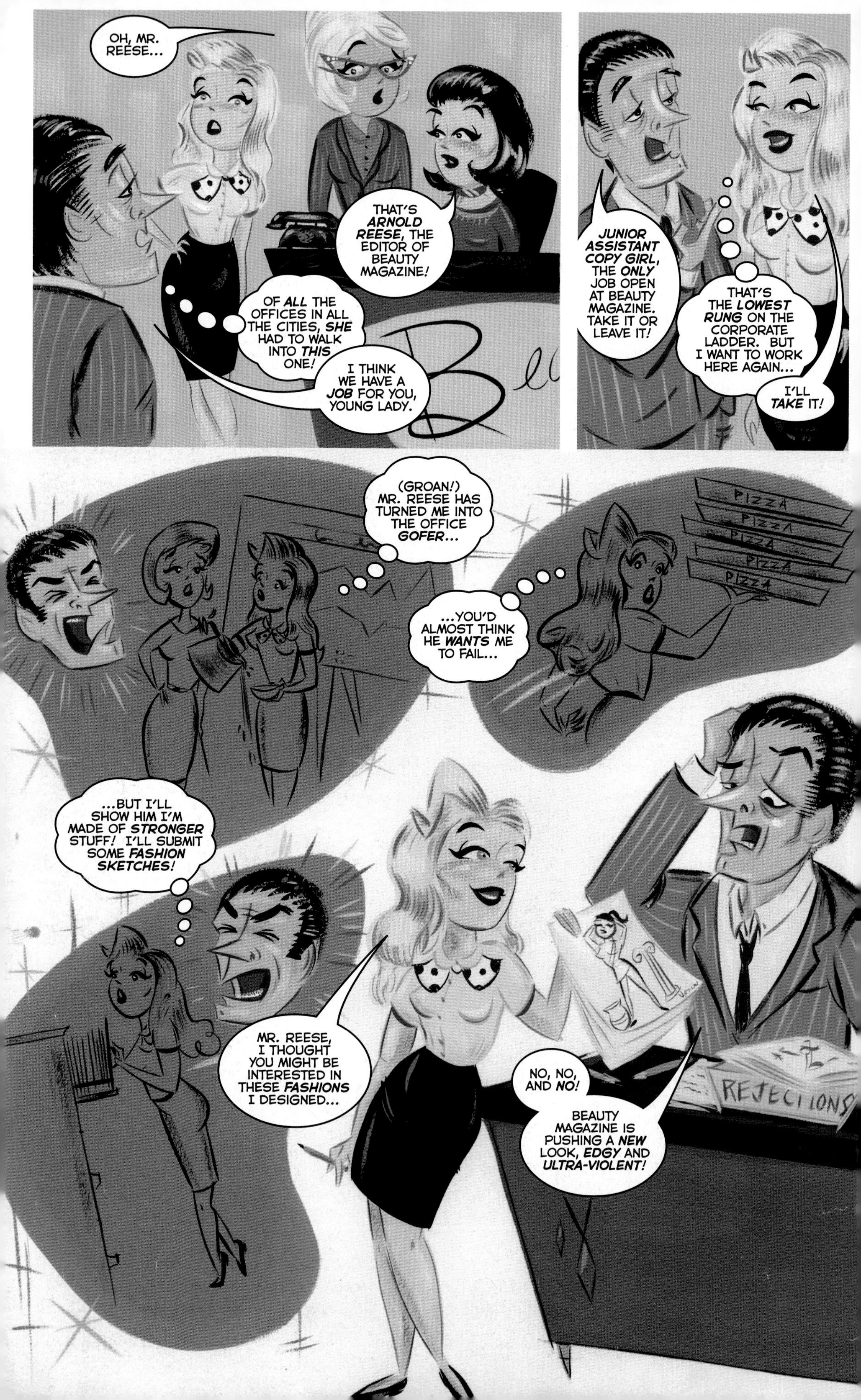
OH, MR. REESE...
THAT'S ARNOLD REESE, THE EDITOR OF BEAUTY MAGAZINE!
OF ALL THE OFFICES IN ALL THE CITIES, SHE HAD TO WALK INTO THIS ONE!
I THINK WE HAVE A JOB FOR YOU, YOUNG LADY.
JUNIOR ASSISTANT COPY GIRL, THE ONLY JOB OPEN AT BEAUTY MAGAZINE. TAKE IT OR LEAVE IT!
THAT'S THE LOWEST RUNG ON THE CORPORATE LADDER. BUT I WANT TO WORK HERE AGAIN...
I'LL TAKE IT!
(GROAN!) MR. REESE HAS TURNED ME INTO THE OFFICE GOFER...
PIZZA
PIZZA
PIZZA
PIZZA
PIZZA
...YOU'D ALMOST THINK HE WANTS ME TO FAIL...
...BUT I'LL SHOW HIM I'M MADE OF STRONGER STUFF! I'LL SUBMIT SOME FASHION SKETCHES!
MR. REESE, I THOUGHT YOU MIGHT BE INTERESTED IN THESE FASHIONS I DESIGNED...
NO, NO, AND NO!
BEAUTY MAGAZINE IS PUSHING A NEW LOOK, EDGY AND ULTRA-VIOLENT!
REJECTIONS

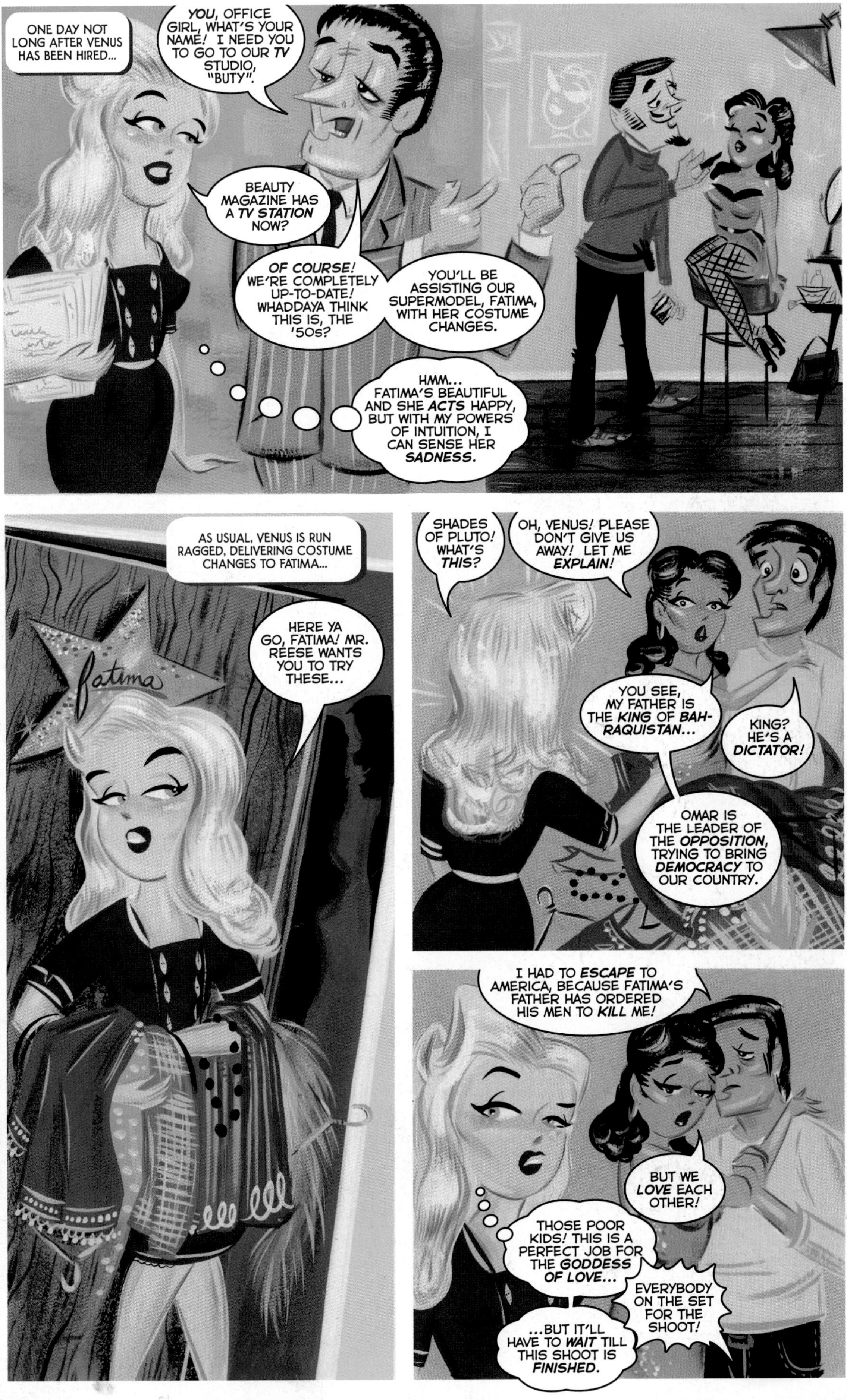
ONE DAY NOT LONG AFTER VENUS HAS BEEN HIRED...
YOU, OFFICE GIRL, WHAT'S YOUR NAME! I NEED YOU TO GO TO OUR TV STUDIO, "BUTY".
BEAUTY MAGAZINE HAS A TV STATION NOW?
OF COURSE! WE'RE COMPLETELY UP-TO-DATE! WHADDAYA THINK THIS IS, THE '50s?
YOU'LL BE ASSISTING OUR SUPERMODEL, FATIMA, WITH HER COSTUME CHANGES.
HMM... FATIMA'S BEAUTIFUL AND SHE ACTS HAPPY, BUT WITH MY POWERS OF INTUITION, I CAN SENSE HER SADNESS.
AS USUAL, VENUS IS RUN RAGGED, DELIVERING COSTUME CHANGES TO FATIMA...
fatima
HERE YA GO, FATIMA! MR. REESE WANTS YOU TO TRY THESE...
SHADES OF PLUTO! WHAT'S THIS?
OH, VENUS! PLEASE DON'T GIVE US AWAY! LET ME EXPLAIN!
YOU SEE, MY FATHER IS THE KING OF BAH-RAQUISTAN...
KING? HE'S A DICTATOR!
OMAR IS THE LEADER OF THE OPPOSITION, TRYING TO BRING DEMOCRACY TO OUR COUNTRY.
I HAD TO ESCAPE TO AMERICA, BECAUSE FATIMA'S FATHER HAS ORDERED HIS MEN TO KILL ME!
BUT WE LOVE EACH OTHER!
THOSE POOR KIDS! THIS IS A PERFECT JOB FOR THE GODDESS OF LOVE...
EVERYBODY ON THE SET FOR THE SHOOT!
...BUT IT'LL HAVE TO WAIT TILL THIS SHOOT IS FINISHED.

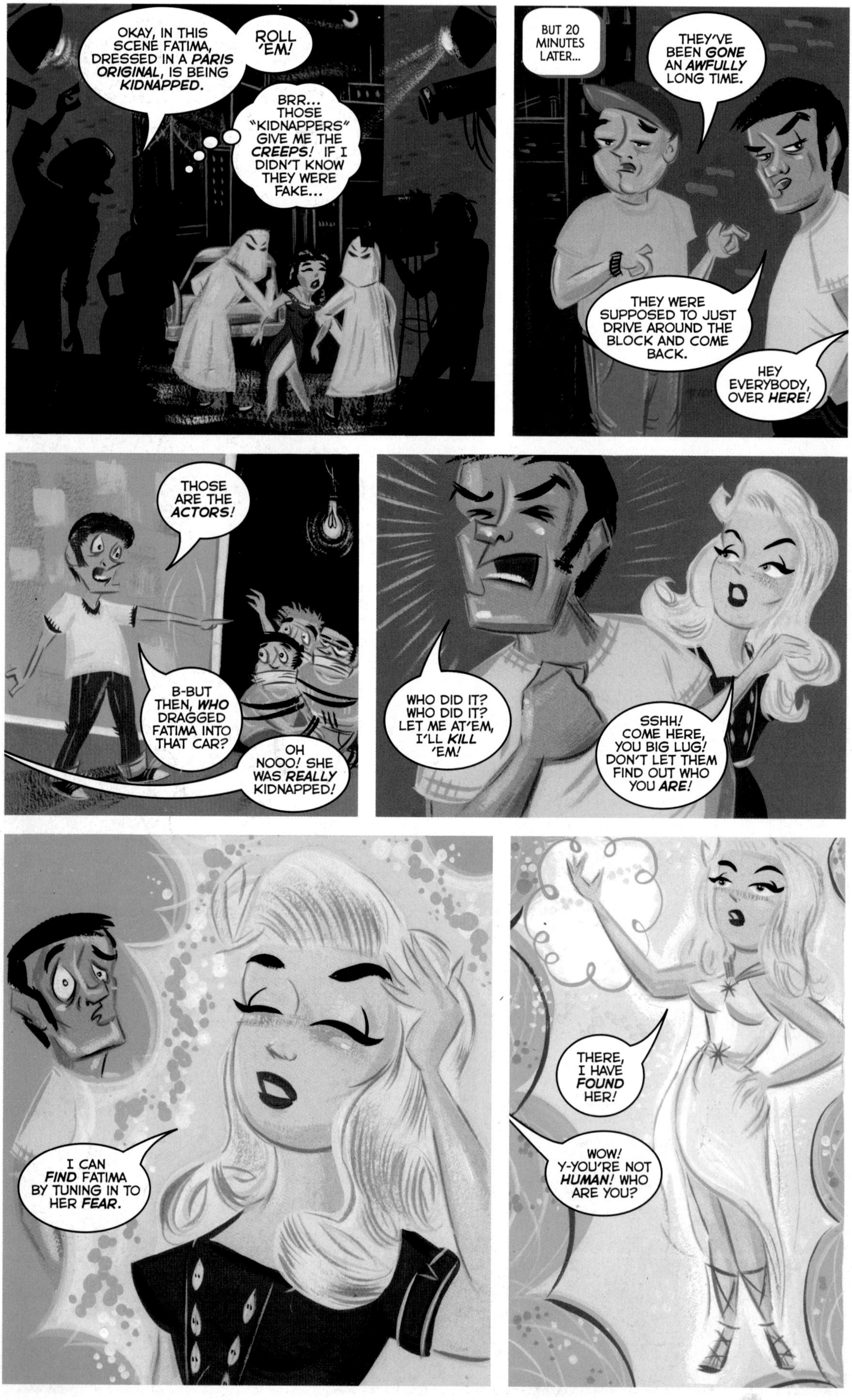
OKAY, IN THIS SCENE FATIMA, DRESSED IN A *PARIS ORIGINAL*, IS BEING *KIDNAPPED*.
ROLL 'EM!
BRR... THOSE "KIDNAPPERS" GIVE ME THE *CREEPS!* IF I DIDN'T KNOW THEY WERE FAKE...
BUT 20 MINUTES LATER...
THEY'VE BEEN *GONE* AN *AWFULLY* LONG TIME.
THEY WERE SUPPOSED TO JUST DRIVE AROUND THE BLOCK AND COME BACK.
HEY EVERYBODY, OVER *HERE!*
THOSE ARE THE *ACTORS!*
B-BUT THEN, *WHO* DRAGGED FATIMA INTO THAT CAR?
OH NOOO! SHE WAS *REALLY* KIDNAPPED!
WHO DID IT? WHO DID IT? LET ME AT'EM, I'LL *KILL* 'EM!
SSHH! COME HERE, YOU BIG LUG! DON'T LET THEM FIND OUT WHO YOU *ARE!*
I CAN *FIND* FATIMA BY TUNING IN TO HER *FEAR*.
THERE, I HAVE *FOUND* HER!
WOW! Y-YOU'RE NOT *HUMAN!* WHO ARE YOU?

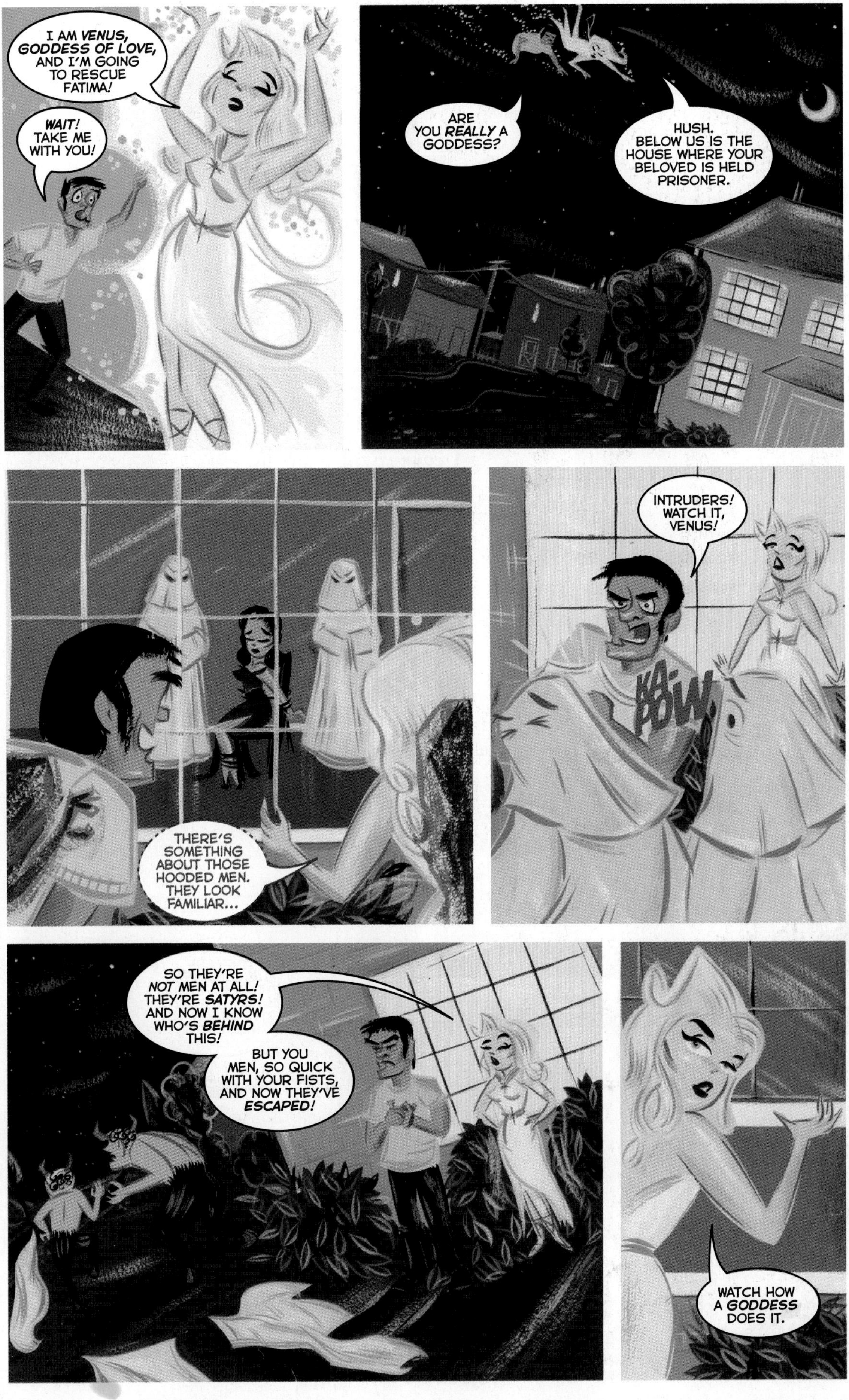

I AM *VENUS*, *GODDESS OF LOVE*, AND I'M GOING TO RESCUE FATIMA!
WAIT! TAKE ME WITH YOU!
ARE YOU *REALLY* A GODDESS?
HUSH. BELOW US IS THE HOUSE WHERE YOUR BELOVED IS HELD PRISONER.
THERE'S SOMETHING ABOUT THOSE HOODED MEN. THEY LOOK FAMILIAR...
INTRUDERS! WATCH IT, VENUS!
KA-POW!
SO THEY'RE *NOT* MEN AT ALL! THEY'RE *SATYRS!* AND NOW I KNOW WHO'S *BEHIND* THIS!
BUT YOU MEN, SO QUICK WITH YOUR FISTS, AND NOW THEY'VE *ESCAPED!*
WATCH HOW A *GODDESS* DOES IT.

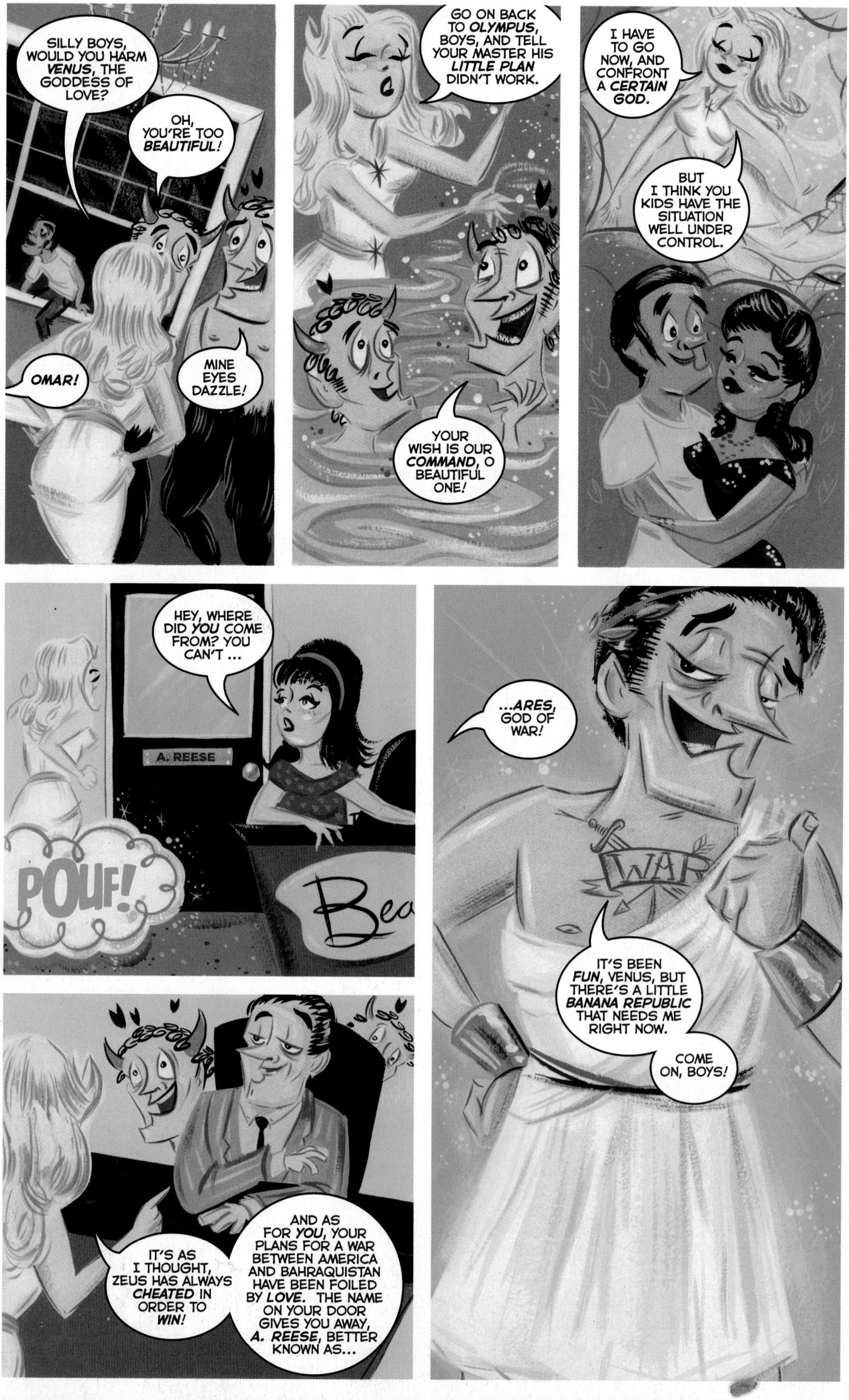
SILLY BOYS, WOULD YOU HARM VENUS, THE GODDESS OF LOVE?
OH, YOU'RE TOO BEAUTIFUL!
OMAR!
MINE EYES DAZZLE!
GO ON BACK TO OLYMPUS, BOYS, AND TELL YOUR MASTER HIS LITTLE PLAN DIDN'T WORK.
YOUR WISH IS OUR COMMAND, O BEAUTIFUL ONE!
I HAVE TO GO NOW, AND CONFRONT A CERTAIN GOD.
BUT I THINK YOU KIDS HAVE THE SITUATION WELL UNDER CONTROL.
HEY, WHERE DID YOU COME FROM? YOU CAN'T ...
A. REESE
POUF!
IT'S AS I THOUGHT, ZEUS HAS ALWAYS CHEATED IN ORDER TO WIN!
AND AS FOR YOU, YOUR PLANS FOR A WAR BETWEEN AMERICA AND BAHRAQUISTAN HAVE BEEN FOILED BY LOVE. THE NAME ON YOUR DOOR GIVES YOU AWAY, A. REESE, BETTER KNOWN AS...
...ARES, GOD OF WAR!
WAR
IT'S BEEN FUN, VENUS, BUT THERE'S A LITTLE BANANA REPUBLIC THAT NEEDS ME RIGHT NOW.
COME ON, BOYS!

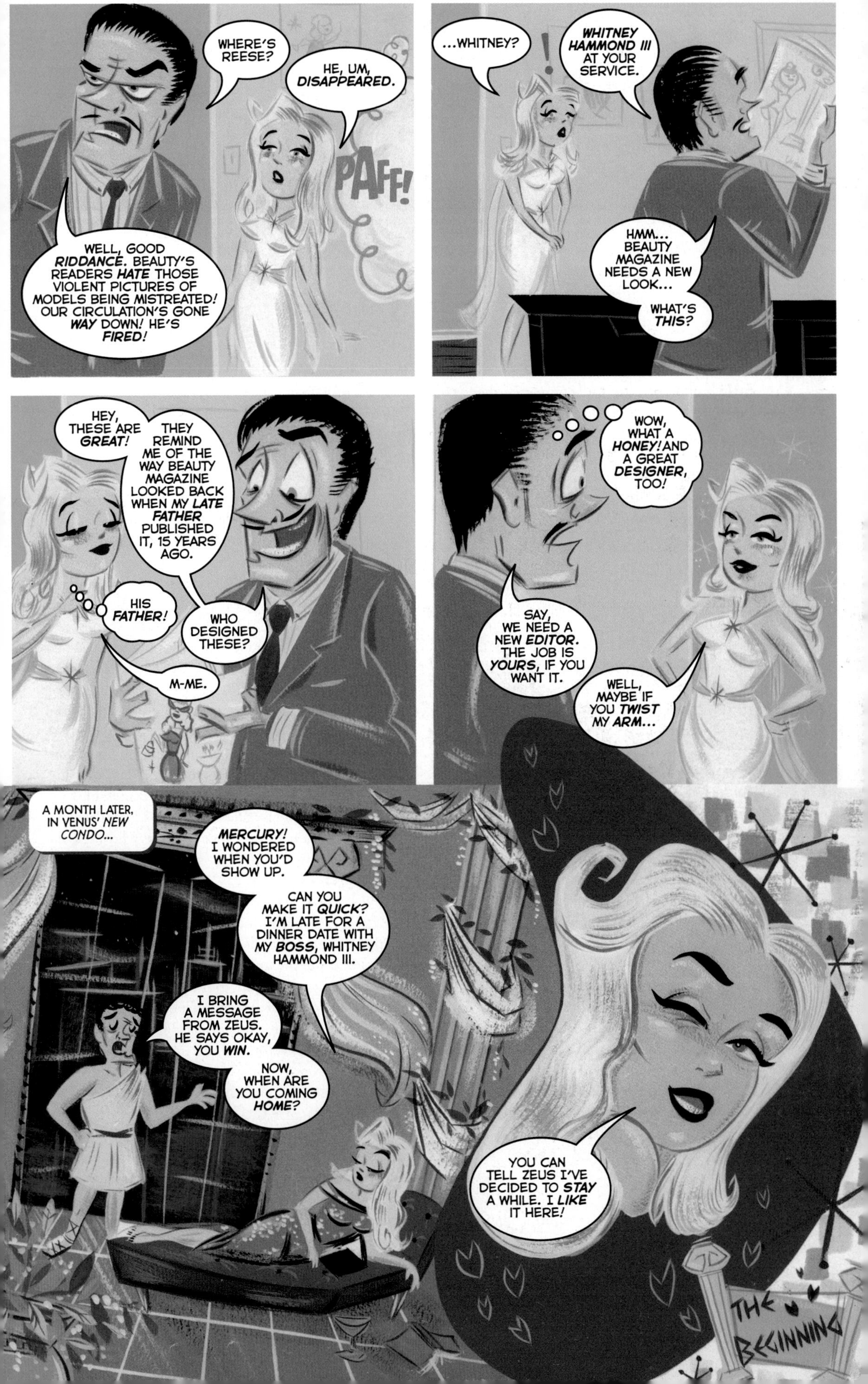
WHERE'S REESE?
HE, UM, DISAPPEARED.
PAFF!
WELL, GOOD RIDDANCE. BEAUTY'S READERS HATE THOSE VIOLENT PICTURES OF MODELS BEING MISTREATED! OUR CIRCULATION'S GONE WAY DOWN! HE'S FIRED!
...WHITNEY?
!
WHITNEY HAMMOND III AT YOUR SERVICE.
HMM... BEAUTY MAGAZINE NEEDS A NEW LOOK...
WHAT'S THIS?
HEY, THESE ARE GREAT!
THEY REMIND ME OF THE WAY BEAUTY MAGAZINE LOOKED BACK WHEN MY LATE FATHER PUBLISHED IT, 15 YEARS AGO.
HIS FATHER!
WHO DESIGNED THESE?
M-ME.
WOW, WHAT A HONEY! AND A GREAT DESIGNER, TOO!
SAY, WE NEED A NEW EDITOR. THE JOB IS YOURS, IF YOU WANT IT.
WELL, MAYBE IF YOU TWIST MY ARM...
A MONTH LATER, IN VENUS' NEW CONDO...
MERCURY! I WONDERED WHEN YOU'D SHOW UP.
CAN YOU MAKE IT QUICK? I'M LATE FOR A DINNER DATE WITH MY BOSS, WHITNEY HAMMOND III.
I BRING A MESSAGE FROM ZEUS. HE SAYS OKAY, YOU WIN.
NOW, WHEN ARE YOU COMING HOME?
YOU CAN TELL ZEUS I'VE DECIDED TO STAY A WHILE. I LIKE IT HERE!
THE BEGINNING

SPOTLIGHT
Flo Steinberg

Fab Flo

If you were a Marvel fan in the 1960s or even remotely connected to the company, then you know exactly who Flo Steinberg is—though chances are you'll know her as "Fabulous Flo," the nickname Stan Lee coined for her in Marvel's Bullpen Bulletins. As Stan Lee's secretary during Marvel's Silver Age, Flo is a big part of the company's history, and a venerable institution unto herself.

Originally from Boston, Flo graduated from the University of Massachusetts, and worked briefly as a service representative at the New England Telephone Company before leaving for New York in 1963. "My job at the time was going nowhere, so I thought why not try New York?" It was a bold move for a woman of her time, but Flo was motivated and spent months job hunting in the city while staying at the YWCA. One fateful day she received an interview at Magazine Management, the publishing company that produced Marvel Comics. There she met Stan Lee, and thereby took her first step to becoming Stan's "Girl Friday" and an integral part of the Marvel family.

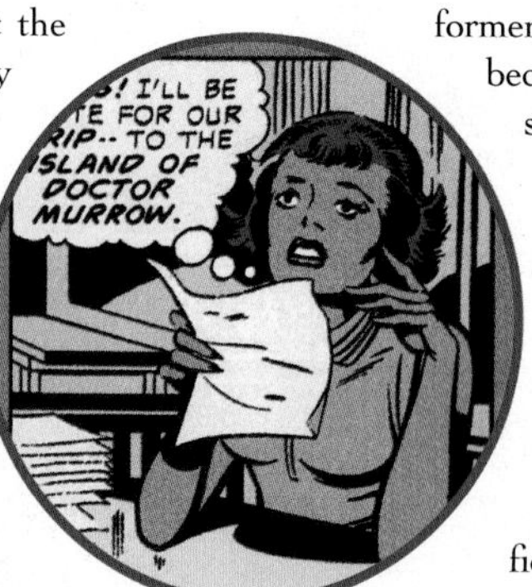
I'LL BE
FOR OUR
TO THE
DOCTOR
MURROW.

As Marvel's corresponding secretary, Flo became the voice of Marvel, providing answers to eager fans' questions about past or upcoming content, as the caretaker of the Merry Marvel Marching Society fan club and acting as the liaison between Stan and the scores of amazing talent that walked through the Marvel offices. At the time Marvel was going through a rapid expansion in publishing. Between 1961 through 1969, they produced about 839 comics, with Stan Lee writing most of them and Flo trafficking much of that content. The sheer amount of books produced, combined with Marvel's increasing popularity, made Flo a jack of all trades, proving her indispensability.

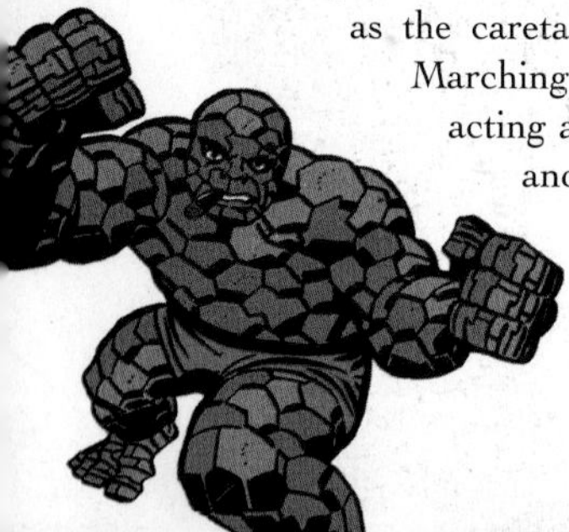

What makes Flo memorable, though, is less about the day-to-day tasks she accomplished with apparent ease, and more about the sweet yet sassy attitude she brought to the Marvel offices. There are few Marvel fans and former employees who don't remember her because of this. Every fan letter they sent she responded to, any office tensions that arose she eased with a joke or calming logic, any crazy fans who stormed the offices she shrewdly deflected—and "sometimes that involved tripping a few." She became an important part of the morale of the company, the cheerleader, the confidante, the tough gatekeeper—all in all, the bona fide Renaissance woman who kept the company running smoothly regardless of the chaos.

By 1968, to Stan and the rest of the office's disappointment, Flo decided it was time to leave Marvel and pursue another career path. Thereafter she began working at the American Petroleum Institute where she learned much of her copy-editing and proofing skills, and then moved to Oregon and San Francisco for a short time. She eventually returned to New York City to head up the Captain Company, the merchandising division of Warren Publishing.

Despite the career change, Flo hadn't gotten comics out of her blood quite yet. While in San Francisco, she was exposed to the underground comix scene through her close friend Trina Robbins and became inspired. Shortly after returning to New York, she

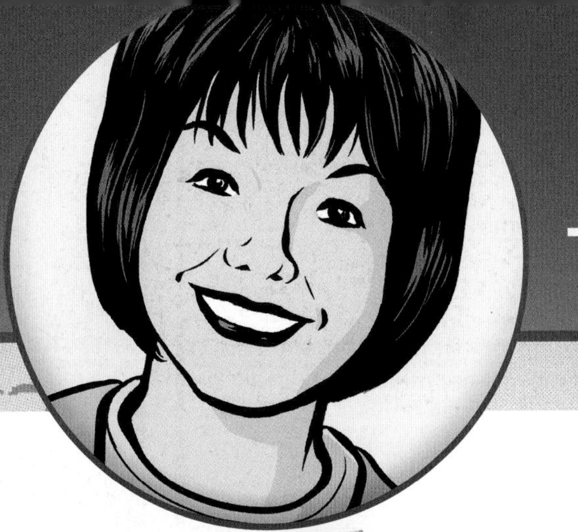

decided to put together an underground comic book about the Big Apple with some of her mainstream comic book artist and writer friends, including Wally Wood, Neal Adams, Herb Trimpe, Linda Fite, Larry Hama, Marie Severin and Archie Goodwin, to name a few. *Big Apple Comix* was published in 1975, with Flo once again playing multi-tasker as editor and publisher. It's considered by many to be one of the first alternative comics of its kind, and to Flo, one of her proudest accomplishments.

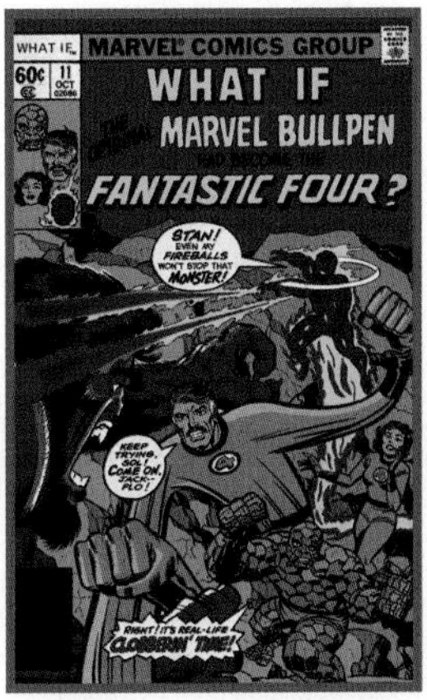
WHAT IF
MARVEL COMICS GROUP
60¢
11 OCT
WHAT IF
MARVEL BULLPEN
FANTASTIC FOUR?
STAN! EVEN MY FIREBALLS WON'T STOP THAT MONSTER!
KEEP TRYING, SOL! COME ON, JACK-- FLO!
RIGHT! IT'S REAL-LIFE CLOBBERIN' TIME!

In 1978, honoring Marvel's first real "Girl Friday," Jack Kirby cast Flo as the Invisible Woman in *What If #11* that asked "What if the original Marvel Bullpen had become the Fantastic Four?" This feature and Mark Millar's brief tribute to her in *Ultimate Fantastic Four #28*, where Flo was secretary to President Thor on a super hero-populated Earth, showed Flo's long-lasting impact on Marvel and those who worked there.

Today you'll find her bustling through the Marvel hallways, just as quick-lipped and loveable as ever, ready to offer a hug or smack-down on a moment's notice. Flo returned to her old stomping ground in the 1990s to work as a proofreader—and yes, she's even proofed this copy even though she laughs at us for featuring her. That's the thing about Flo—she's worked alongside some of the greatest in the industry and doesn't quite realize that she, too, is one of them.

...ready to offer a hug or smack-down on a moment's notice.

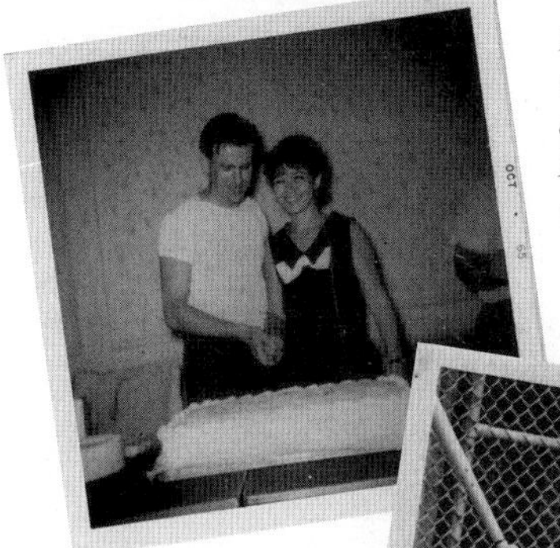

Flo and former Marvel writer Dave Kaler cutting a cake at a New York Comic Con (c.1965)

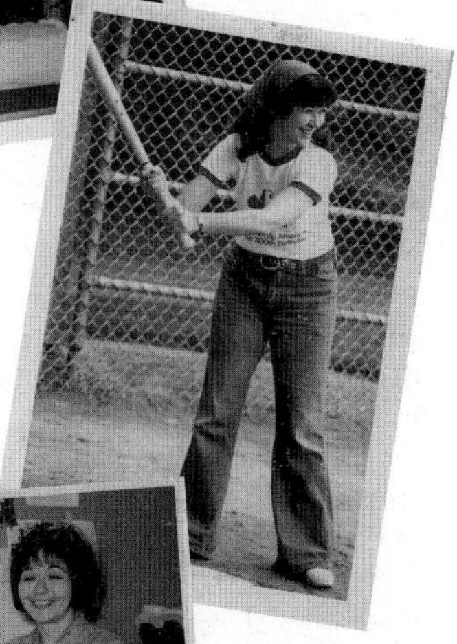

Sporty Flo in 1974

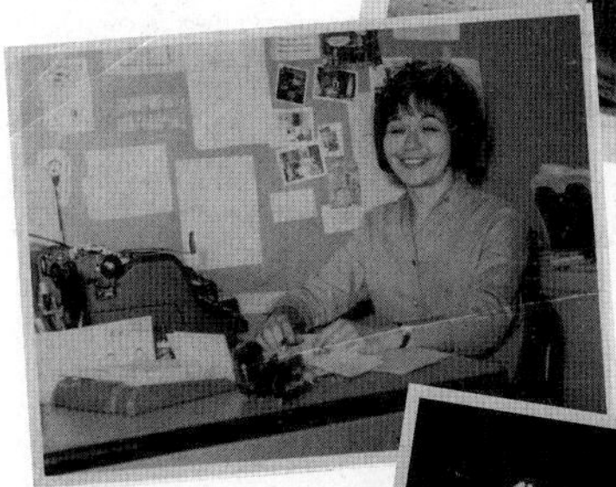

An exhausted, but cheerful Flo at the Marvel offices in the '60's

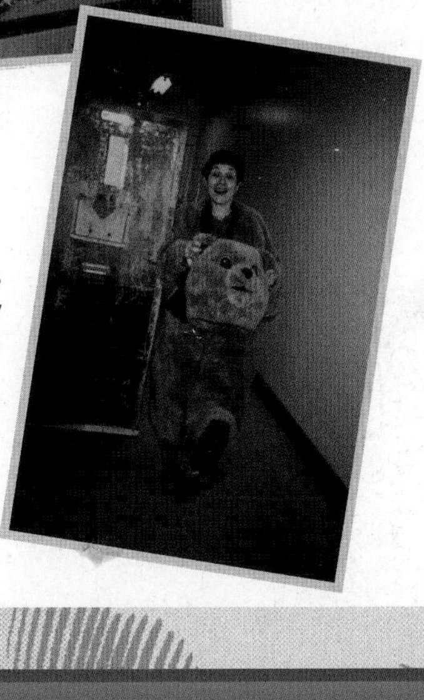

Flo all dressed up for a holiday gig!

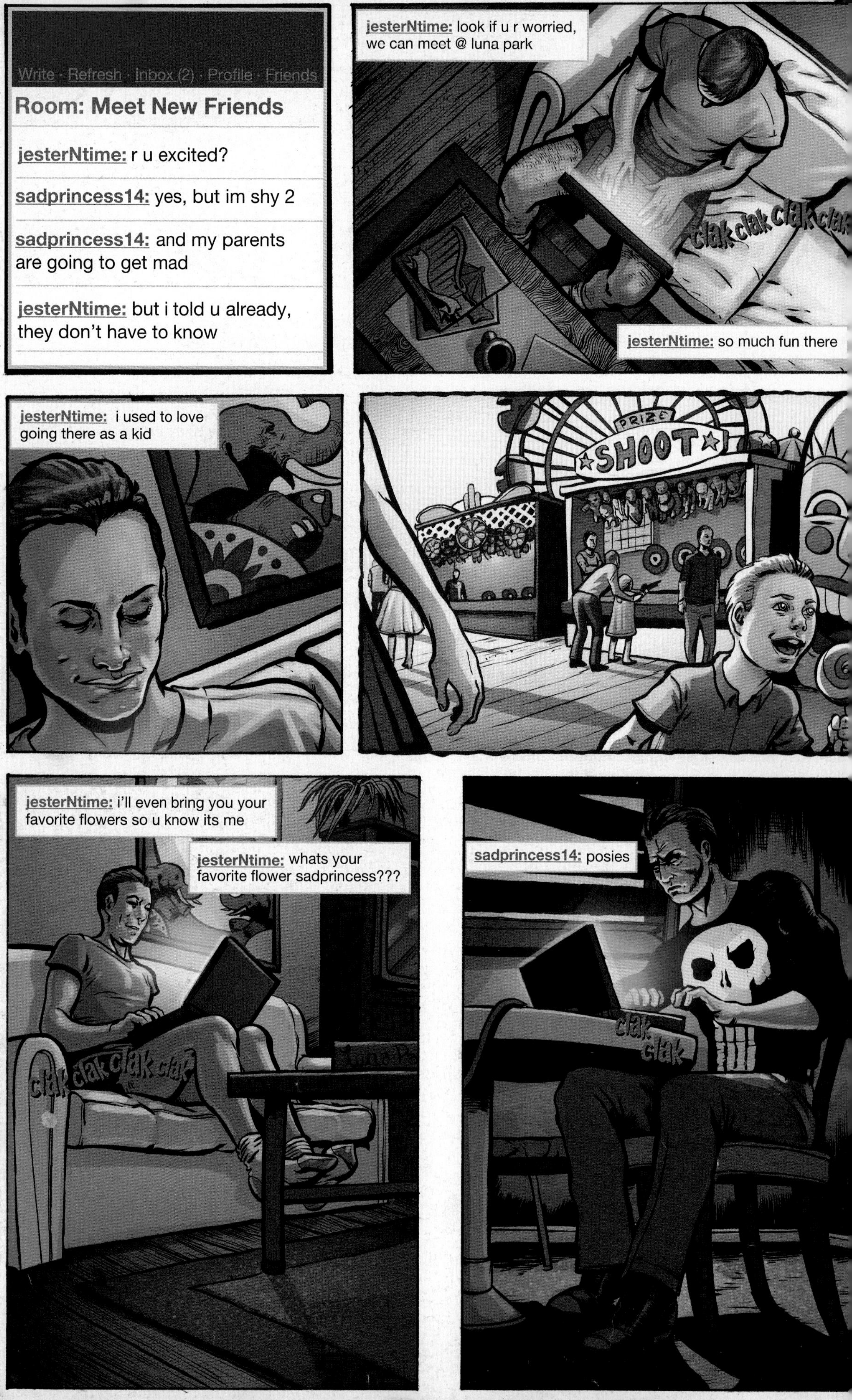
Write · Refresh · Inbox (2) · Profile · Friends
Room: Meet New Friends
jesterNtime: r u excited?
sadprincess14: yes, but im shy 2
sadprincess14: and my parents are going to get mad
jesterNtime: but i told u already, they don't have to know
jesterNtime: look if u r worried, we can meet @ luna park
clak clak clak clak
jesterNtime: so much fun there
jesterNtime: i used to love going there as a kid
PRIZE
SHOOT
jesterNtime: i'll even bring you your favorite flowers so u know its me
jesterNtime: whats your favorite flower sadprincess???
clak clak clak clak
sadprincess14: posies
clak clak

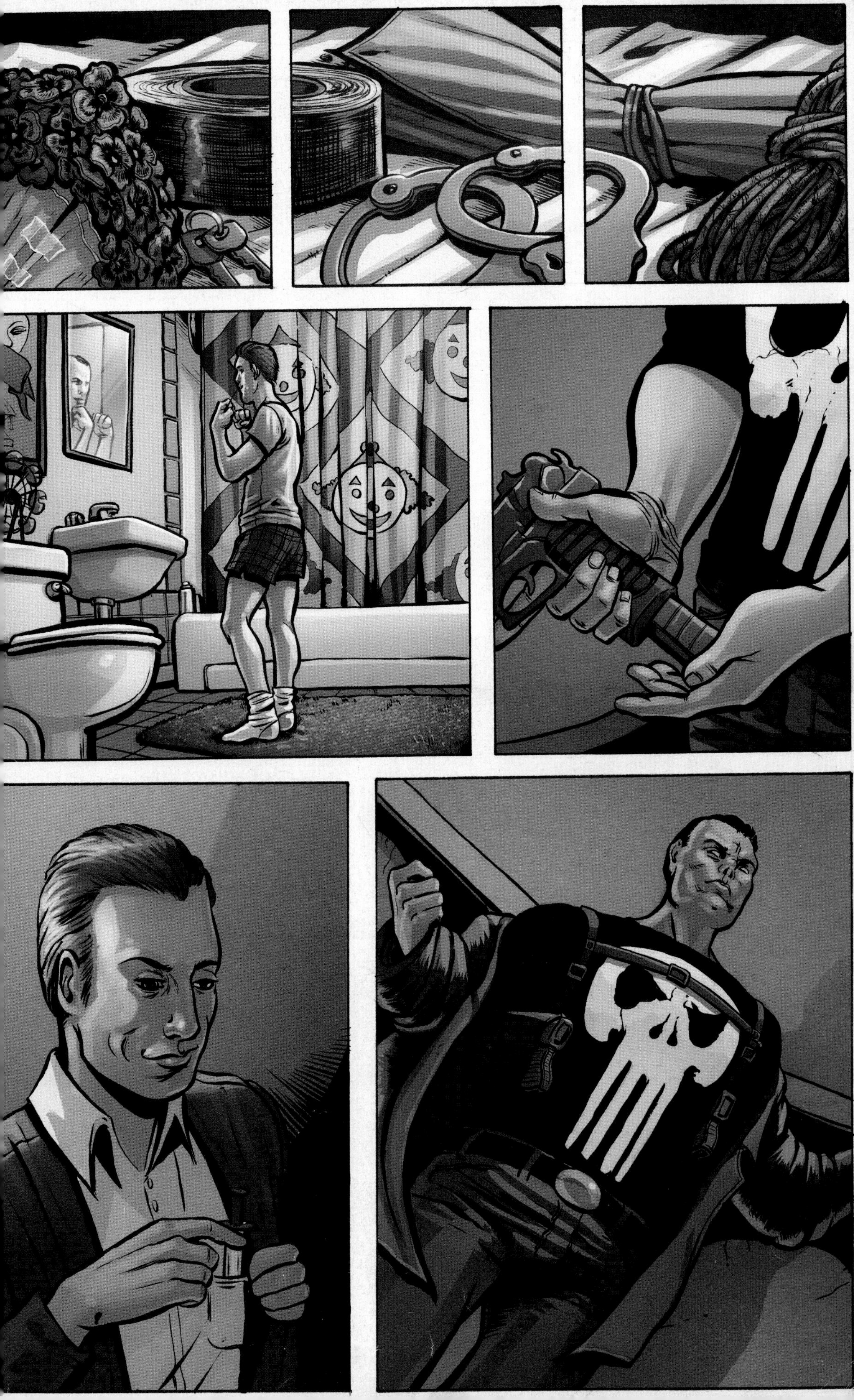

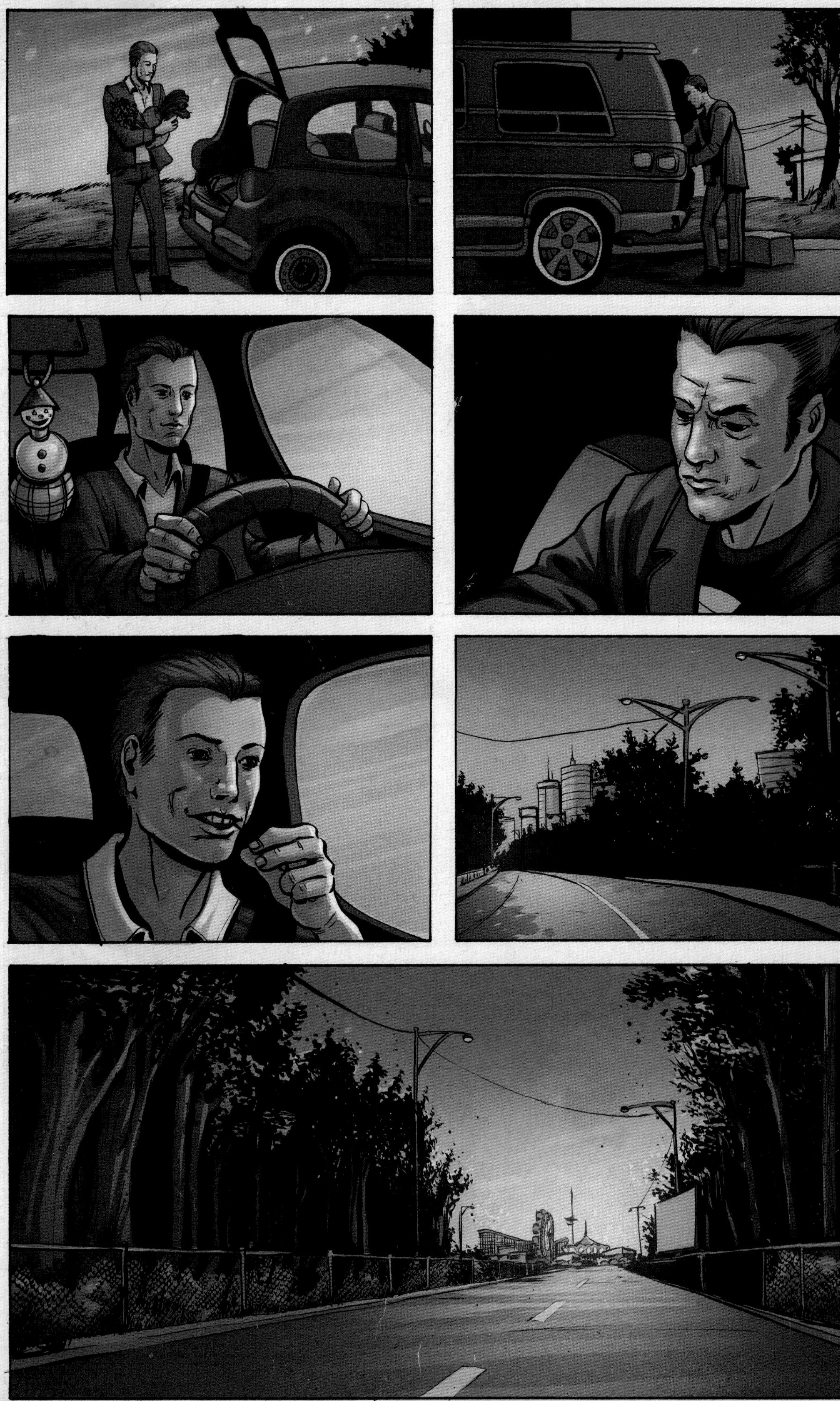

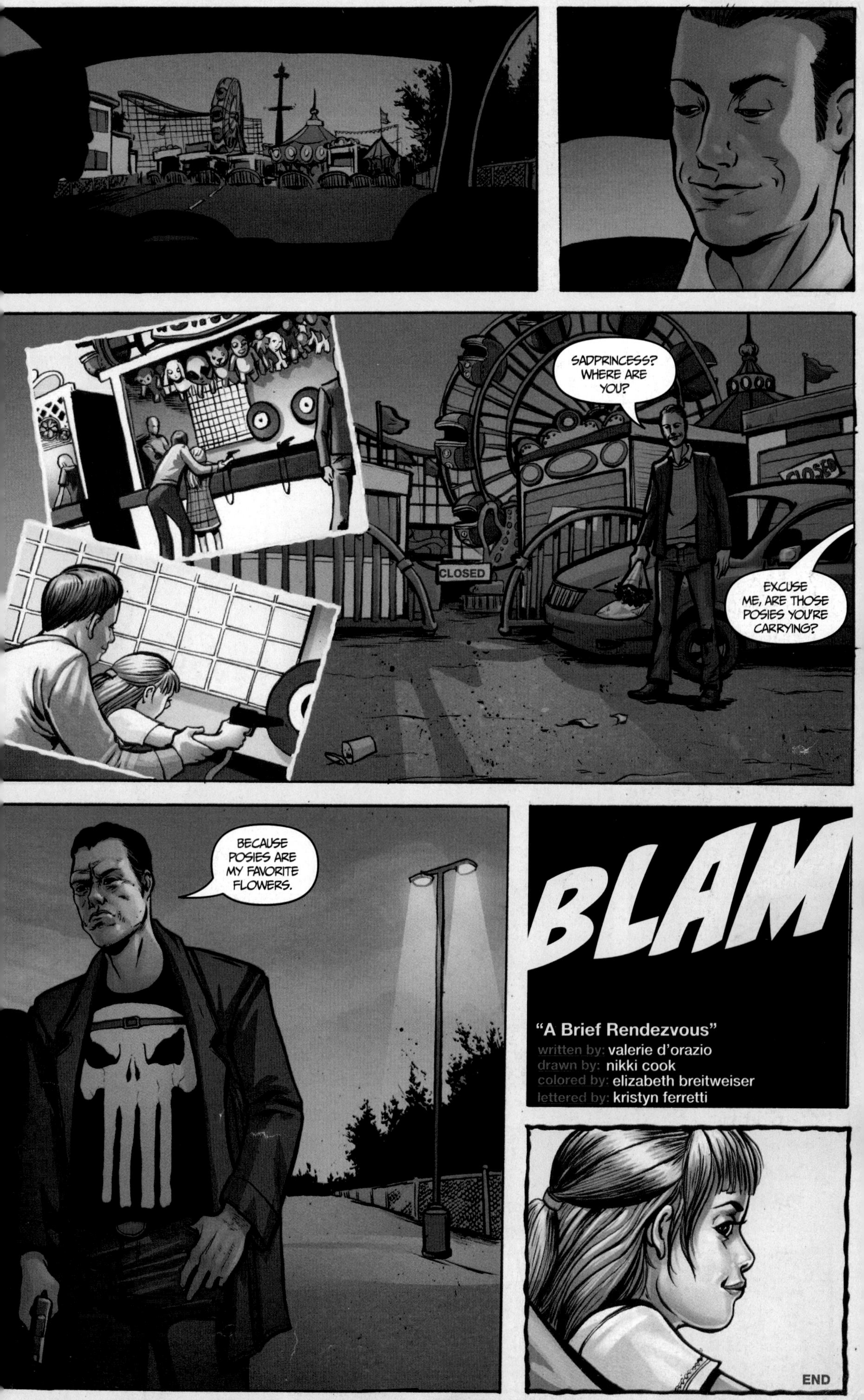

SADPRINCESS? WHERE ARE YOU?
CLOSED
CLOSED
EXCUSE ME, ARE THOSE POSIES YOU'RE CARRYING?
BECAUSE POSIES ARE MY FAVORITE FLOWERS.
BLAM
"A Brief Rendezvous"
written by: valerie d'orazio
drawn by: nikki cook
colored by: elizabeth breitweiser
lettered by: kristyn ferretti
END

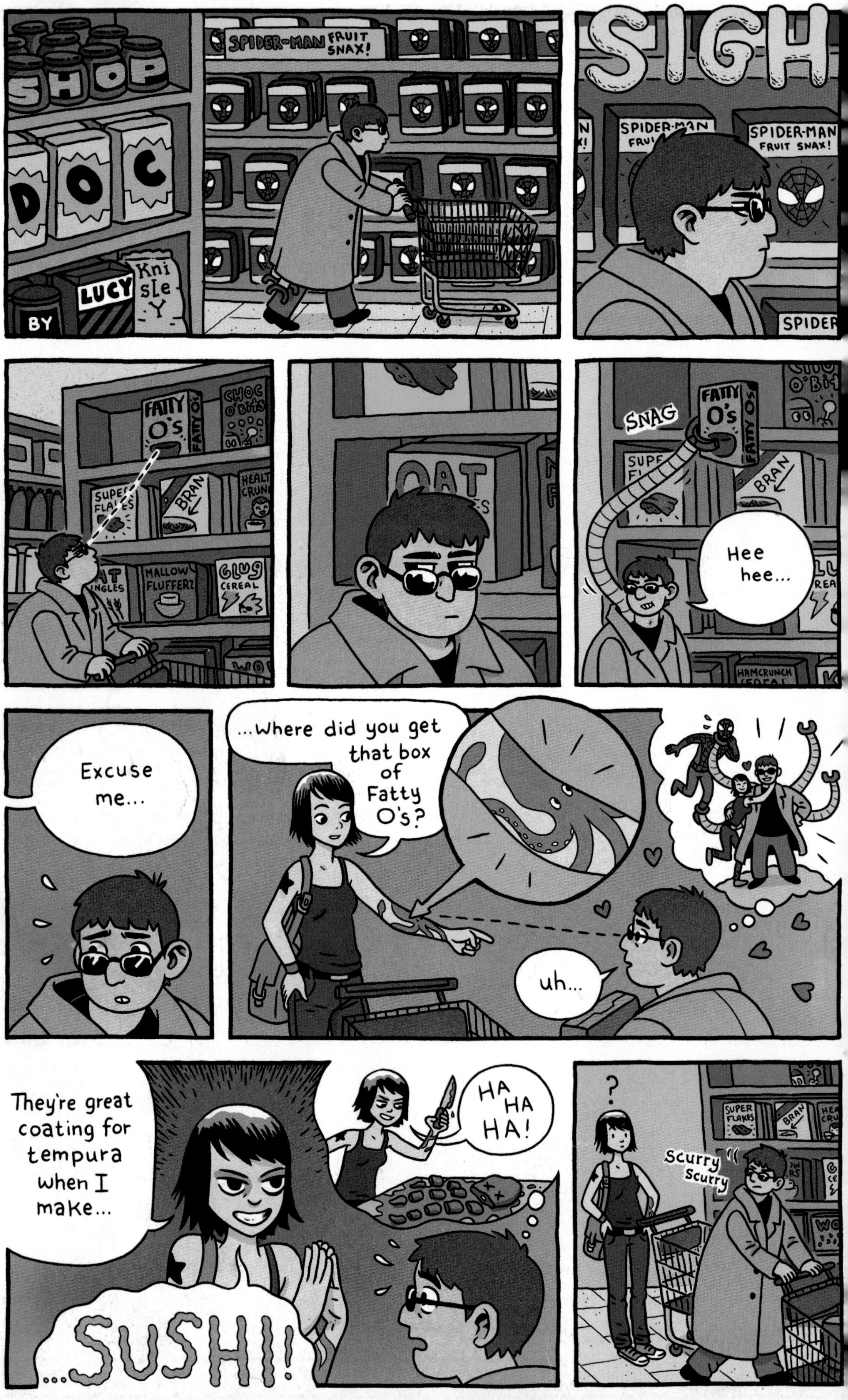
SHOP
DOC
BY
LUCY
Knisley
SPIDER-MAN FRUIT SNAX!
SIGH
SPIDER-MAN FRUIT SNAX!
FATTY O's
CHOC O'BITS
SUPER FLAKES
BRAN
HEALTH CRUNCH
MALLOW FLUFFERZ
GLUG CEREAL
OAT
SNAG
Hee hee...
HAMCRUNCH CEREAL
Excuse me...
...Where did you get that box of Fatty O's?
uh...
They're great coating for tempura when I make...
HA HA HA!
...SUSHI!
?
Scurry Scurry

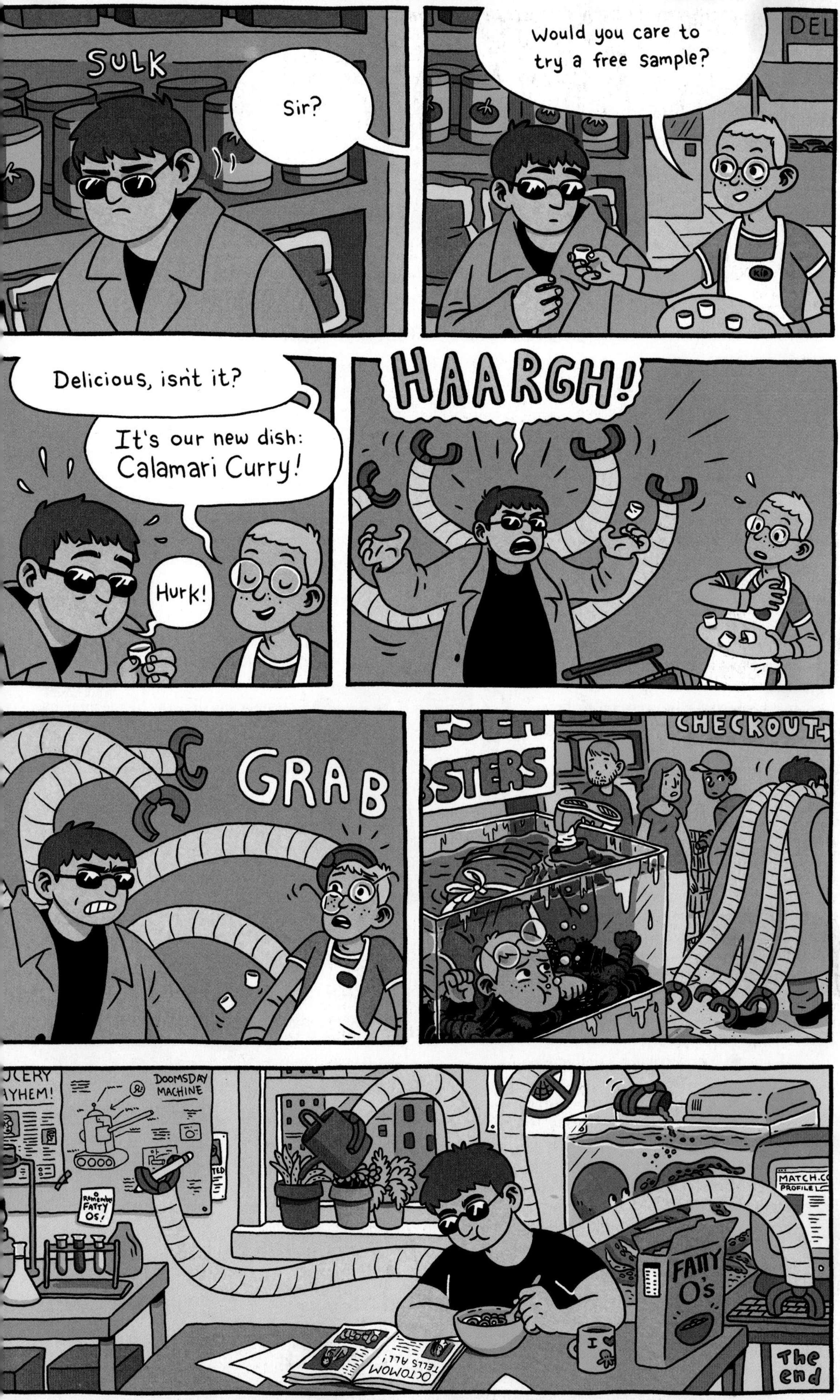
SULK
Sir?
Would you care to try a free sample?
Delicious, isn't it?
It's our new dish: Calamari Curry!
Hurk!
HAARGH!
GRAB
CHECKOUT
DOOMSDAY MACHINE
Remember FATTY Os!
MATCH.CO
PROFILE
FATTY O's
OCTOMOM TELLS ALL!
The end

SPOTLIGHT
Marie Severin

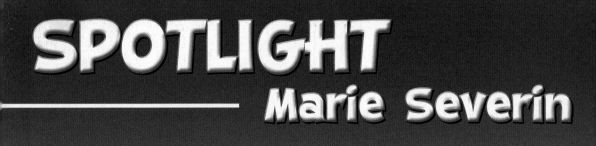

Marvel-ous Marie

Of all the creators that have graced the pages of Marvel history, Marie Severin has probably been one of the most prolific. In her tenure at Marvel, she has worked on almost every character in Marvel's database. Whether through colors, pencils, inks or production, Marie's sheer artistic omnipresence during Marvel's Silver Age is quite a feat. And that has nothing to do with her being one of the only women in the bullpen at the time.

Born to a family of artists, Marie was naturally artistically inclined and further developed her skills because of her family's encouragement. Her father was a designer for Elizabeth Arden, and her brother, John Severin, was also an artist who went on to be an important part of the Marvel family as well. After John's service in the army during World War II, he joined the Charles William and Harvey studio, a studio where comic artists came to work on their various industry assignments. The studio was in need of a colorist, and John encouraged his sister to join. Though she enrolled at Pratt Institute for a short time, Marie decided a more practical approach would benefit her talents more—and of course it was a bit more convenient to "make money while drawing instead of spending money to do the same thing." When Harvey Kurtzman, one of the studio's founders, became an editor at Entertainment Comics, he asked John and Marie to join his staff in 1949.

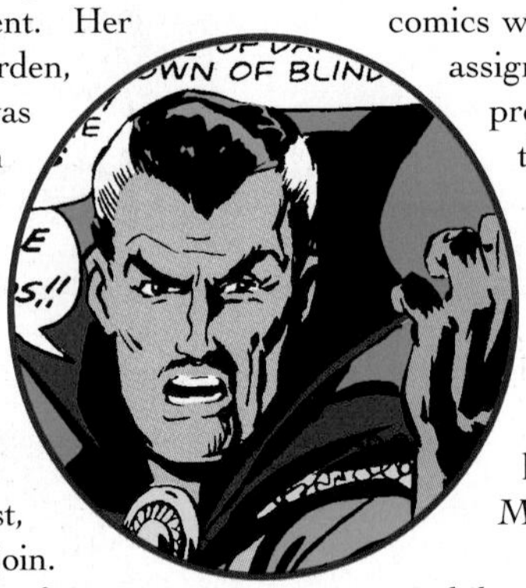

While at EC Comics, Marie learned the ins and outs of lettering, inking, coloring, and production, in addition to honing on her skills as a penciler. "I worked to learn, and ended up enjoying my work at the same time, so I stayed." Much of her work at EC was on the production end, but eventually she became the company's resident colorist—and resident female, as the sole woman in a group of male artists. Oddly enough though, Marie didn't seem to mind. "I was the only gal, but they all loved it when I colored their stuff. They didn't see my work as competition, but rather as a complement to theirs. It was wonderful." Her colleagues challenged and inspired her, and the work itself helped her style evolve. It was while she was working on Mad Magazine, one of EC's more prominent titles, that she perfected her ability to draw satire and humor, which she later became known for.

As EC Comics began to shift its focus to less mainstream content, Marie sought more traditional comics work and found freelance production assignments with Atlas Comics, Marvel's precursor. The industry as a whole was thrown into disarray by the infamous Comics Code ruling that put severe restrictions on acceptable content, and so work became limited. During this time Marie worked briefly for the Federal Reserve Bank, but by 1964 Stan Lee offered her a full-time production job at Marvel.

While at Marvel, Marie handled much of the in-house coloring, but her skills as an inker and penciler couldn't be ignored and Stan offered her the opportunity to take over from Steve Ditko on the "Doctor Strange" feature in *Strange Tales*. From there, she went on to draw titles like *Sub-Mariner*, *The Incredible Hulk*, *Tales to Astonish* and *Kull the Conquerer*, where she

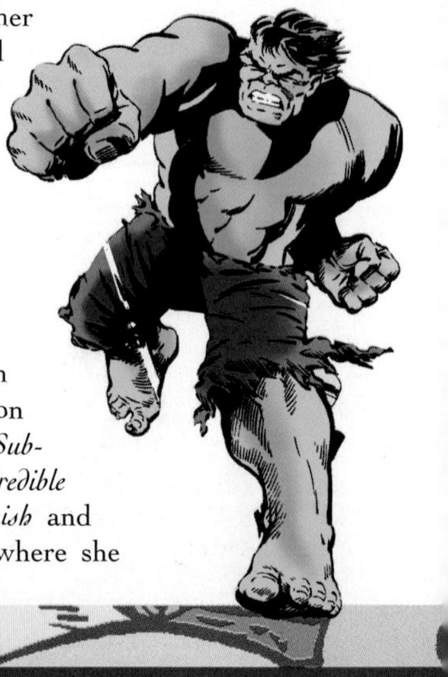

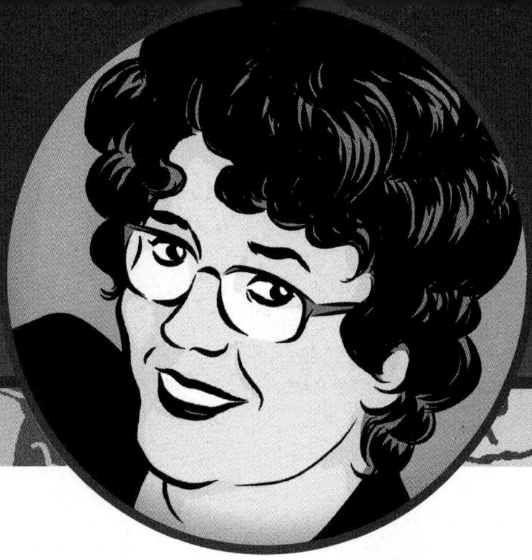

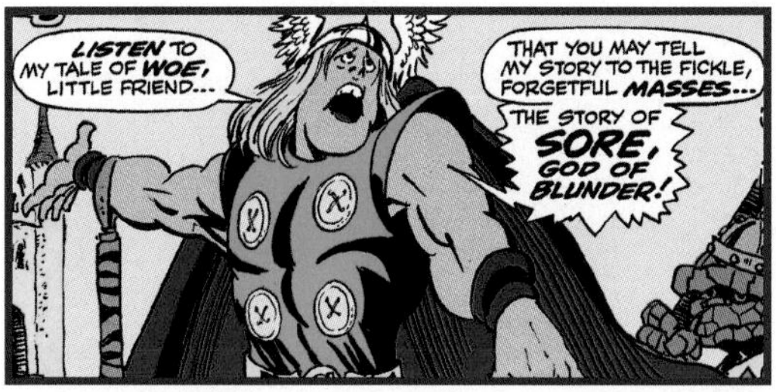
LISTEN TO MY TALE OF WOE, LITTLE FRIEND---
THAT YOU MAY TELL MY STORY TO THE FICKLE, FORGETFUL MASSES---
THE STORY OF SORE, GOD OF BLUNDER!

finally got to collaborate with her brother, John, who inked her pencils. Her flexibility and artistic diversity compelled the company to rely on her so heavily that at one point she became de facto art director, drawing the concepts for most of Marvel's covers.

In Marvel's parody series of itself, *Not Brand Echh*, Marie once again showcased her comedic sensibility. But Marvel's characters weren't the only ones subject to Marie's satiric wit; she became notorious for sketching caricatures of Marvel staffers, most famously a picture of Flo being bitten by a bunch of pit bulls characterized as Stan Lee, Roy Thomas, Sol Brodsky and Marie herself. These images relay the chaos of the times, but also the amusement and inside jokes they shared. "Oh, there were times I wanted to rip people's heads off, but we just had a good time teasing each other," she's said, chuckling.

"I was the only gal, but they all loved it when I colored their stuff. They didn't see my work as competition, but rather as a complement to theirs. It was wonderful."

As the years of Marvel's Silver Age came to a close, Marie stayed on in the special projects division working on licensing. Though she's no longer at Marvel, her presence has been long felt in the company and the industry as a whole, not only as one of its first female artists, but simply as one of its most prominent creators.

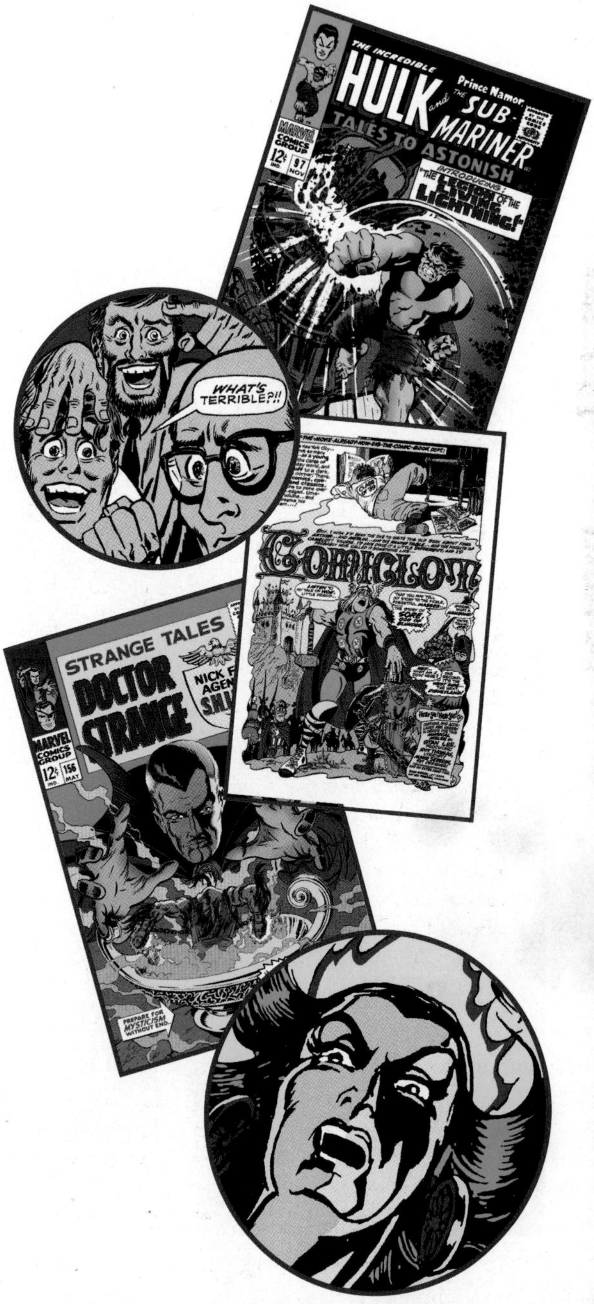
THE INCREDIBLE HULK and THE SUB-MARINER
Prince Namor
TALES TO ASTONISH
MARVEL COMICS GROUP
12¢ 97 NOV
WHAT'S TERRIBLE?!!
STRANGE TALES
DOCTOR STRANGE
MARVEL COMICS GROUP
12¢ 156 MAY
PREPARE FOR MYSTICISM WITHOUT END...

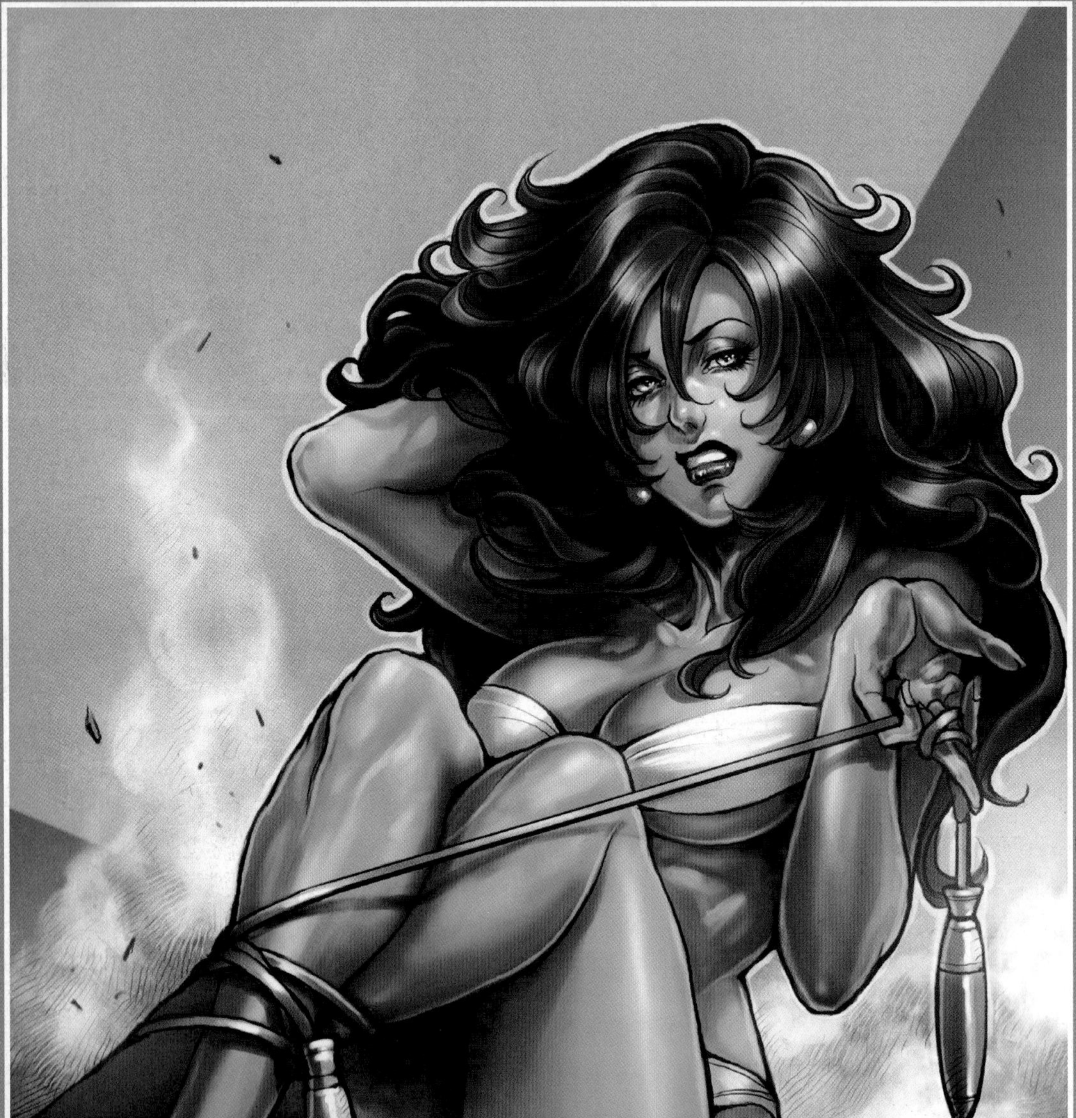

HAPPY ANNIVERSARY,
SHE-HULK!
PIN-UP BY SANA TAKEDA

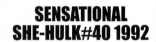

SENSATIONAL SHE-HULK#40 1992

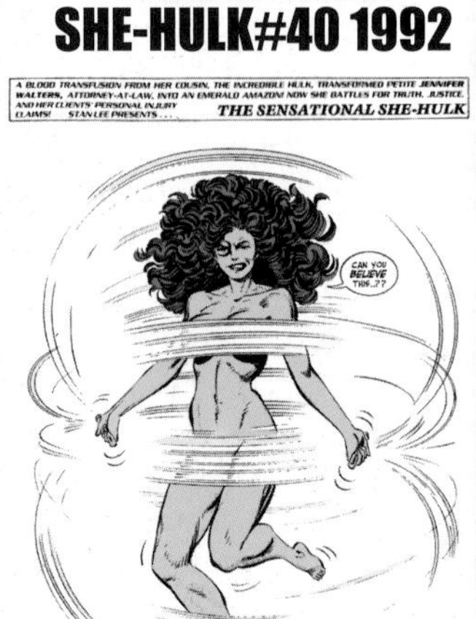
A BLOOD TRANSFUSION FROM HER COUSIN, THE INCREDIBLE HULK, TRANSFORMED PETITE JENNIFER WALTERS, ATTORNEY-AT-LAW, INTO AN EMERALD AMAZON! NOW SHE BATTLES FOR TRUTH, JUSTICE, AND HER CLIENTS' PERSONAL INJURY CLAIMS! STAN LEE PRESENTS . . .
THE SENSATIONAL SHE-HULK
CAN YOU BELIEVE THIS..??
JOHN BYRNE
WRITER/ARTIST
GLYNIS OLIVER
COLORIST
RENÉE WITTERSTAETTER
EDITOR
TOM DEFALCO
EDITOR IN CHIEF

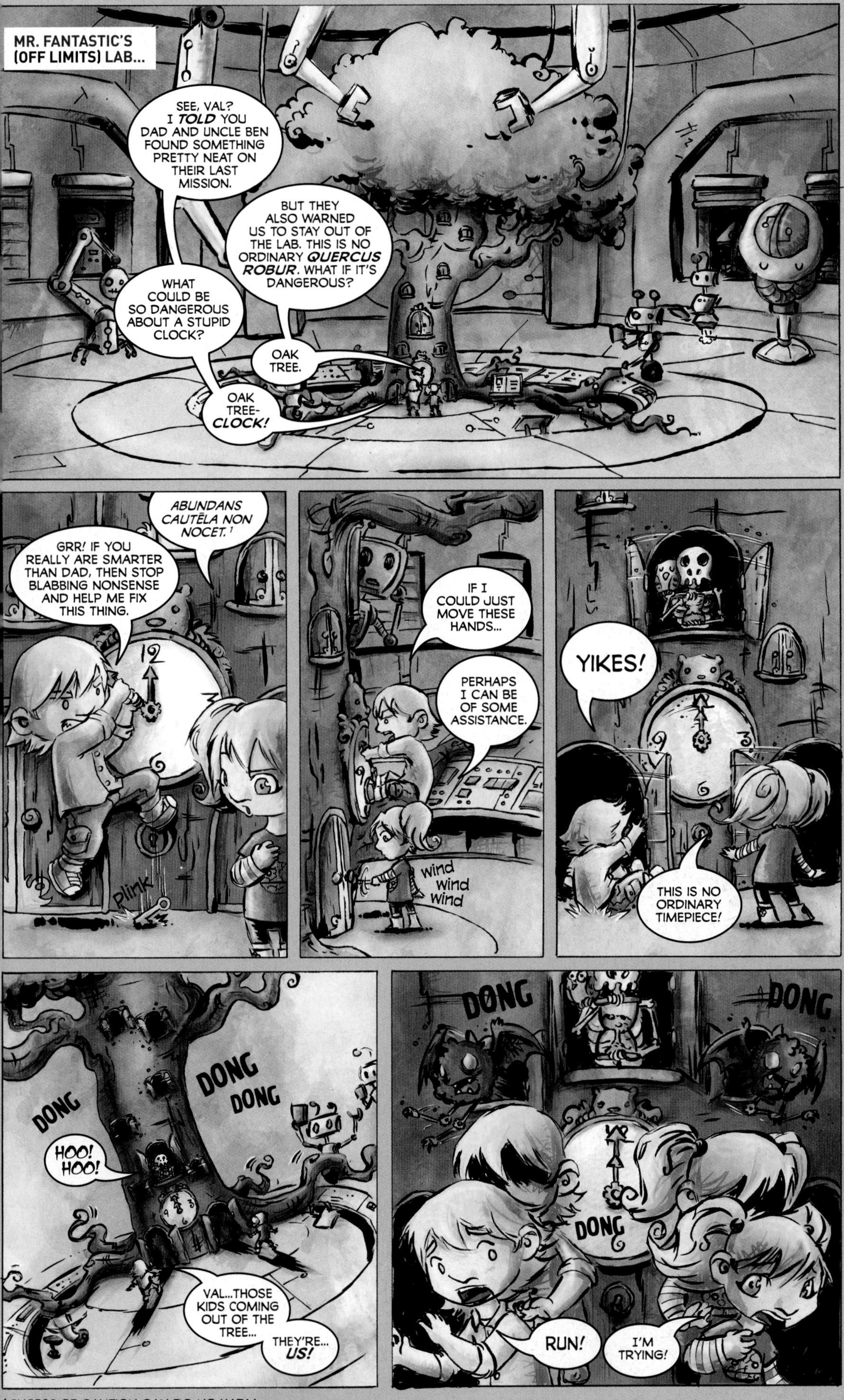
MR. FANTASTIC'S (OFF LIMITS) LAB...
SEE, VAL? I TOLD YOU DAD AND UNCLE BEN FOUND SOMETHING PRETTY NEAT ON THEIR LAST MISSION.
BUT THEY ALSO WARNED US TO STAY OUT OF THE LAB. THIS IS NO ORDINARY QUERCUS ROBUR. WHAT IF IT'S DANGEROUS?
WHAT COULD BE SO DANGEROUS ABOUT A STUPID CLOCK?
OAK TREE.
OAK TREE-CLOCK!
ABUNDANS CAUTĒLA NON NOCET.[1]
GRR! IF YOU REALLY ARE SMARTER THAN DAD, THEN STOP BLABBING NONSENSE AND HELP ME FIX THIS THING.
plink
IF I COULD JUST MOVE THESE HANDS...
PERHAPS I CAN BE OF SOME ASSISTANCE.
wind wind wind
YIKES!
THIS IS NO ORDINARY TIMEPIECE!
DONG
DONG DONG
HOO! HOO!
VAL...THOSE KIDS COMING OUT OF THE TREE...
THEY'RE... US!
DONG
DONG
DONG
RUN!
I'M TRYING!

[1] EXCESS OF CAUTION CAN DO NO HARM.

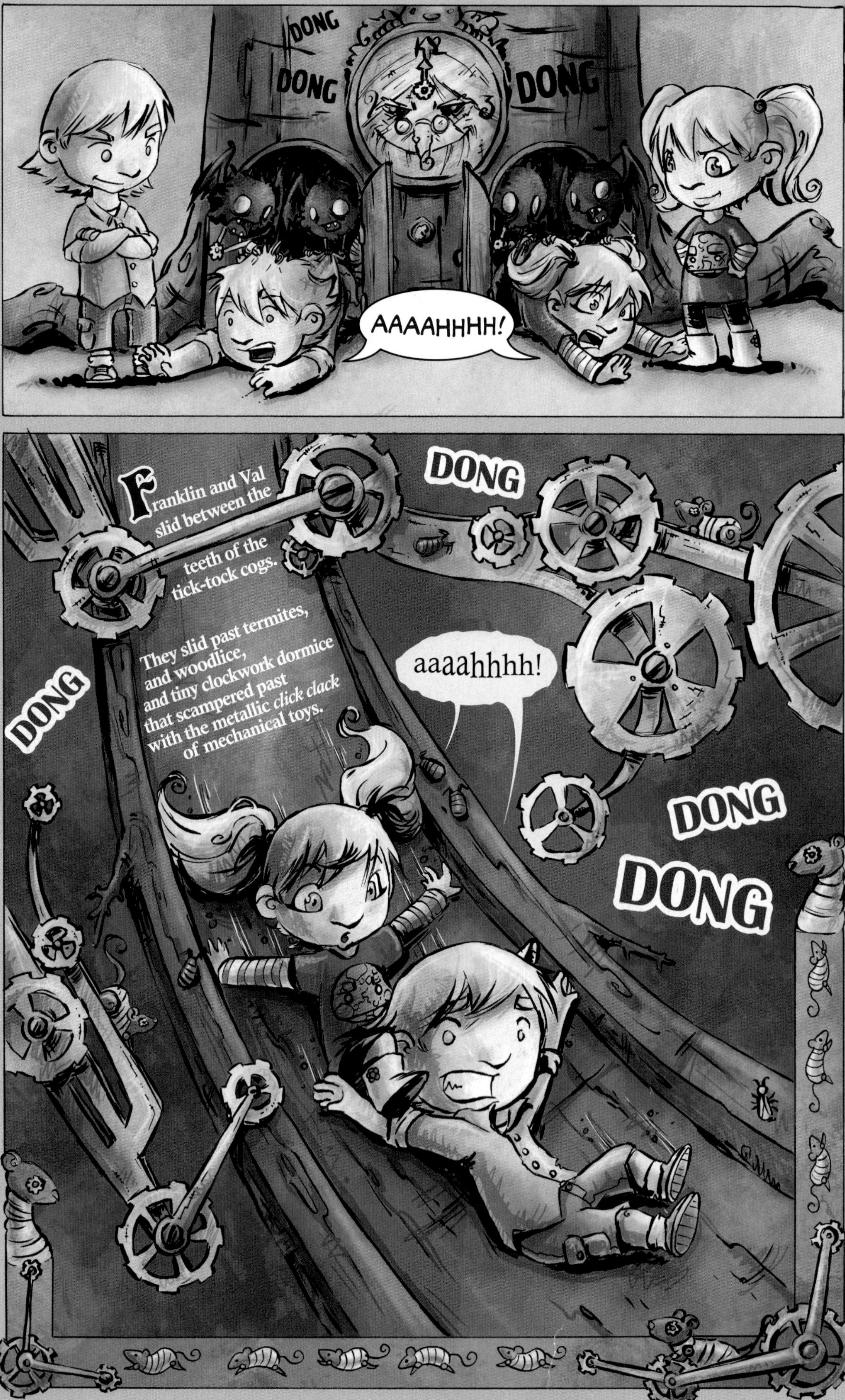
DONG
DONG
DONG
AAAAHHHH!
Franklin and Val slid between the teeth of the tick-tock cogs.
They slid past termites, and woodlice, and tiny clockwork dormice that scampered past with the metallic *click clack* of mechanical toys.
DONG
DONG
aaaahhhh!
DONG
DONG

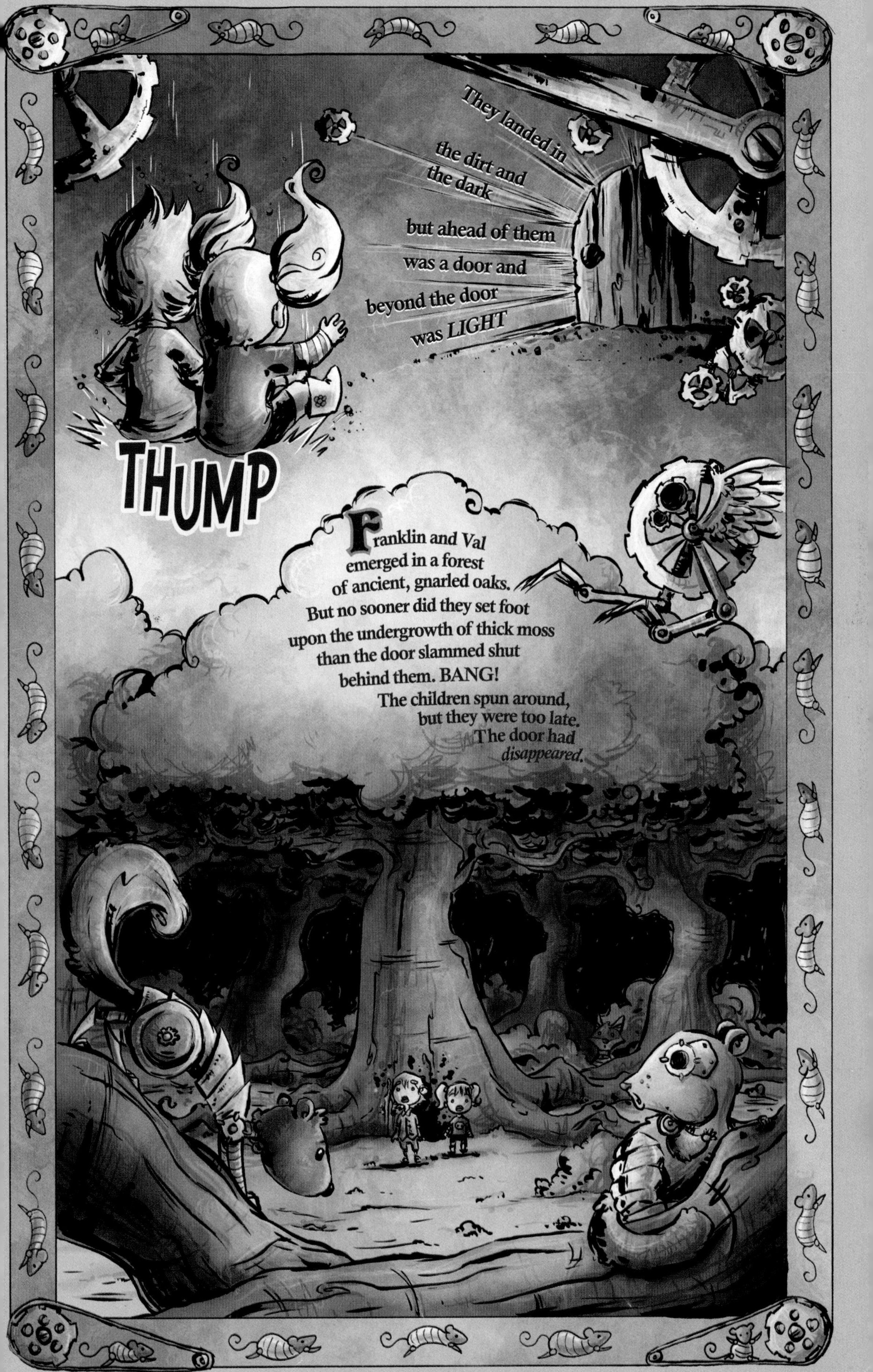

They landed in
the dirt and
the dark
but ahead of them
was a door and
beyond the door
was *LIGHT*
THUMP
Franklin and Val
emerged in a forest
of ancient, gnarled oaks.
But no sooner did they set foot
upon the undergrowth of thick moss
than the door slammed shut
behind them. BANG!
The children spun around,
but they were too late.
The door had
disappeared.

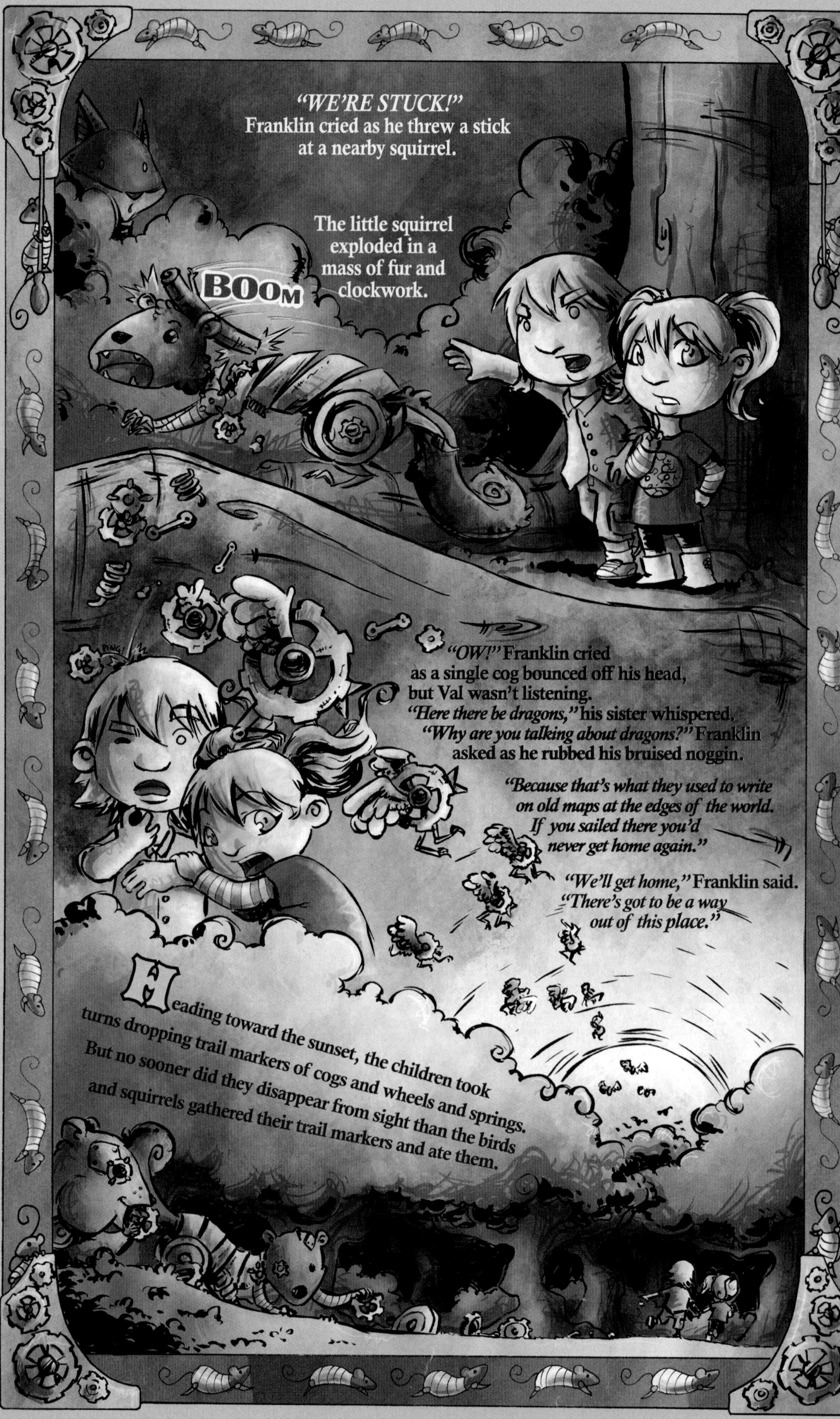

"WE'RE STUCK!"
Franklin cried as he threw a stick at a nearby squirrel.
The little squirrel exploded in a mass of fur and clockwork.
BOOM
PING!
"OW!" Franklin cried as a single cog bounced off his head, but Val wasn't listening.
"Here there be dragons," his sister whispered.
"Why are you talking about dragons?" Franklin asked as he rubbed his bruised noggin.
"Because that's what they used to write on old maps at the edges of the world. If you sailed there you'd never get home again."
"We'll get home," Franklin said. *"There's got to be a way out of this place."*
Heading toward the sunset, the children took turns dropping trail markers of cogs and wheels and springs. But no sooner did they disappear from sight than the birds and squirrels gathered their trail markers and ate them.

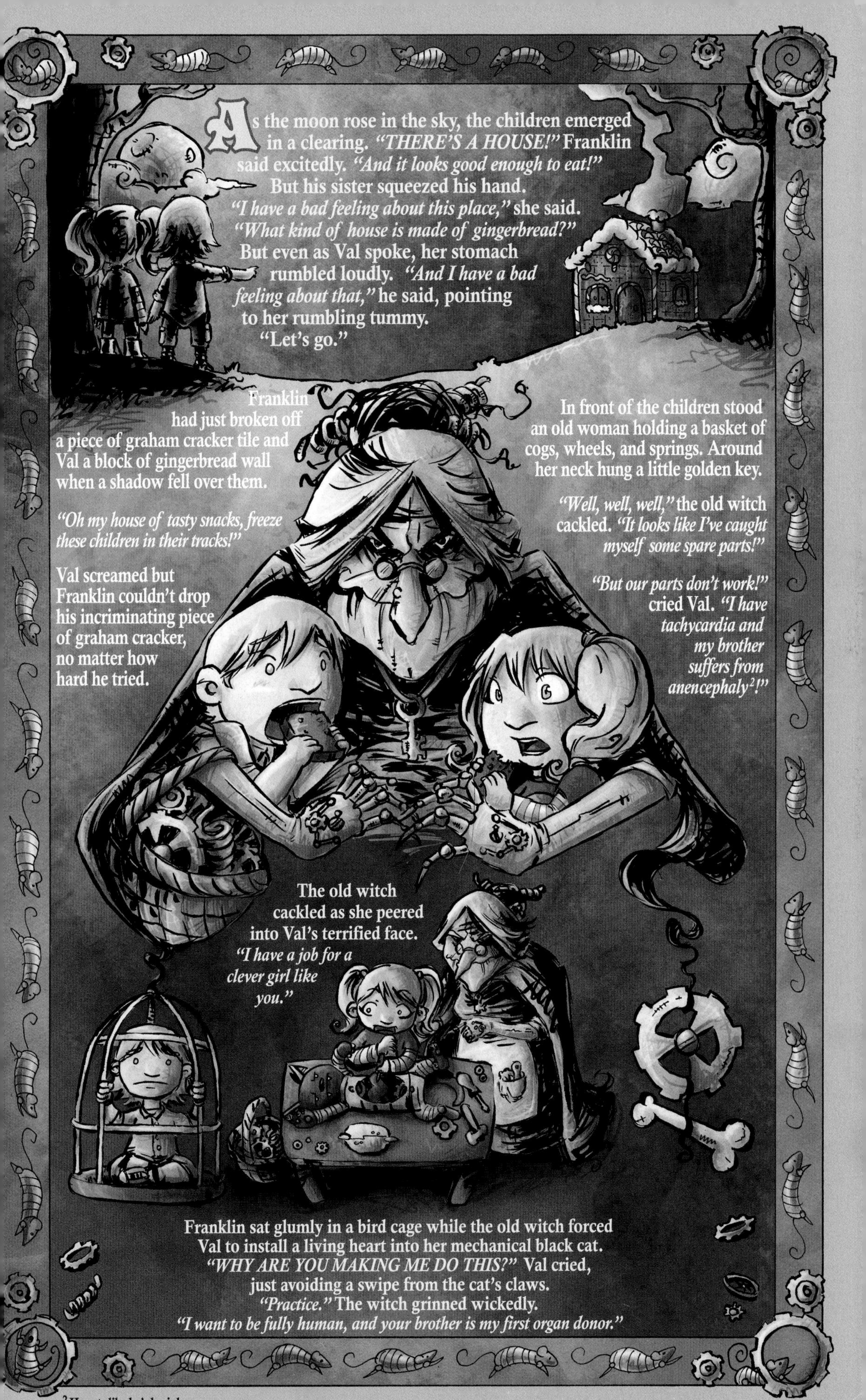
As the moon rose in the sky, the children emerged in a clearing. *"THERE'S A HOUSE!"* Franklin said excitedly. *"And it looks good enough to eat!"*
But his sister squeezed his hand.
"I have a bad feeling about this place," she said. *"What kind of house is made of gingerbread?"*
But even as Val spoke, her stomach rumbled loudly. *"And I have a bad feeling about that,"* he said, pointing to her rumbling tummy.
"Let's go."
Franklin had just broken off a piece of graham cracker tile and Val a block of gingerbread wall when a shadow fell over them.
"Oh my house of tasty snacks, freeze these children in their tracks!"
Val screamed but Franklin couldn't drop his incriminating piece of graham cracker, no matter how hard he tried.
In front of the children stood an old woman holding a basket of cogs, wheels, and springs. Around her neck hung a little golden key.
"Well, well, well," the old witch cackled. *"It looks like I've caught myself some spare parts!"*
"But our parts don't work!" cried Val. *"I have tachycardia and my brother suffers from anencephaly[2]!"*
The old witch cackled as she peered into Val's terrified face.
"I have a job for a clever girl like you."
Franklin sat glumly in a bird cage while the old witch forced Val to install a living heart into her mechanical black cat.
"WHY ARE YOU MAKING ME DO THIS?" Val cried, just avoiding a swipe from the cat's claws.
"Practice." The witch grinned wickedly.
"I want to be fully human, and your brother is my first organ donor."

[2] He acts like he's brainless.

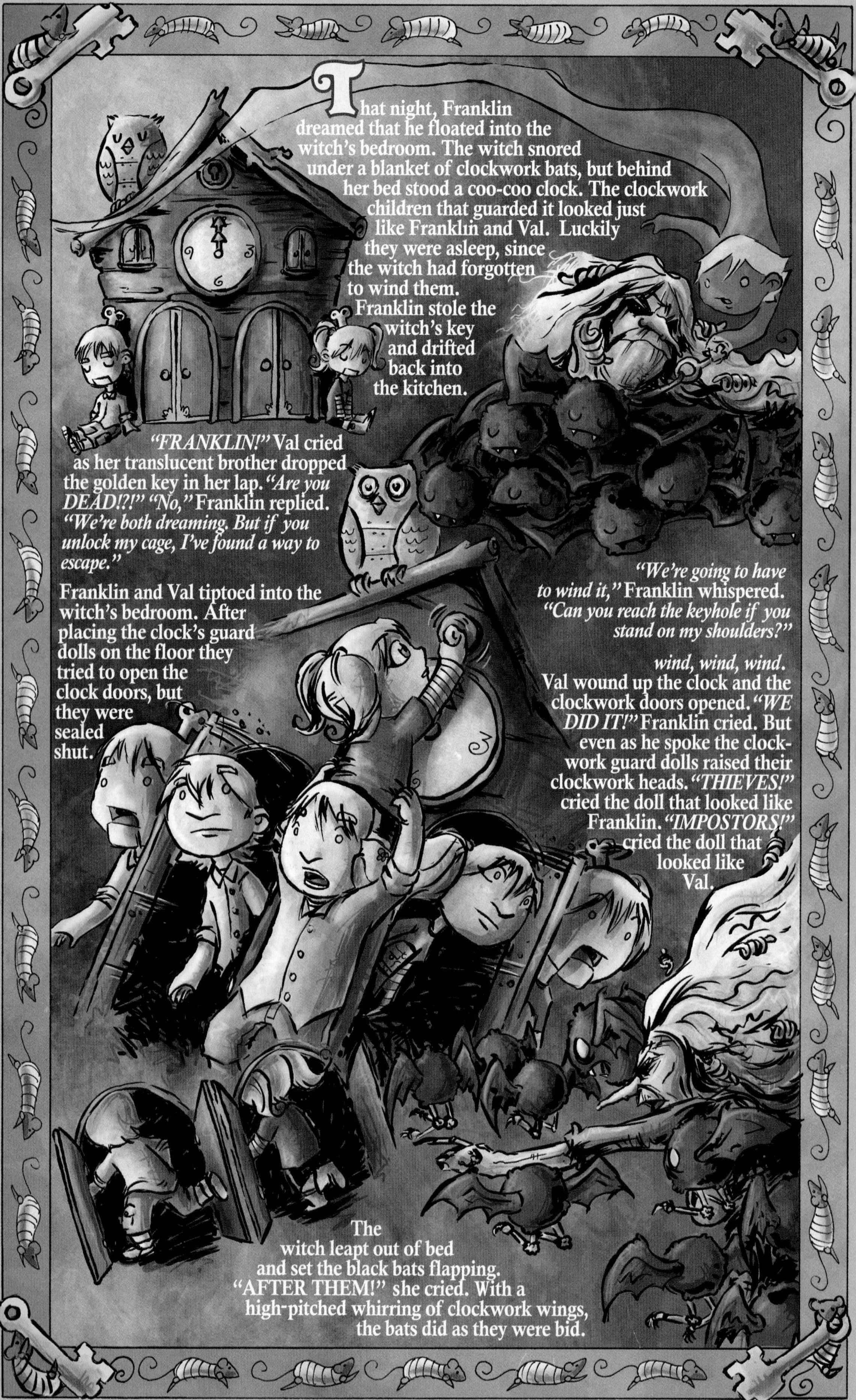
That night, Franklin dreamed that he floated into the witch's bedroom. The witch snored under a blanket of clockwork bats, but behind her bed stood a coo-coo clock. The clockwork children that guarded it looked just like Franklin and Val. Luckily they were asleep, since the witch had forgotten to wind them. Franklin stole the witch's key and drifted back into the kitchen.
"FRANKLIN!" Val cried as her translucent brother dropped the golden key in her lap. *"Are you DEAD!?!"* *"No,"* Franklin replied. *"We're both dreaming. But if you unlock my cage, I've found a way to escape."*
Franklin and Val tiptoed into the witch's bedroom. After placing the clock's guard dolls on the floor they tried to open the clock doors, but they were sealed shut.
"We're going to have to wind it," Franklin whispered. *"Can you reach the keyhole if you stand on my shoulders?"*
wind, wind, wind.
Val wound up the clock and the clockwork doors opened. *"WE DID IT!"* Franklin cried. But even as he spoke the clock-work guard dolls raised their clockwork heads. *"THIEVES!"* cried the doll that looked like Franklin. *"IMPOSTORS!"* cried the doll that looked like Val.
The witch leapt out of bed and set the black bats flapping. "AFTER THEM!" she cried. With a high-pitched whirring of clockwork wings, the bats did as they were bid.

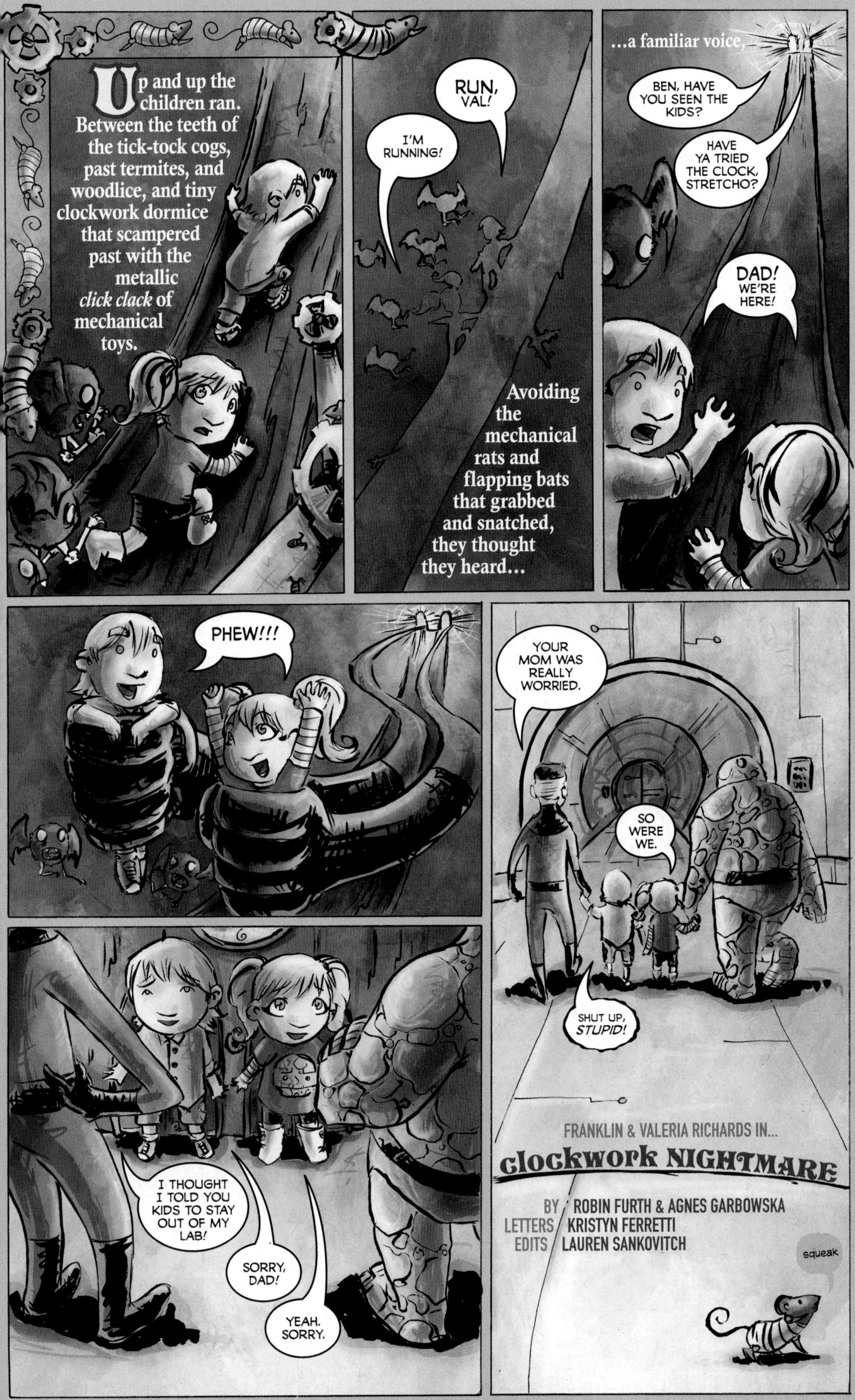
Up and up the children ran. Between the teeth of the tick-tock cogs, past termites, and woodlice, and tiny clockwork dormice that scampered past with the metallic *click clack* of mechanical toys.
RUN, VAL!
I'M RUNNING!
Avoiding the mechanical rats and flapping bats that grabbed and snatched, they thought they heard...
...a familiar voice,
BEN, HAVE YOU SEEN THE KIDS?
HAVE YA TRIED THE CLOCK, STRETCHO?
DAD! WE'RE HERE!
PHEW!!!
YOUR MOM WAS REALLY WORRIED.
SO WERE WE.
SHUT UP, *STUPID!*
I THOUGHT I TOLD YOU KIDS TO STAY OUT OF MY LAB!
SORRY, DAD!
YEAH. SORRY.
FRANKLIN & VALERIA RICHARDS IN...
Clockwork NIGHTMARE
BY ROBIN FURTH & AGNES GARBOWSKA
LETTERS KRISTYN FERRETTI
EDITS LAUREN SANKOVITCH
squeak

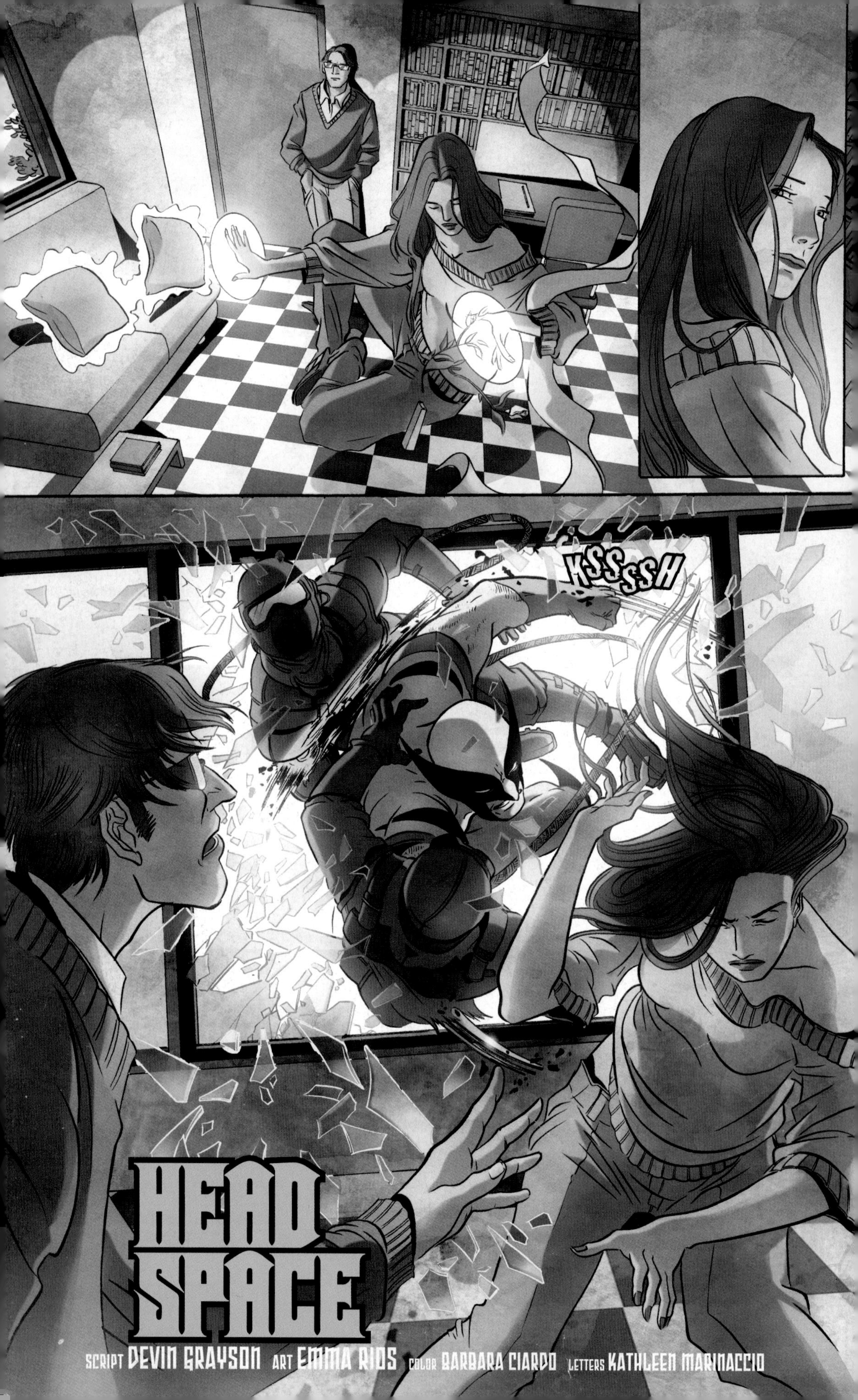
KSSSSH
HEAD SPACE
SCRIPT DEVIN GRAYSON ART EMMA RIOS COLOR BARBARA CIARDO LETTERS KATHLEEN MARINACCIO

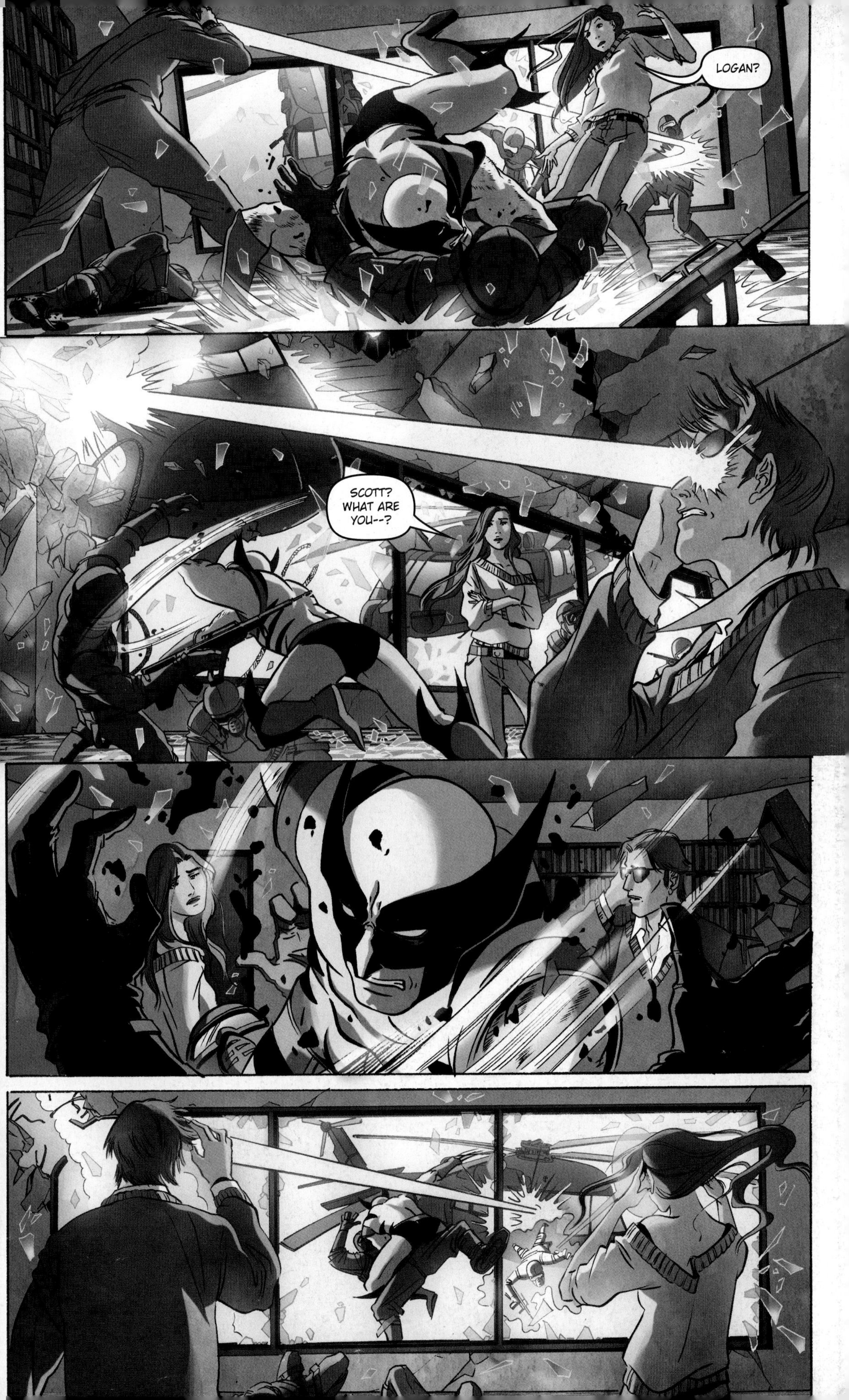
LOGAN?
SCOTT? WHAT ARE YOU--?

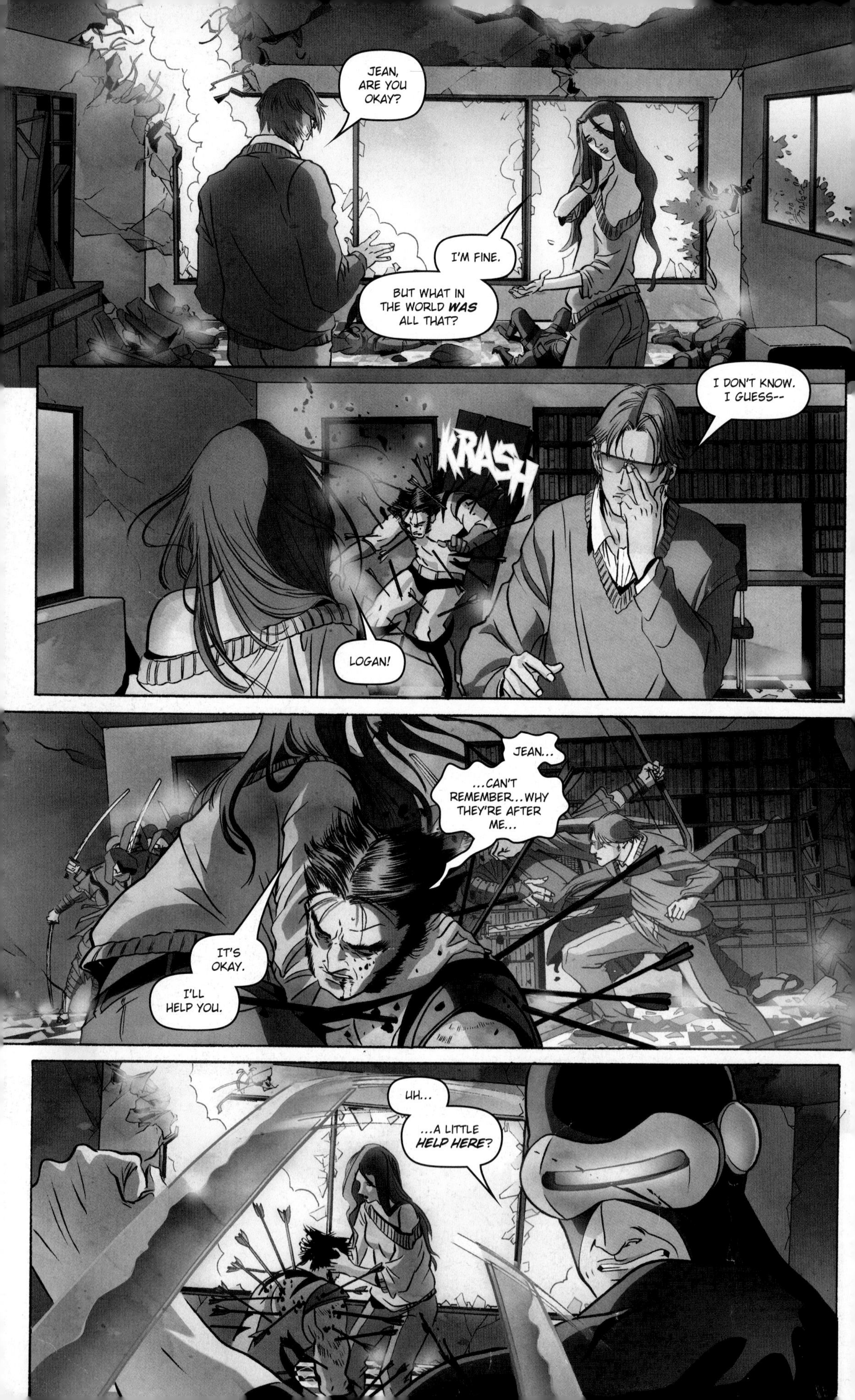

JEAN, ARE YOU OKAY?
I'M FINE.
BUT WHAT IN THE WORLD WAS ALL THAT?
I DON'T KNOW. I GUESS--
KRASH
LOGAN!
JEAN...
...CAN'T REMEMBER...WHY THEY'RE AFTER ME...
IT'S OKAY.
I'LL HELP YOU.
UH...
...A LITTLE HELP HERE?

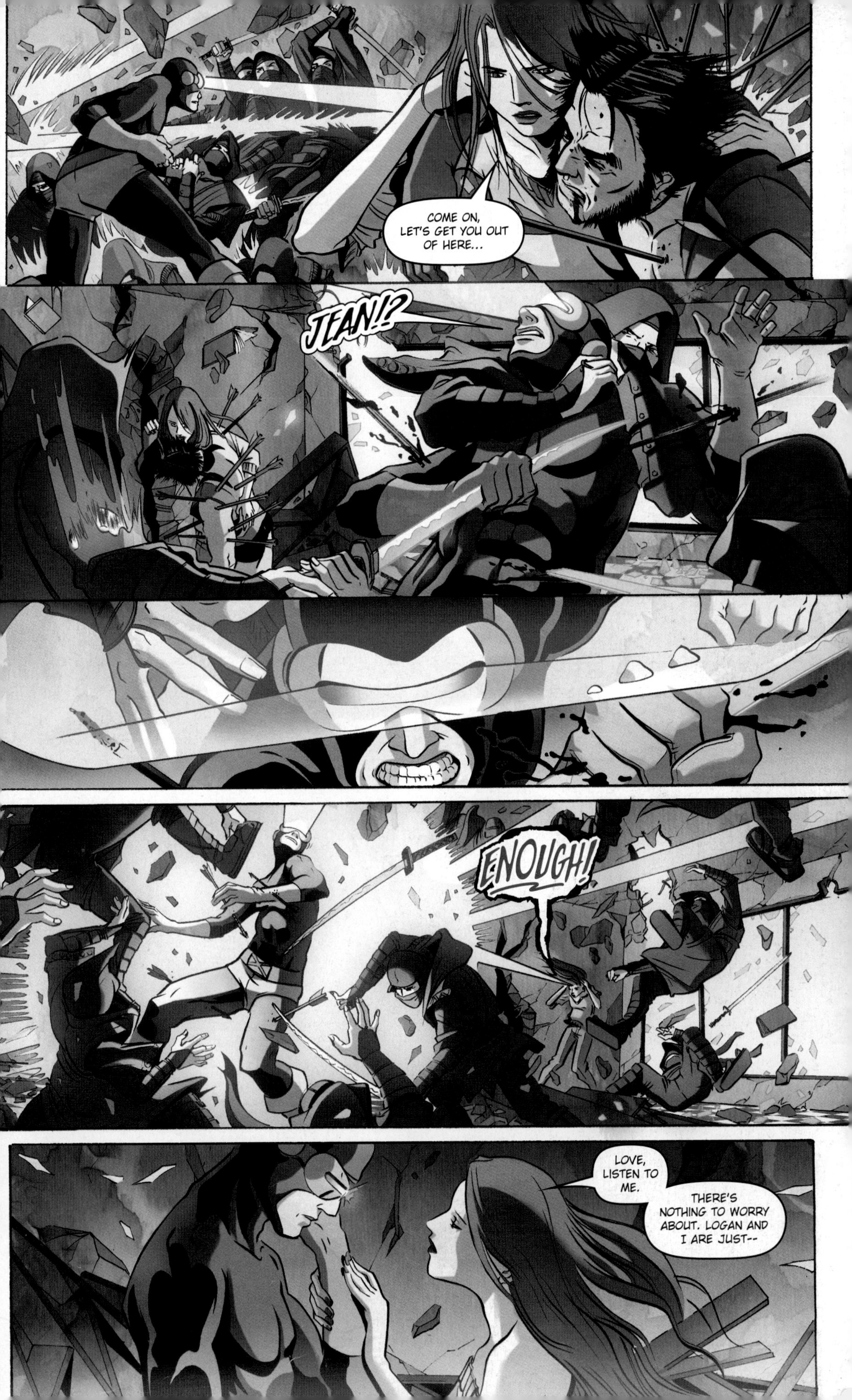
COME ON, LET'S GET YOU OUT OF HERE...
JEAN!?
ENOUGH!
LOVE, LISTEN TO ME.
THERE'S NOTHING TO WORRY ABOUT. LOGAN AND I ARE JUST--

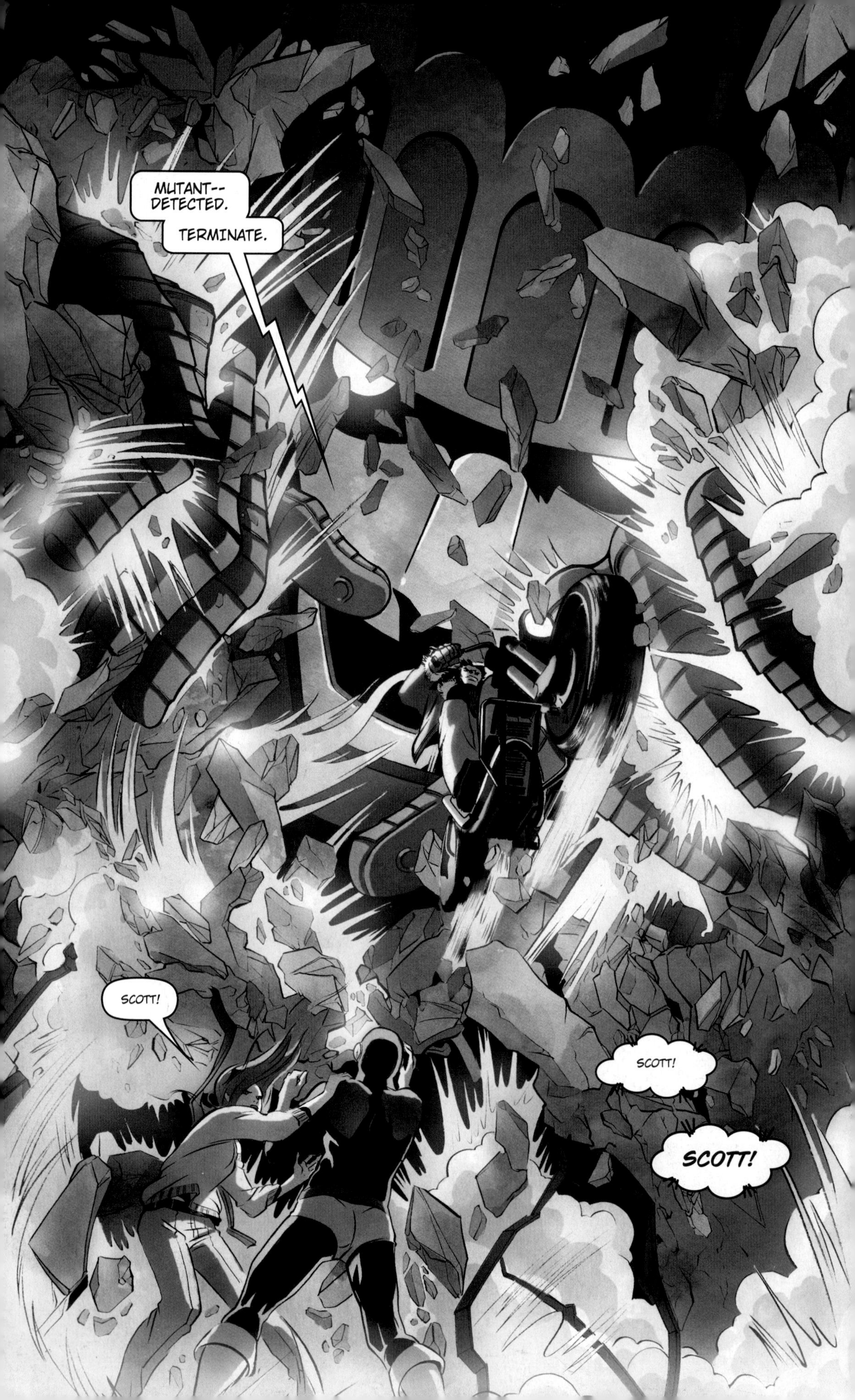
MUTANT--
DETECTED.
TERMINATE.
SCOTT!
SCOTT!
SCOTT!

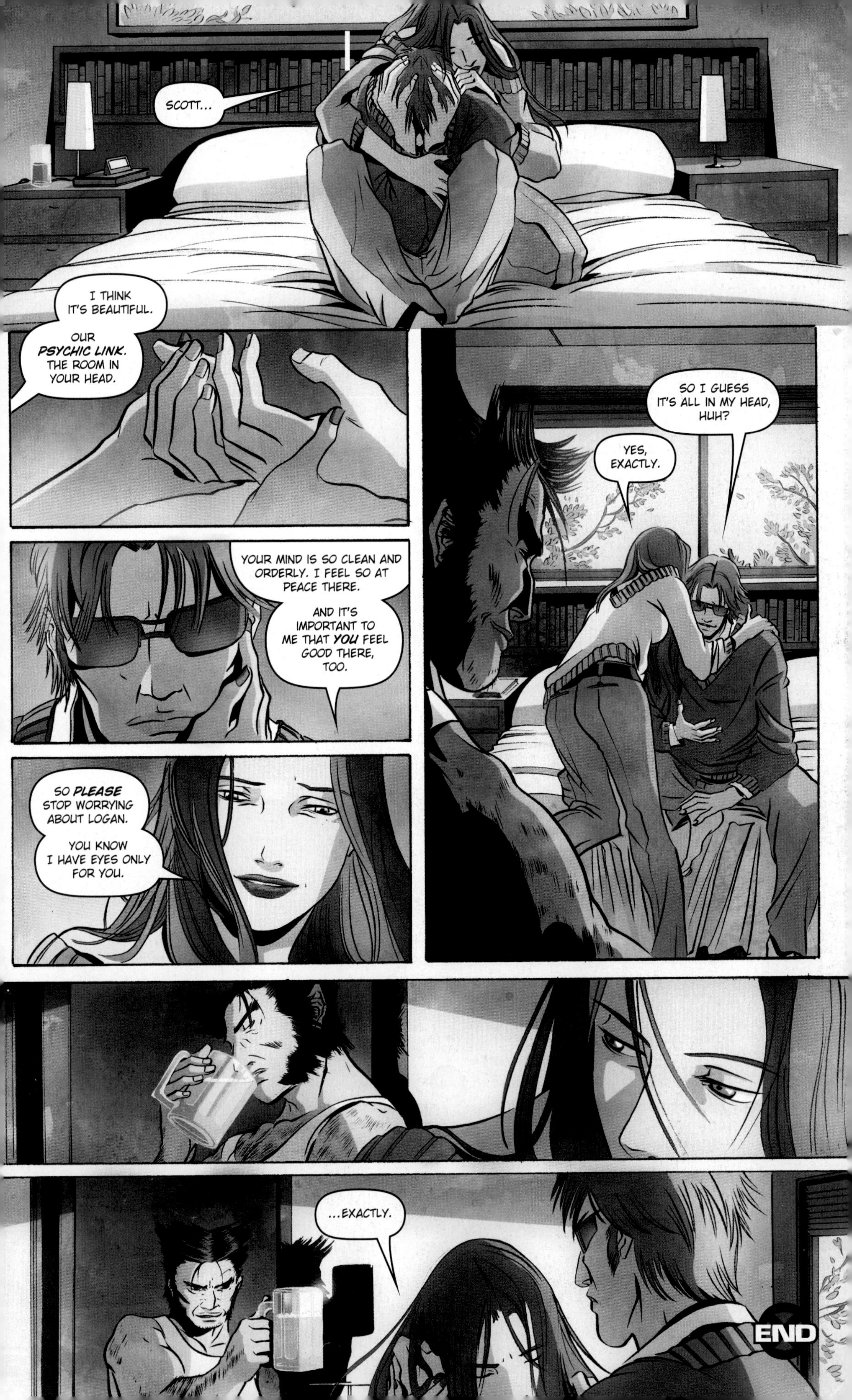
SCOTT...
I THINK IT'S BEAUTIFUL.
OUR PSYCHIC LINK. THE ROOM IN YOUR HEAD.
YOUR MIND IS SO CLEAN AND ORDERLY. I FEEL SO AT PEACE THERE.
AND IT'S IMPORTANT TO ME THAT YOU FEEL GOOD THERE, TOO.
SO PLEASE STOP WORRYING ABOUT LOGAN.
YOU KNOW I HAVE EYES ONLY FOR YOU.
SO I GUESS IT'S ALL IN MY HEAD, HUH?
YES, EXACTLY.
...EXACTLY.
END

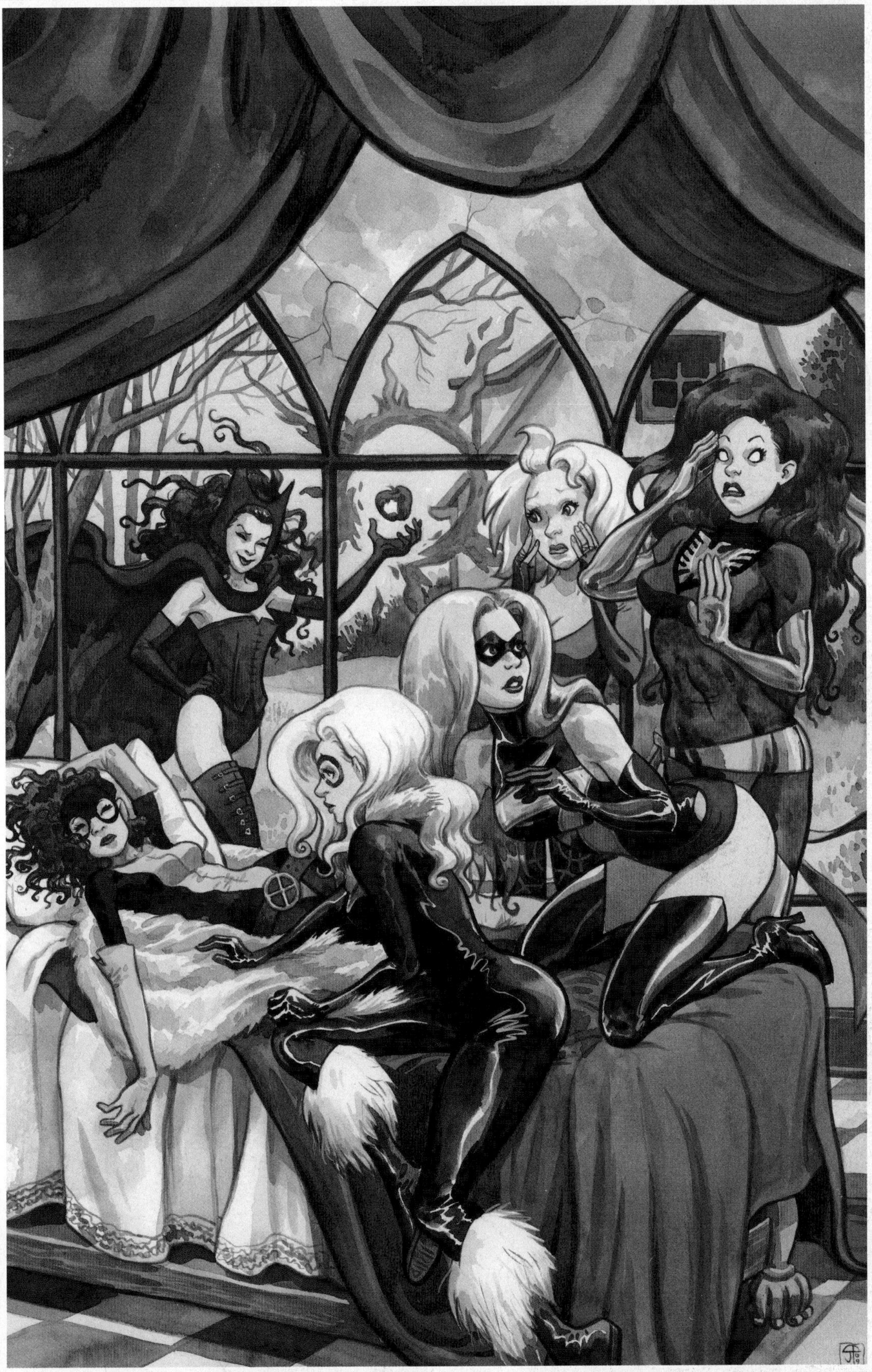

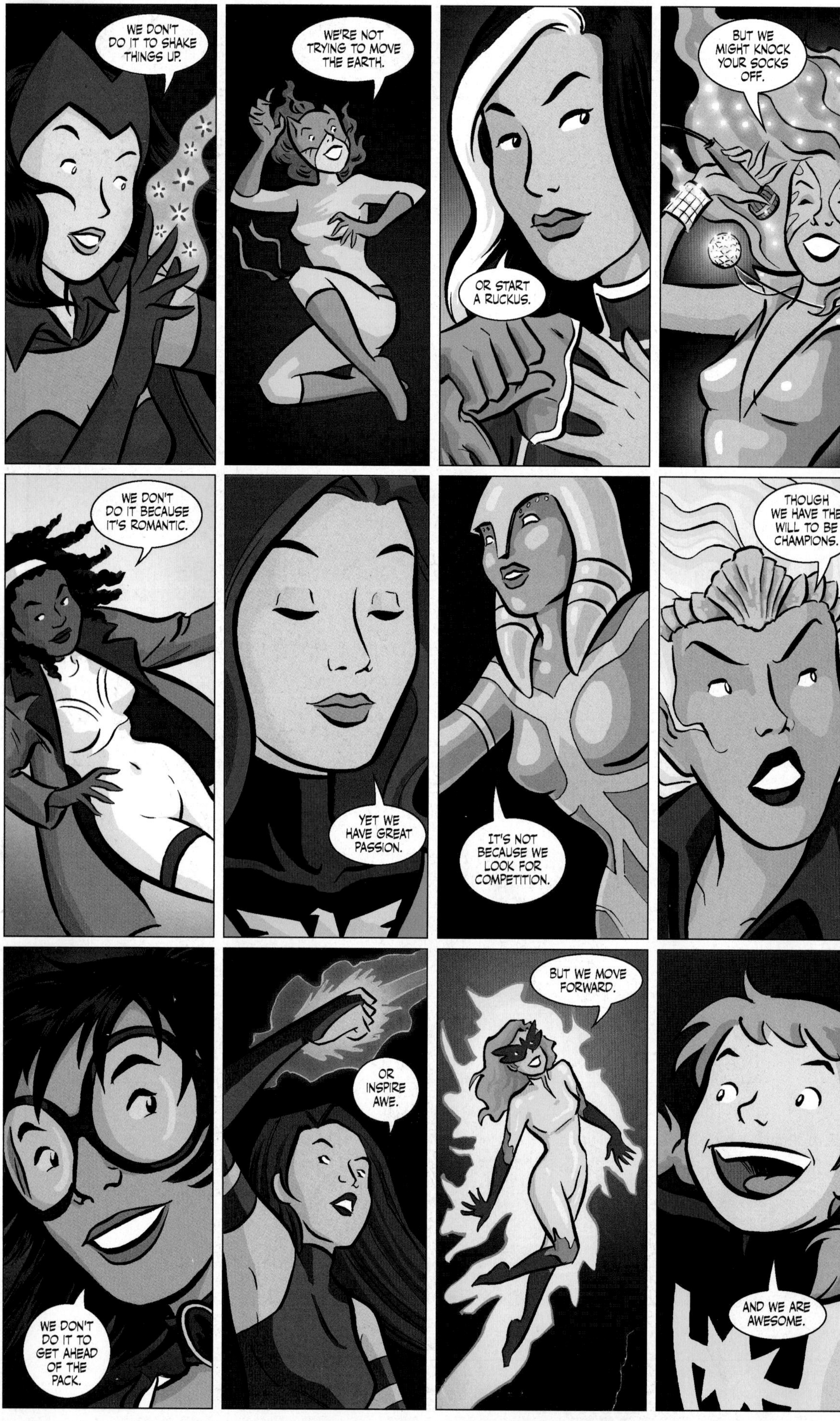
WE DON'T DO IT TO SHAKE THINGS UP.
WE'RE NOT TRYING TO MOVE THE EARTH.
OR START A RUCKUS.
BUT WE MIGHT KNOCK YOUR SOCKS OFF.
WE DON'T DO IT BECAUSE IT'S ROMANTIC.
YET WE HAVE GREAT PASSION.
IT'S NOT BECAUSE WE LOOK FOR COMPETITION.
THOUGH WE HAVE THE WILL TO BE CHAMPIONS.
WE DON'T DO IT TO GET AHEAD OF THE PACK.
OR INSPIRE AWE.
BUT WE MOVE FORWARD.
AND WE ARE AWESOME.

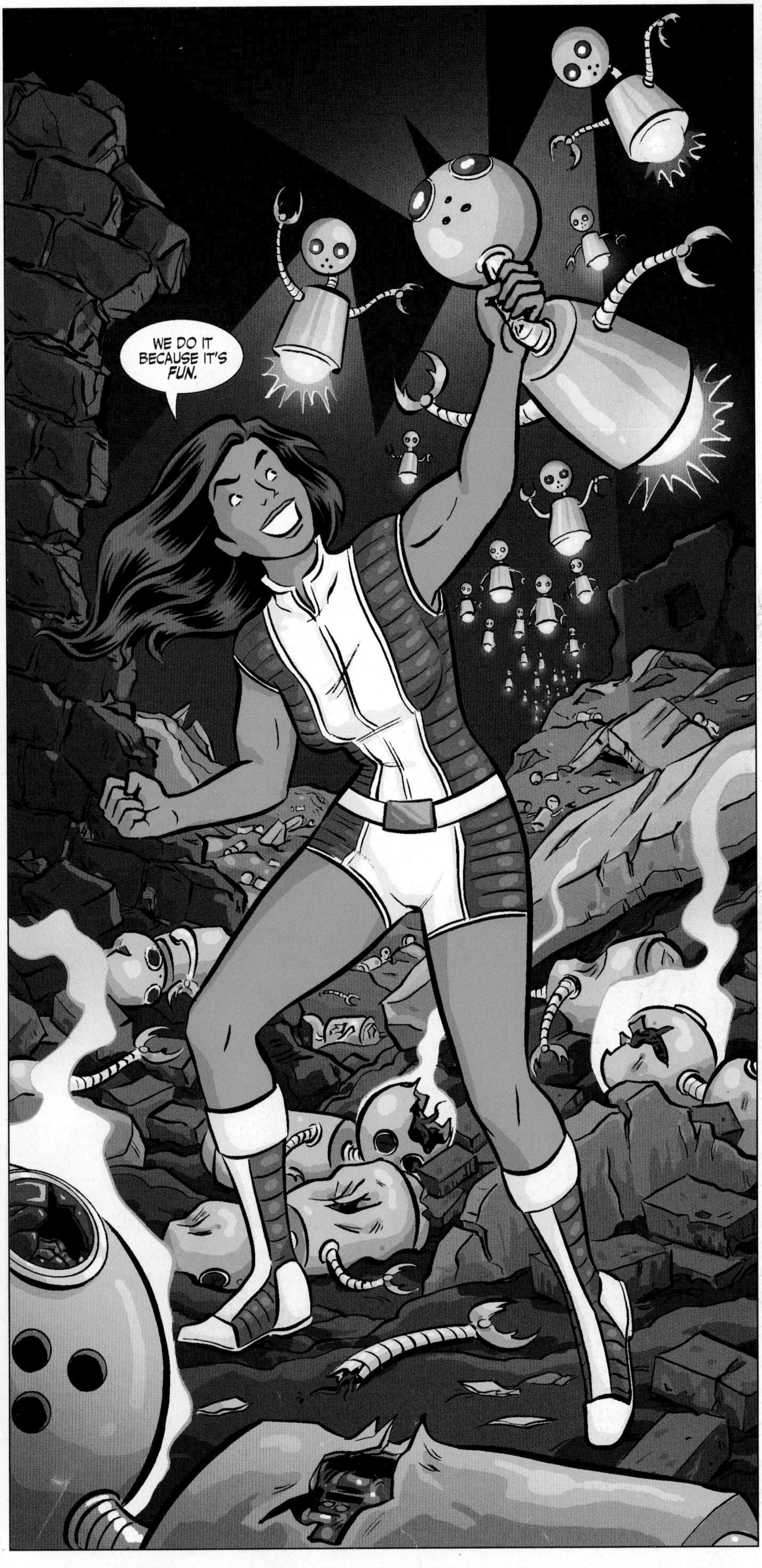
WE DO IT BECAUSE IT'S FUN.

GIRL COMICS

Part Two of Three

INTRODUCTION:
COLLEEN COOVER

COVER ART:
JILL THOMPSON

PRODUCTION:
IRENE LEE

ASSISTANT EDITORS:
SANA AMANAT & RACHEL PINNELAS

ASSOCIATE EDITOR:
LAUREN SANKOVITCH

EDITOR:
JEANINE SCHAEFER

EDITOR IN CHIEF:
JOE QUESADA

PUBLISHER:
DAN BUCKLEY

EXEC. PRODUCER:
ALAN FINE

SPECIAL THANKS:
SPRING HOTELING

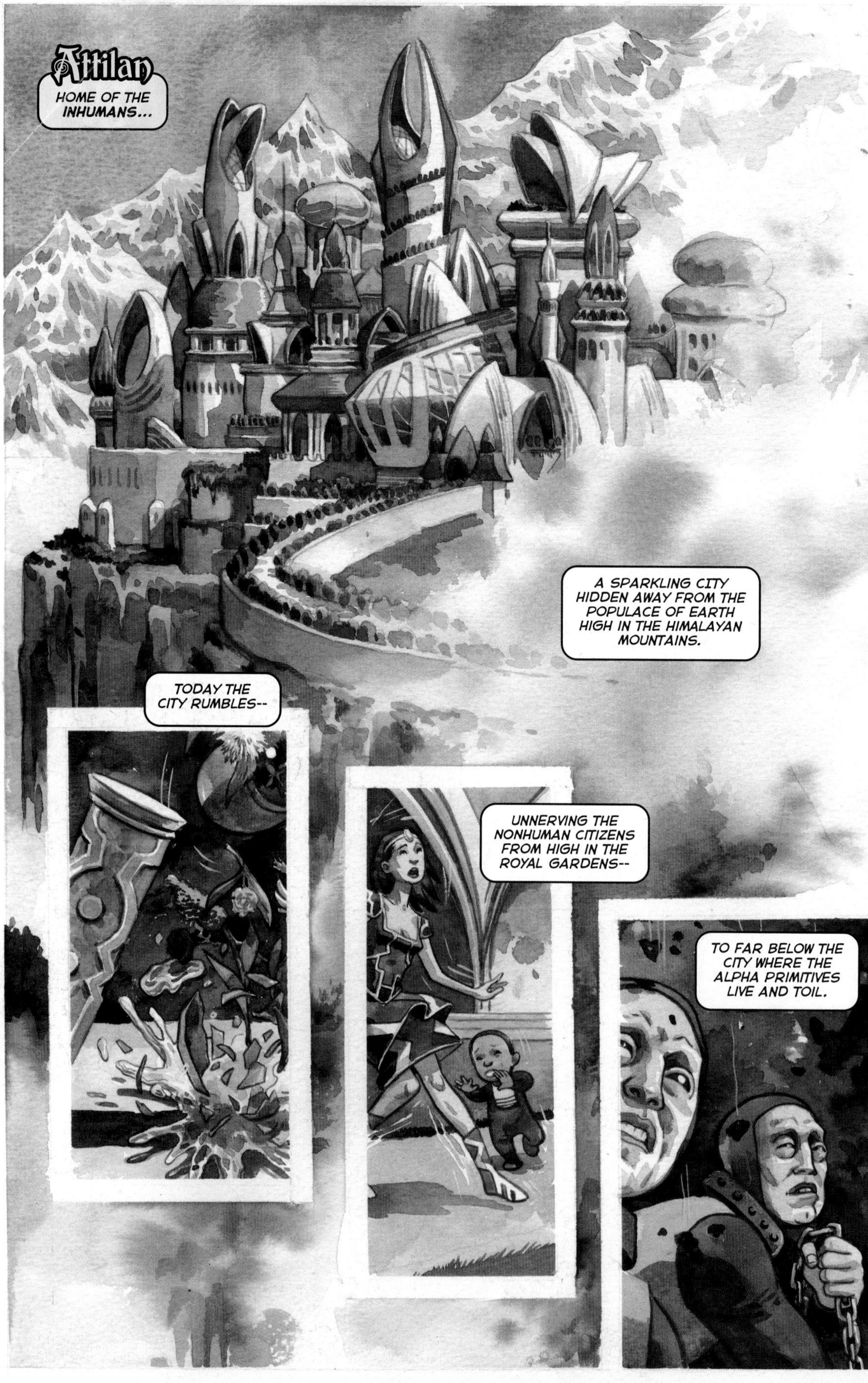
Attilan
HOME OF THE INHUMANS...
A SPARKLING CITY HIDDEN AWAY FROM THE POPULACE OF EARTH HIGH IN THE HIMALAYAN MOUNTAINS.
TODAY THE CITY RUMBLES--
UNNERVING THE NONHUMAN CITIZENS FROM HIGH IN THE ROYAL GARDENS--
TO FAR BELOW THE CITY WHERE THE ALPHA PRIMITIVES LIVE AND TOIL.

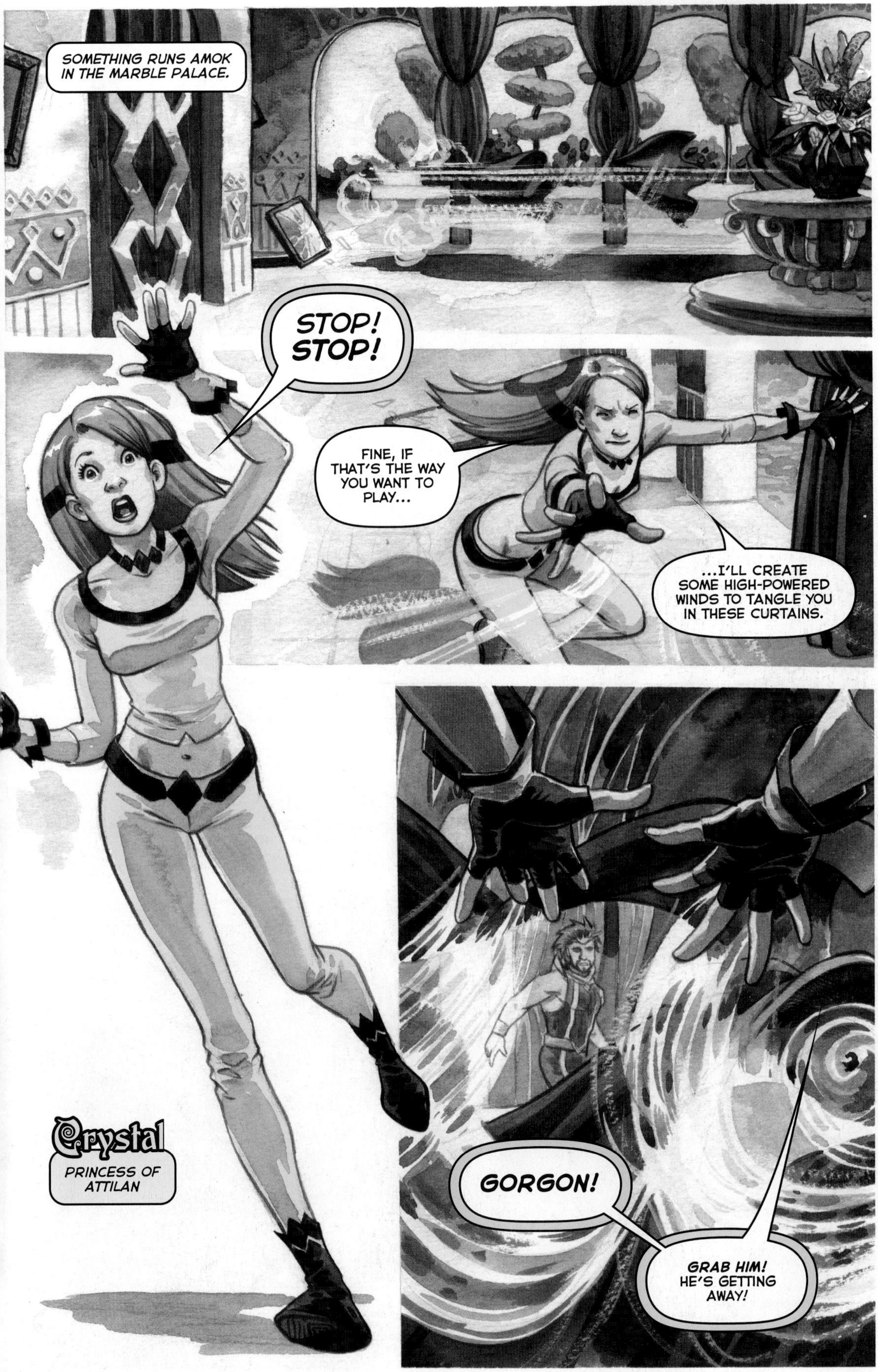
SOMETHING RUNS AMOK IN THE MARBLE PALACE.
STOP! STOP!
FINE, IF THAT'S THE WAY YOU WANT TO PLAY...
...I'LL CREATE SOME HIGH-POWERED WINDS TO TANGLE YOU IN THESE CURTAINS.
Crystal
PRINCESS OF ATTILAN
GORGON!
GRAB HIM! HE'S GETTING AWAY!

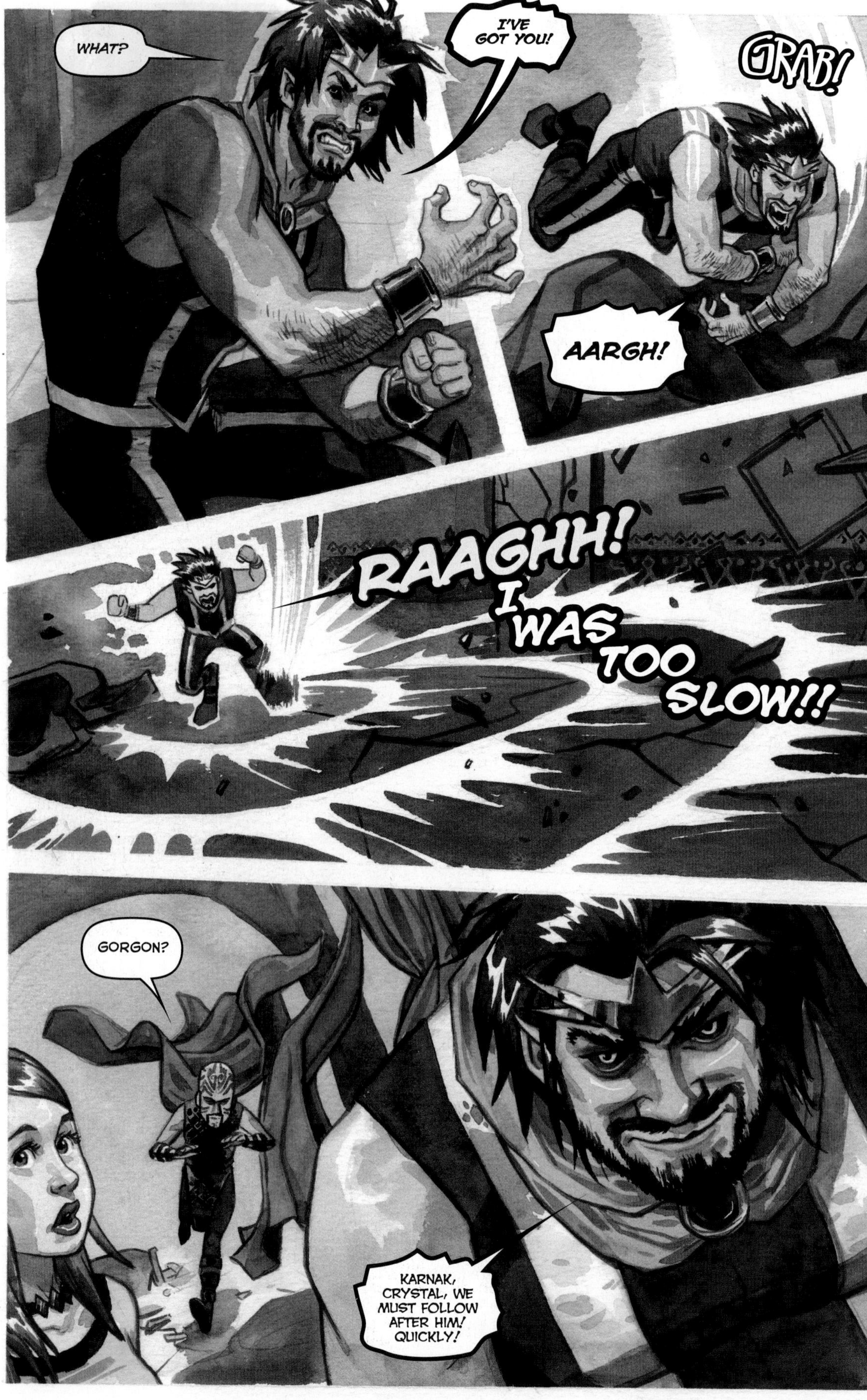
WHAT?
I'VE GOT YOU!
GRAB!
AARGH!
RAAGHH! I WAS TOO SLOW!!
GORGON?
KARNAK, CRYSTAL, WE MUST FOLLOW AFTER HIM! QUICKLY!

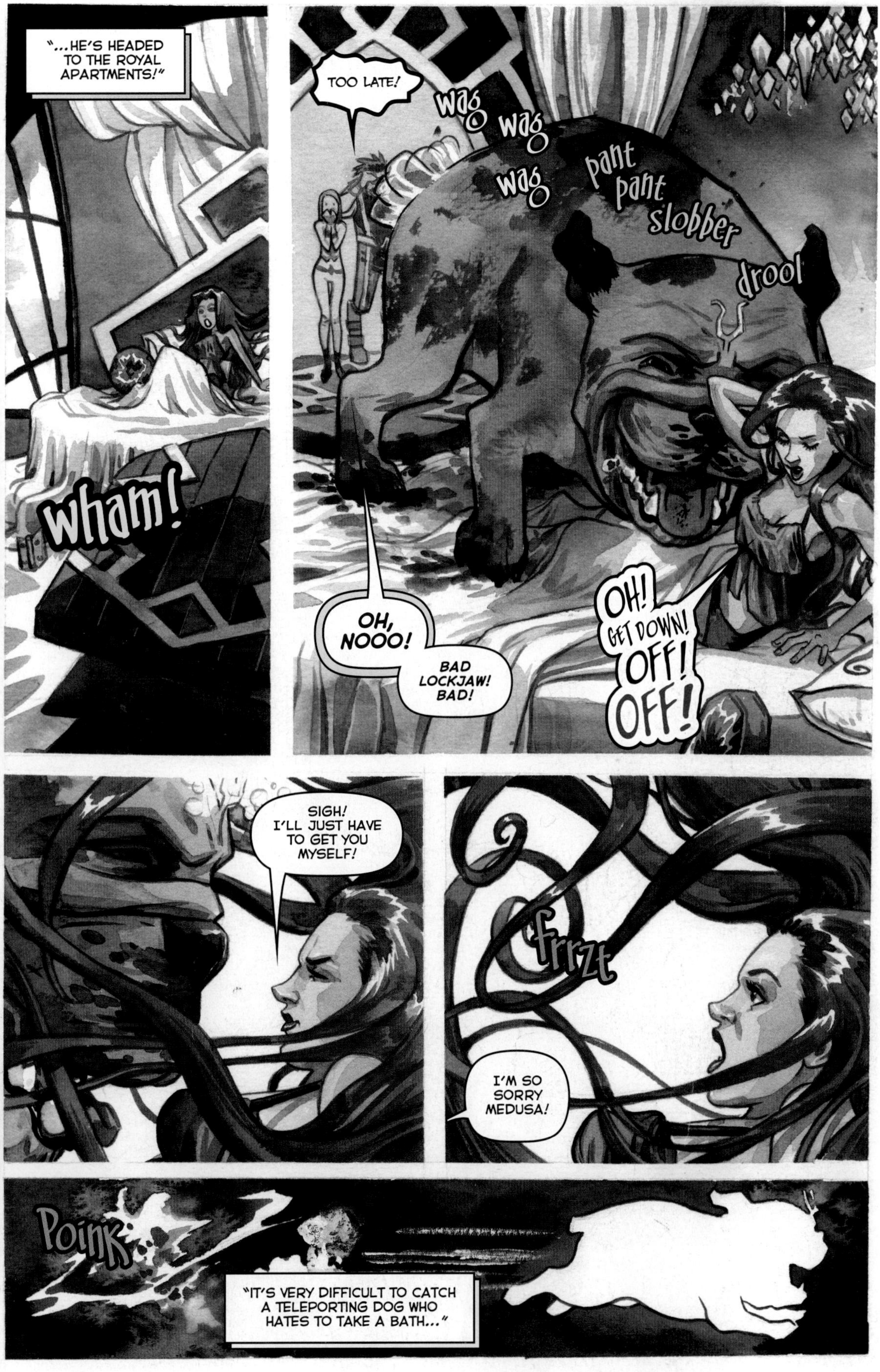
"...HE'S HEADED TO THE ROYAL APARTMENTS!"
WHAM!
TOO LATE!
WAG WAG WAG
PANT PANT SLOBBER
DROOL
OH, NOOO!
BAD LOCKJAW! BAD!
OH! GET DOWN! OFF! OFF!
SIGH! I'LL JUST HAVE TO GET YOU MYSELF!
FRRZT
I'M SO SORRY MEDUSA!
POINK
"IT'S VERY DIFFICULT TO CATCH A TELEPORTING DOG WHO HATES TO TAKE A BATH..."

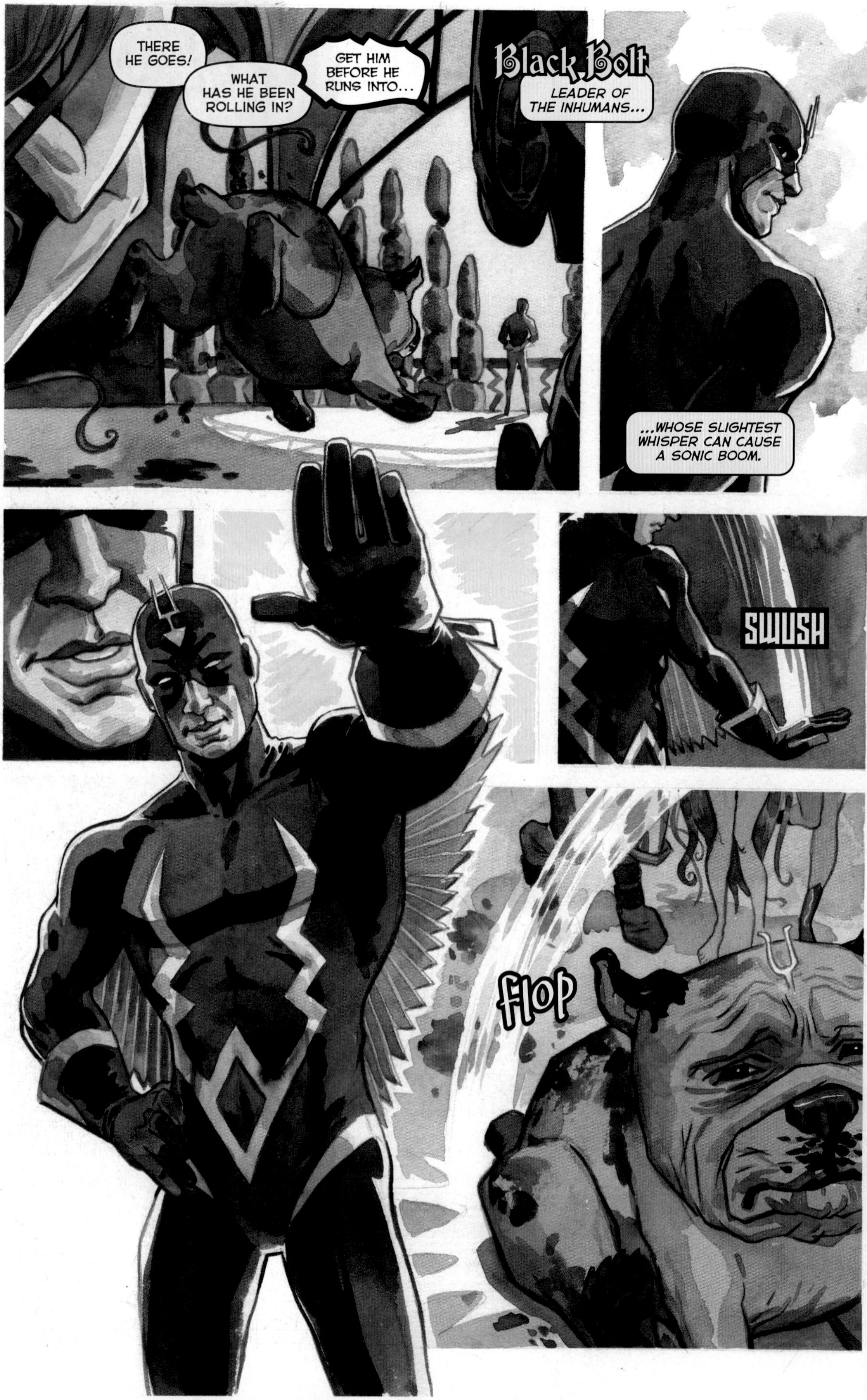
THERE HE GOES!
WHAT HAS HE BEEN ROLLING IN?
GET HIM BEFORE HE RUNS INTO...
Black Bolt
LEADER OF THE INHUMANS...
...WHOSE SLIGHTEST WHISPER CAN CAUSE A SONIC BOOM.
SWUSH
flop

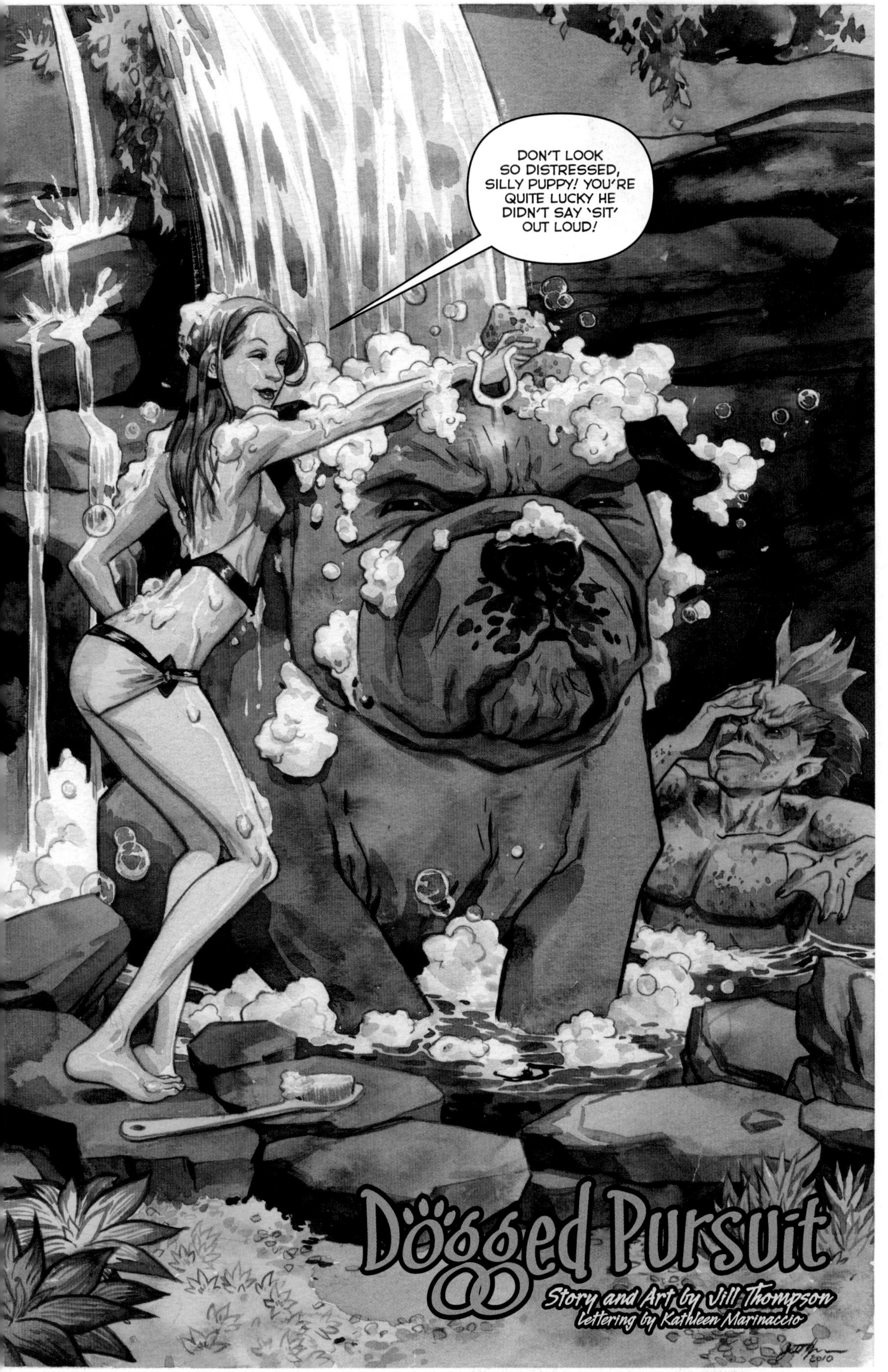

DON'T LOOK SO DISTRESSED, SILLY PUPPY! YOU'RE QUITE LUCKY HE DIDN'T SAY 'SIT' OUT LOUD!
Dogged Pursuit
Story and Art by Jill Thompson
lettering by Kathleen Marinaccio

SPOTLIGHT

June Tarpe Mills

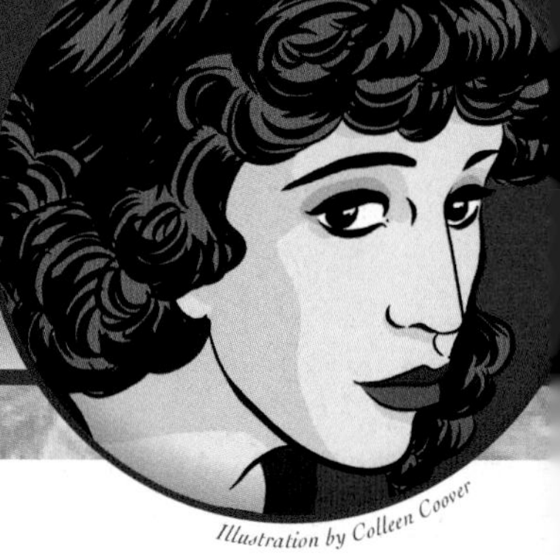
Illustration by Colleen Coover

During the Golden Age of comic book production it was not industry standard to provide detailed credits for each strip, making the creator-tree a bit difficult to navigate. The business' brisk general turnover combined with the fact that few women even worked in comics makes the hunt for female creators in particular quite a task. What further complicates matters is when a creator shied away from acknowledging his or her gender in the credits. Like many female writers and artists before her, June Tarpe Mills signed her stories with her gender-neutral middle name, Tarpe, in case her first name caused inadvertent sexual discrimination. But hide it or not, June Tarpe Mills was in fact Marvel's first prominent female creator.

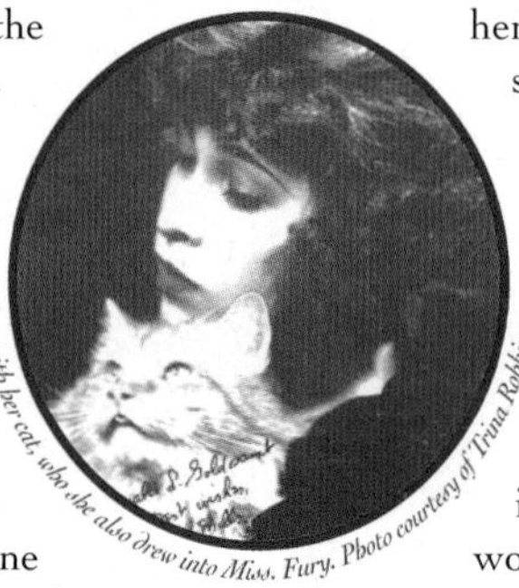
June with her cat, who she also drew into Miss. Fury. Photo courtesy of Trina Robbins

Educated at the Pratt Institute, Mills worked as a Sunday comic strip artist, creating characters like The Cat Man, The Purple Zombie and Daredevil Barry Fin before conceiving her most notable character: Miss Fury. Launched in 1941 as the *Black Fury* in the *Bell Syndicate*, the series is one of the first of its kind: a comic with a female super hero as its lead and a female at the creator's reins. Mills created, wrote and illustrated the strip, which eventually took the name of its title character, Miss Fury. The comic featured Marla Drake, a wealthy socialite who donned a panther-like costume to fight evil-doers as an escape from her mundane life. Though she had no significant powers of her own, the costume was said to be cursed, causing the wearer to have unusual abilities. It's been noted Mills fashioned the character's physical attributes after her own appearance, and the few public pictures that exist of Mills actually show that similarity. Marla Drake was fashionable, beautiful and brazen, much like Mills herself.

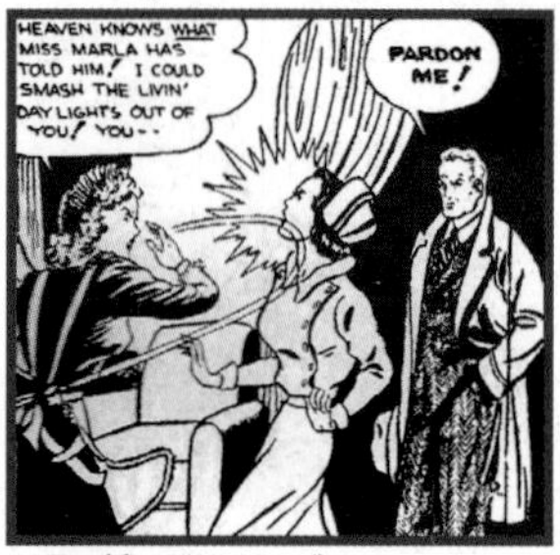
HEAVEN KNOWS WHAT MISS MARLA HAS TOLD HIM! I COULD SMASH THE LIVIN' DAYLIGHTS OUT OF YOU! YOU--
PARDON ME!
Panel from "Miss Fury"

As the popularity of the strip increased, Mills agreed to start doing interviews, finally exposing her true identity to audiences—and surprisingly having no apparent effect on its sales. Its continued popularity attracted the attention of Marvel, and from 1942-1946 the company published her strips in a series of 8 comic books. The strip itself ran until 1952, after which Mills retired from the comics industry. Until 1971 that is, when she came back to Marvel to work on the romance title, *Our Love Story.*

Though Mills might have chosen a relatively conservative garb for her super hero (the fully covered albeit form-fitting costume only showed a bit of her face), the content of the strip was quite risqué for the times. With scantily-clad women, violence and sensitive subject matter that touched upon the political climate at the time, Mills portrayed a very untraditional and sometimes controversial spin on popular culture. A few decades ago, she might have been thwarted by society's inner circles, but it's that same nonconformist creative spirit that has us at Marvel celebrating Mills and her amazing contribution to the field. Her tenure at the company may have been short, but she unknowingly set the standard for future women of Marvel to come.

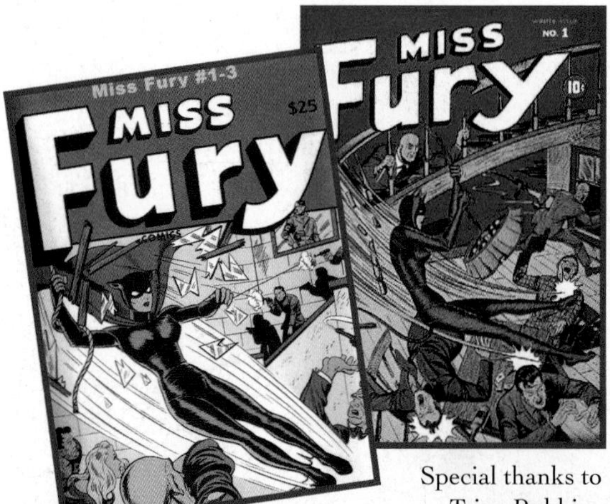
Miss Fury #1-3
MISS Fury
$25
MISS Fury
NO. 1
10¢

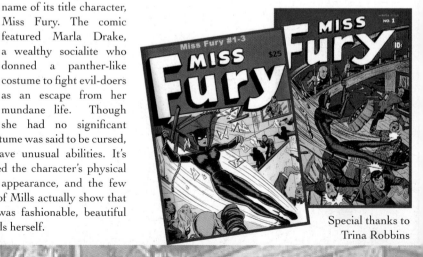

Special thanks to Trina Robbins

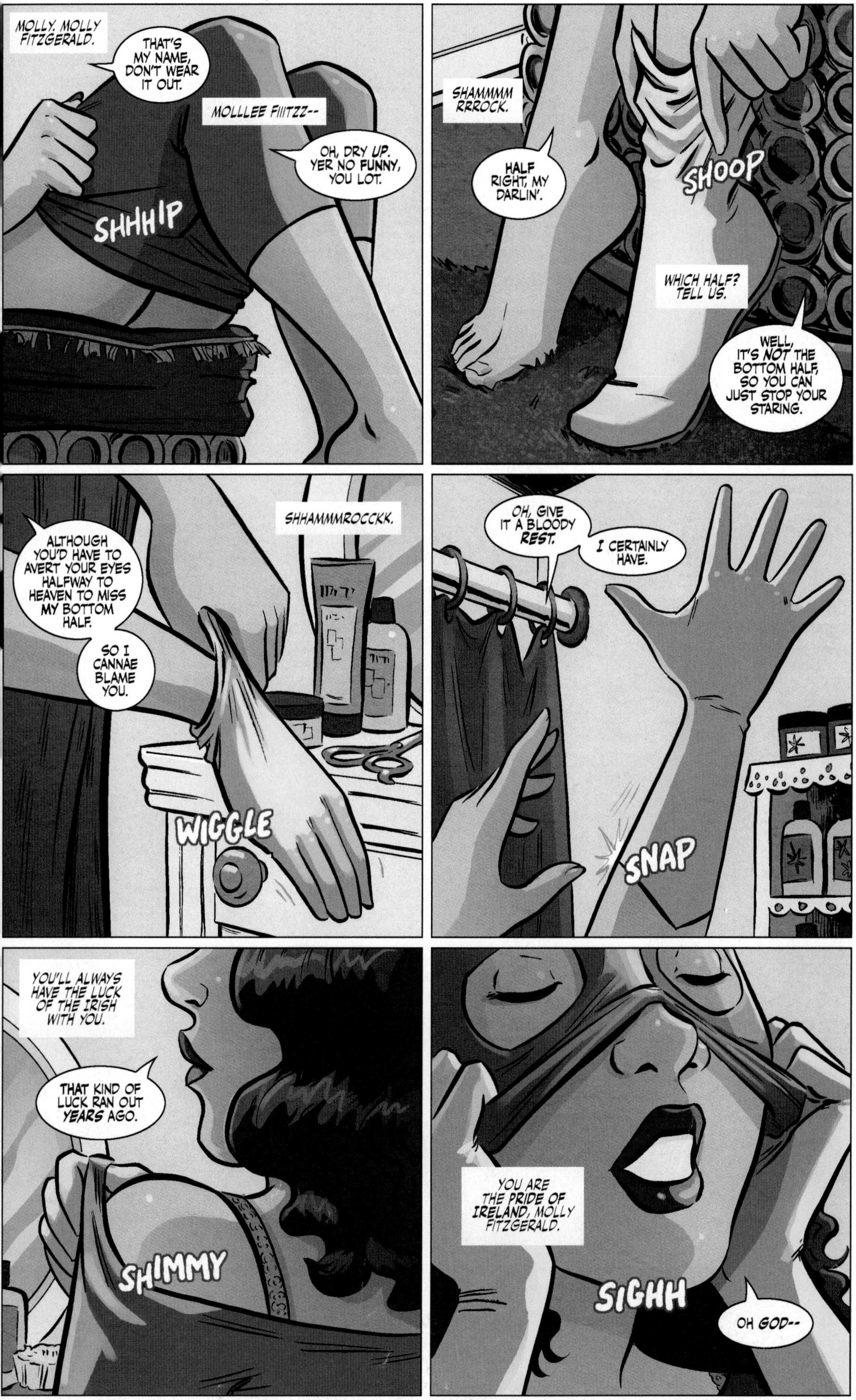

MOLLY. MOLLY FITZGERALD.
THAT'S MY NAME, DON'T WEAR IT OUT.
MOLLLEE FIIITZZ--
OH, DRY UP. YER NO FUNNY, YOU LOT.
SHHHIP
SHAMMMM RRROCK.
HALF RIGHT, MY DARLIN'.
SHOOP
WHICH HALF? TELL US.
WELL, IT'S NOT THE BOTTOM HALF, SO YOU CAN JUST STOP YOUR STARING.
SHHAMMMROCCKK.
ALTHOUGH YOU'D HAVE TO AVERT YOUR EYES HALFWAY TO HEAVEN TO MISS MY BOTTOM HALF.
SO I CANNAE BLAME YOU.
WIGGLE
OH, GIVE IT A BLOODY REST.
I CERTAINLY HAVE.
SNAP
YOU'LL ALWAYS HAVE THE LUCK OF THE IRISH WITH YOU.
THAT KIND OF LUCK RAN OUT YEARS AGO.
SHIMMY
YOU ARE THE PRIDE OF IRELAND, MOLLY FITZGERALD.
SIGHH
OH GOD--

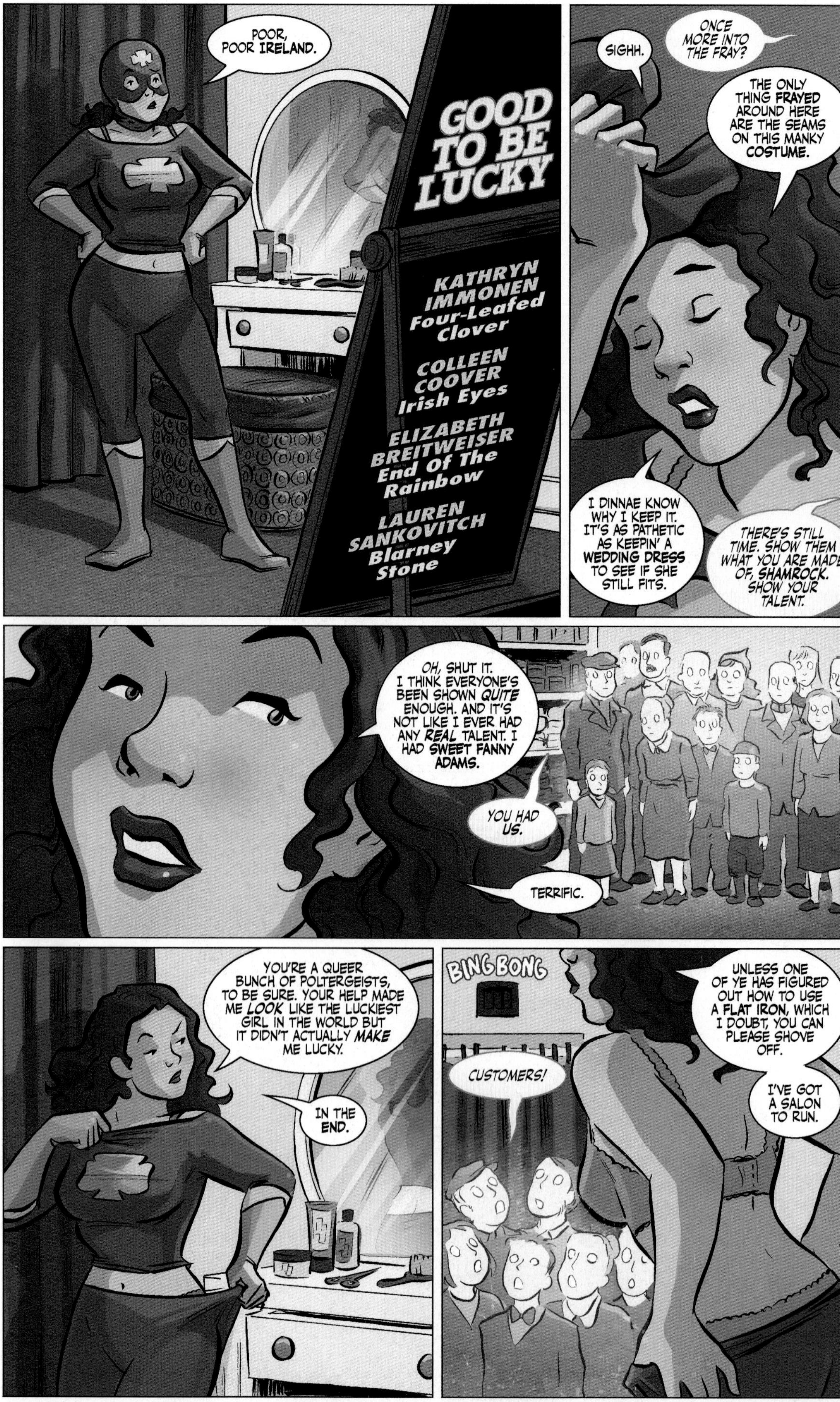
POOR, POOR IRELAND.
GOOD TO BE LUCKY
KATHRYN IMMONEN Four-Leafed Clover
COLLEEN COOVER Irish Eyes
ELIZABETH BREITWEISER End Of The Rainbow
LAUREN SANKOVITCH Blarney Stone
SIGHH.
ONCE MORE INTO THE FRAY?
THE ONLY THING FRAYED AROUND HERE ARE THE SEAMS ON THIS MANKY COSTUME.
I DINNAE KNOW WHY I KEEP IT. IT'S AS PATHETIC AS KEEPIN' A WEDDING DRESS TO SEE IF SHE STILL FITS.
THERE'S STILL TIME. SHOW THEM WHAT YOU ARE MADE OF, SHAMROCK. SHOW YOUR TALENT.
OH, SHUT IT. I THINK EVERYONE'S BEEN SHOWN QUITE ENOUGH. AND IT'S NOT LIKE I EVER HAD ANY REAL TALENT. I HAD SWEET FANNY ADAMS.
YOU HAD US.
TERRIFIC.
YOU'RE A QUEER BUNCH OF POLTERGEISTS, TO BE SURE. YOUR HELP MADE ME LOOK LIKE THE LUCKIEST GIRL IN THE WORLD BUT IT DIDN'T ACTUALLY MAKE ME LUCKY.
IN THE END.
BING BONG
CUSTOMERS!
UNLESS ONE OF YE HAS FIGURED OUT HOW TO USE A FLAT IRON, WHICH I DOUBT, YOU CAN PLEASE SHOVE OFF.
I'VE GOT A SALON TO RUN.

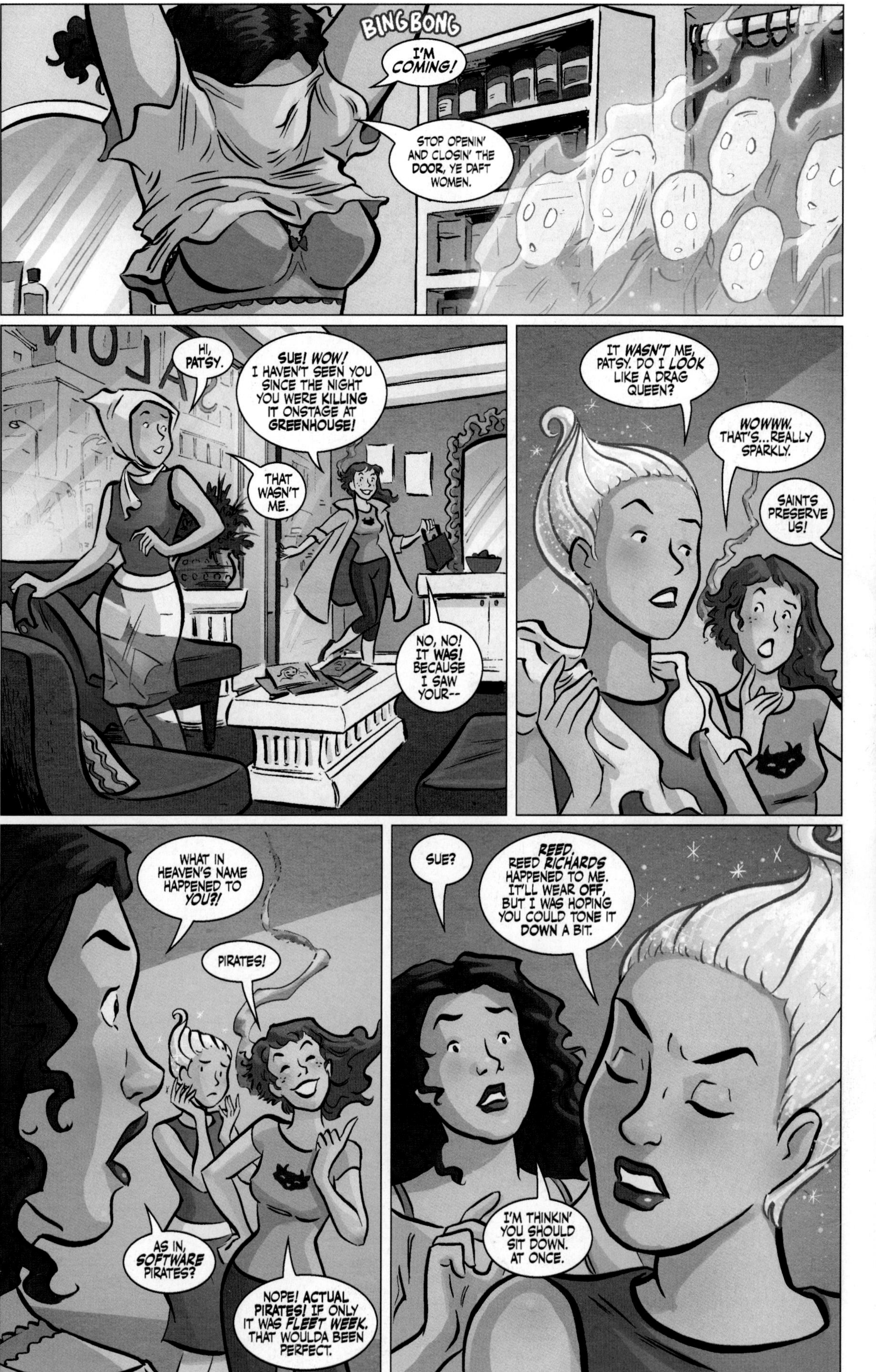
BING BONG
I'M COMING!
STOP OPENIN' AND CLOSIN' THE DOOR, YE DAFT WOMEN.
HI, PATSY.
SUE! WOW! I HAVEN'T SEEN YOU SINCE THE NIGHT YOU WERE KILLING IT ONSTAGE AT GREENHOUSE!
THAT WASN'T ME.
NO, NO! IT WAS! BECAUSE I SAW YOUR--
IT WASN'T ME, PATSY. DO I LOOK LIKE A DRAG QUEEN?
WOWWW. THAT'S...REALLY SPARKLY.
SAINTS PRESERVE US!
WHAT IN HEAVEN'S NAME HAPPENED TO YOU?!
PIRATES!
AS IN, SOFTWARE PIRATES?
NOPE! ACTUAL PIRATES! IF ONLY IT WAS FLEET WEEK. THAT WOULDA BEEN PERFECT.
SUE?
REED. REED RICHARDS HAPPENED TO ME. IT'LL WEAR OFF, BUT I WAS HOPING YOU COULD TONE IT DOWN A BIT.
I'M THINKIN' YOU SHOULD SIT DOWN. AT ONCE.

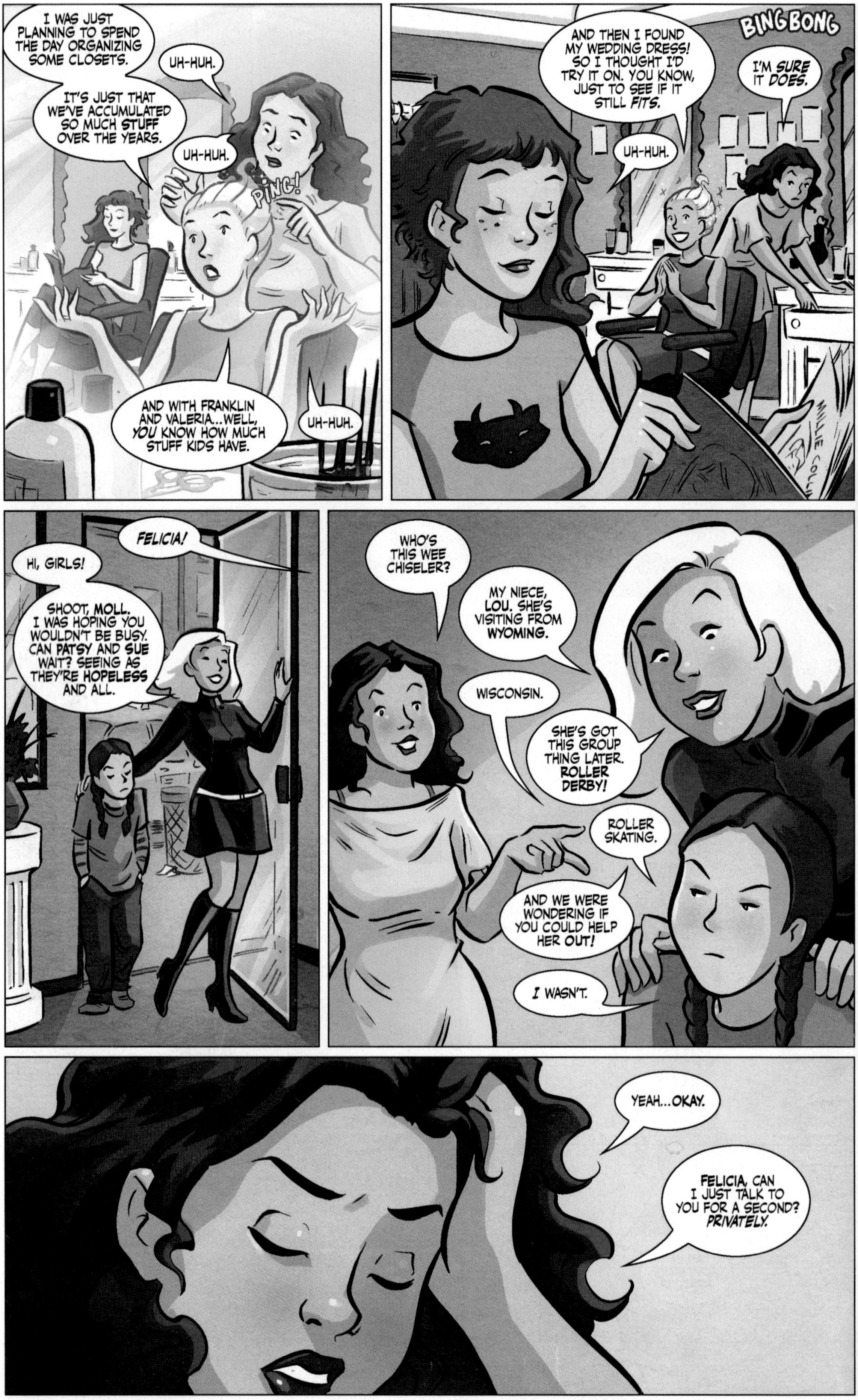
I WAS JUST PLANNING TO SPEND THE DAY ORGANIZING SOME CLOSETS.
UH-HUH.
IT'S JUST THAT WE'VE ACCUMULATED SO MUCH STUFF OVER THE YEARS.
UH-HUH.
PING!
AND WITH FRANKLIN AND VALERIA...WELL, YOU KNOW HOW MUCH STUFF KIDS HAVE.
UH-HUH.
BING BONG
AND THEN I FOUND MY WEDDING DRESS! SO I THOUGHT I'D TRY IT ON. YOU KNOW, JUST TO SEE IF IT STILL FITS.
UH-HUH.
I'M SURE IT DOES.
FELICIA!
HI, GIRLS!
SHOOT, MOLL. I WAS HOPING YOU WOULDN'T BE BUSY. CAN PATSY AND SUE WAIT? SEEING AS THEY'RE HOPELESS AND ALL.
WHO'S THIS WEE CHISELER?
MY NIECE, LOU. SHE'S VISITING FROM WYOMING.
WISCONSIN.
SHE'S GOT THIS GROUP THING LATER. ROLLER DERBY!
ROLLER SKATING.
AND WE WERE WONDERING IF YOU COULD HELP HER OUT!
I WASN'T.
YEAH...OKAY.
FELICIA, CAN I JUST TALK TO YOU FOR A SECOND? PRIVATELY.

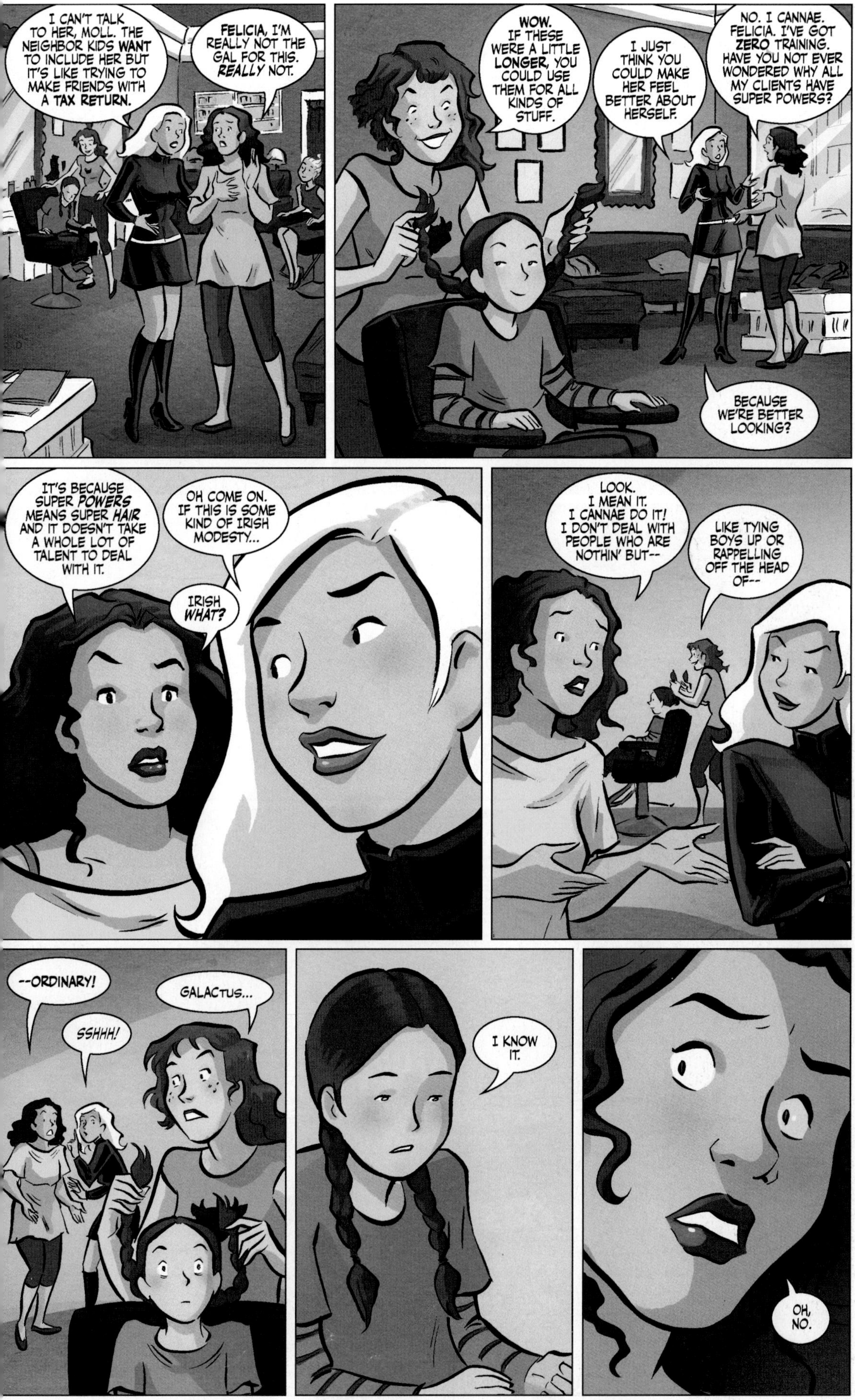
I CAN'T TALK TO HER, MOLL. THE NEIGHBOR KIDS WANT TO INCLUDE HER BUT IT'S LIKE TRYING TO MAKE FRIENDS WITH A TAX RETURN.
FELICIA, I'M REALLY NOT THE GAL FOR THIS. REALLY NOT.
WOW. IF THESE WERE A LITTLE LONGER, YOU COULD USE THEM FOR ALL KINDS OF STUFF.
I JUST THINK YOU COULD MAKE HER FEEL BETTER ABOUT HERSELF.
NO. I CANNAE. FELICIA. I'VE GOT ZERO TRAINING. HAVE YOU NOT EVER WONDERED WHY ALL MY CLIENTS HAVE SUPER POWERS?
BECAUSE WE'RE BETTER LOOKING?
IT'S BECAUSE SUPER POWERS MEANS SUPER HAIR AND IT DOESN'T TAKE A WHOLE LOT OF TALENT TO DEAL WITH IT.
OH COME ON. IF THIS IS SOME KIND OF IRISH MODESTY...
IRISH WHAT?
LOOK. I MEAN IT. I CANNAE DO IT! I DON'T DEAL WITH PEOPLE WHO ARE NOTHIN' BUT--
LIKE TYING BOYS UP OR RAPPELLING OFF THE HEAD OF--
--ORDINARY!
SSHHH!
GALACTUS...
I KNOW IT.
OH, NO.

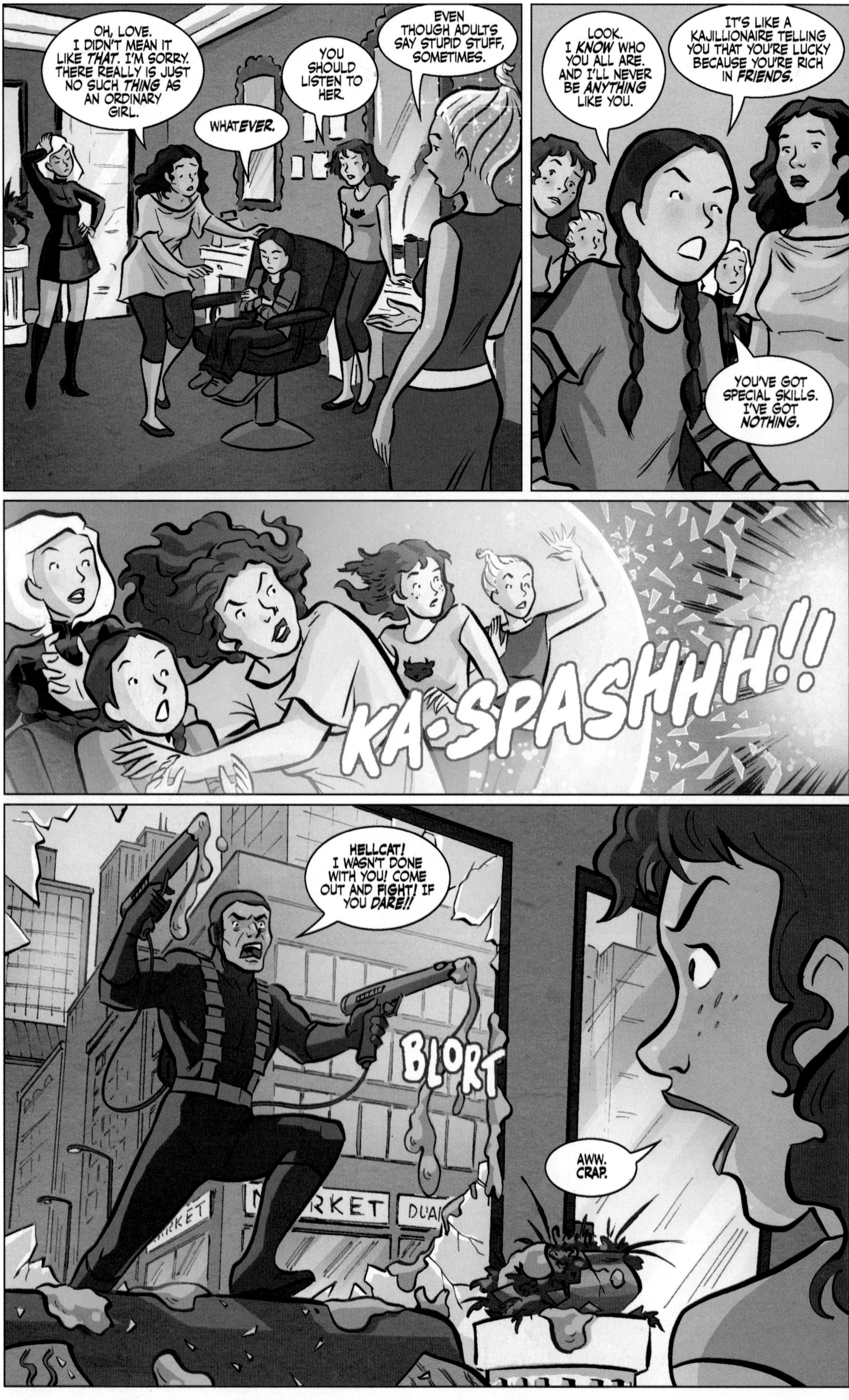

OH, LOVE. I DIDN'T MEAN IT LIKE THAT. I'M SORRY. THERE REALLY IS JUST NO SUCH THING AS AN ORDINARY GIRL.
WHATEVER.
YOU SHOULD LISTEN TO HER.
EVEN THOUGH ADULTS SAY STUPID STUFF, SOMETIMES.
LOOK. I KNOW WHO YOU ALL ARE. AND I'LL NEVER BE ANYTHING LIKE YOU.
IT'S LIKE A KAJILLIONAIRE TELLING YOU THAT YOU'RE LUCKY BECAUSE YOU'RE RICH IN FRIENDS.
YOU'VE GOT SPECIAL SKILLS. I'VE GOT NOTHING.
KA-SPASHHH!!
HELLCAT! I WASN'T DONE WITH YOU! COME OUT AND FIGHT! IF YOU DARE!!
BLORT
AWW. CRAP.

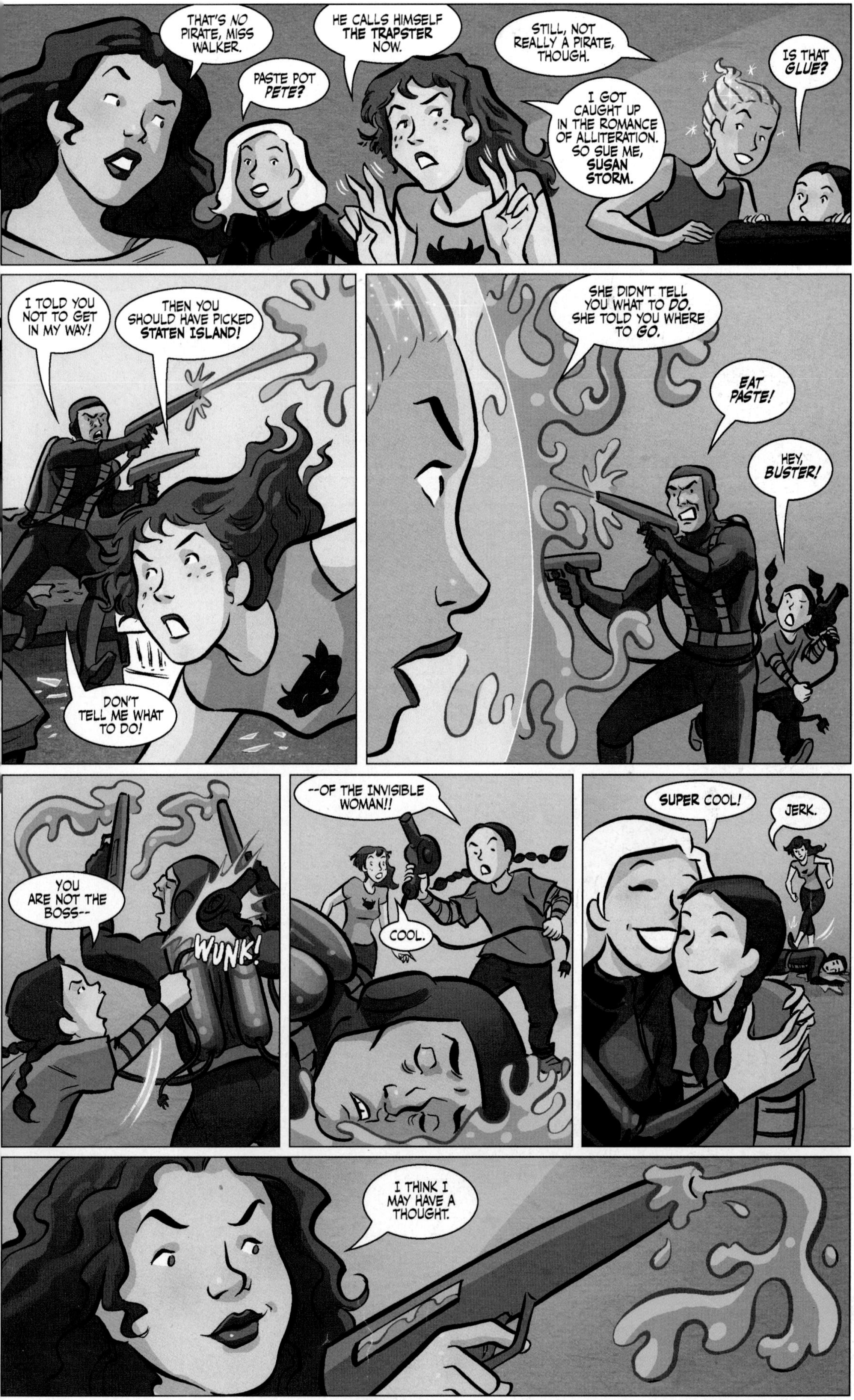
THAT'S NO PIRATE, MISS WALKER.
PASTE POT PETE?
HE CALLS HIMSELF THE TRAPSTER NOW.
STILL, NOT REALLY A PIRATE, THOUGH.
I GOT CAUGHT UP IN THE ROMANCE OF ALLITERATION. SO SUE ME, SUSAN STORM.
IS THAT GLUE?
I TOLD YOU NOT TO GET IN MY WAY!
THEN YOU SHOULD HAVE PICKED STATEN ISLAND!
DON'T TELL ME WHAT TO DO!
SHE DIDN'T TELL YOU WHAT TO DO. SHE TOLD YOU WHERE TO GO.
EAT PASTE!
HEY, BUSTER!
YOU ARE NOT THE BOSS--
WUNK!
--OF THE INVISIBLE WOMAN!!
COOL.
SUPER COOL!
JERK.
I THINK I MAY HAVE A THOUGHT.

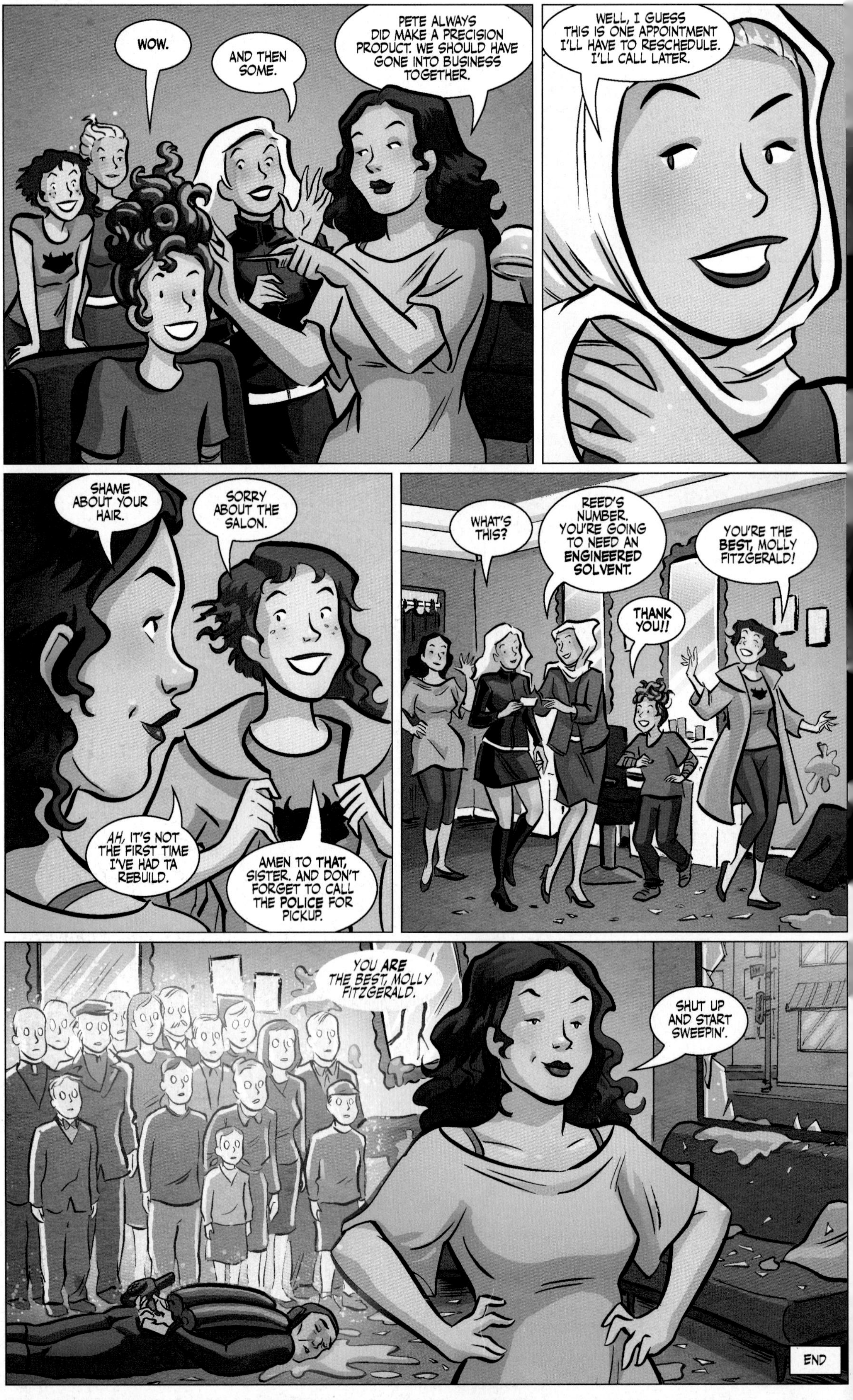

WOW.
AND THEN SOME.
PETE ALWAYS DID MAKE A PRECISION PRODUCT. WE SHOULD HAVE GONE INTO BUSINESS TOGETHER.
WELL, I GUESS THIS IS ONE APPOINTMENT I'LL HAVE TO RESCHEDULE. I'LL CALL LATER.
SHAME ABOUT YOUR HAIR.
SORRY ABOUT THE SALON.
AH, IT'S NOT THE FIRST TIME I'VE HAD TA REBUILD.
AMEN TO THAT, SISTER. AND DON'T FORGET TO CALL THE POLICE FOR PICKUP.
WHAT'S THIS?
REED'S NUMBER. YOU'RE GOING TO NEED AN **ENGINEERED SOLVENT.**
THANK YOU!!
YOU'RE THE **BEST,** MOLLY FITZGERALD!
*YOU **ARE** THE BEST, MOLLY FITZGERALD.*
SHUT UP AND START SWEEPIN'.
END

SPOTLIGHT

Ruth Atkinson

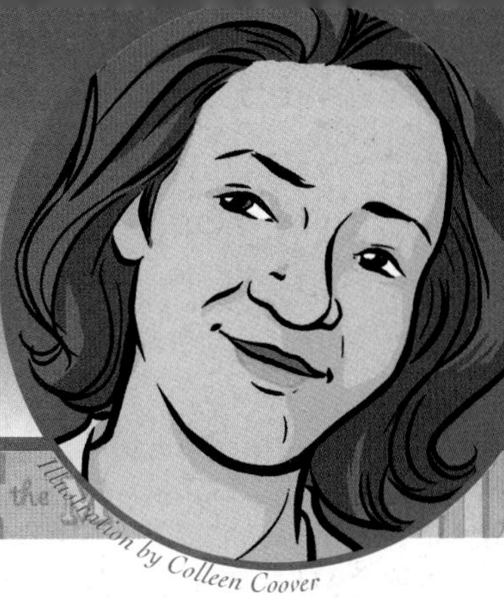

Illustration by Colleen Coover

The title *Girl Comics* has had its fair share of critics and supporters. But love it or hate it, those familiar with Marvel's history will know that the title is a throwback, referencing a series that sought the attention of the female marketplace. Atlas Comics (Marvel's predecessor) published a romance series in the early '50s entitled *Girl Comics,* which eventually became *Girl Confessions.* In the spirit of bringing in more of a female readership Atlas produced a series of romance and female-centric comics. At the helm of this venture was one of the industry's pioneering female illustrators, Ruth Atkinson.

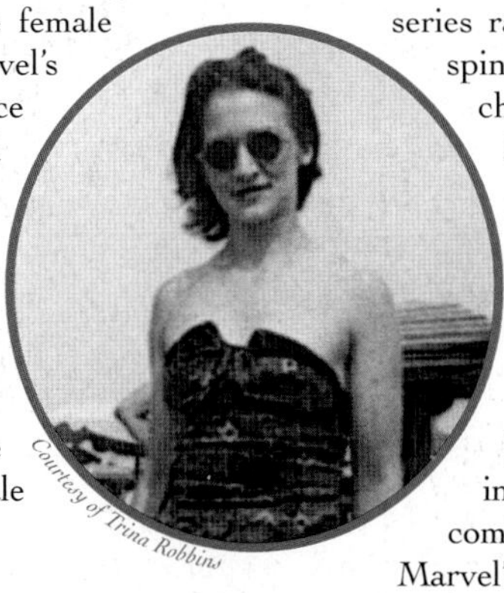

Courtesy of Trina Robbins

Originally from Toronto, Canada, Ruth was raised in upstate New York and entered the comics field through Fiction House, a comic publishing company, and Iger Studio, a comic-book packaging company. At Fiction House she freelanced as a penciler and inker on multiple titles, with her first credited work, *Wing Tips,* published in *Wing Comics* in 1944. It featured an airplane called The Hellcat, a name which would have later significance in Ruth's comic career.

Author and herstorian Trina Robbins noted in *The Great Women Superheroes* that many of Fiction House's stories featured "strong, beautiful, competent heroines...that did not need rescuing." It was an innovative point of view for an entertainment company at that time, but seems as though it might have had an indirect influence on Ruth's creative process. When she left her position as art director at Fiction House, she freelanced for Timely Comics and co-created the red-headed teen sensation, Patsy Walker. Patsy premiered in *Miss America* #2 in 1944, eventually earning her own series in 1945. It became one of Marvel's most successful series featuring a female lead, with Ruth penciling and inking on it for about 2 years. By the '70s, Patsy went on to assume the super hero persona of Hellcat, establishing herself as one of Marvel's longest-running female characters.

Ruth might have hit the jackpot with Patsy, but she wasn't done yet. Around the same time as Patsy's inception, Ruth created *Millie the Model,* a humor series about a fashion model in New York City. The series ran from 1945 to 1973, with numerous spin-off titles as well. Most recently the character was revived in *Models Inc.,* honoring the original title by featuring Millie and her model gal pals, with a guest appearance by fashion guru, Tim Gunn—proving the timelessness of Ruth's creations.

Though she passed in 1996 after a battle with cancer, Ruth has left an indelible mark at Marvel and across the comics industry. Her creations have spanned Marvel's pages, establishing Ruth as one of the company's preeminent and most influential creators—and one of its favorite girls in comics.

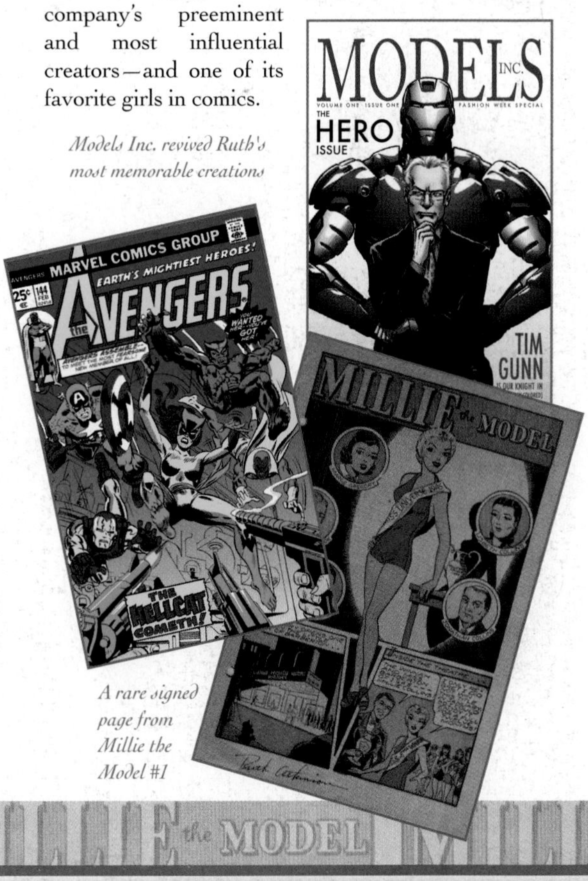

MODELS INC.
THE HERO ISSUE
TIM GUNN
MARVEL COMICS GROUP
EARTH'S MIGHTIEST HEROES!
AVENGERS
THE HELLCAT COMETH!
MILLIE the MODEL

Models Inc. revived Ruth's most memorable creations

A rare signed page from Millie the Model #1

Special thanks to Trina Robbins

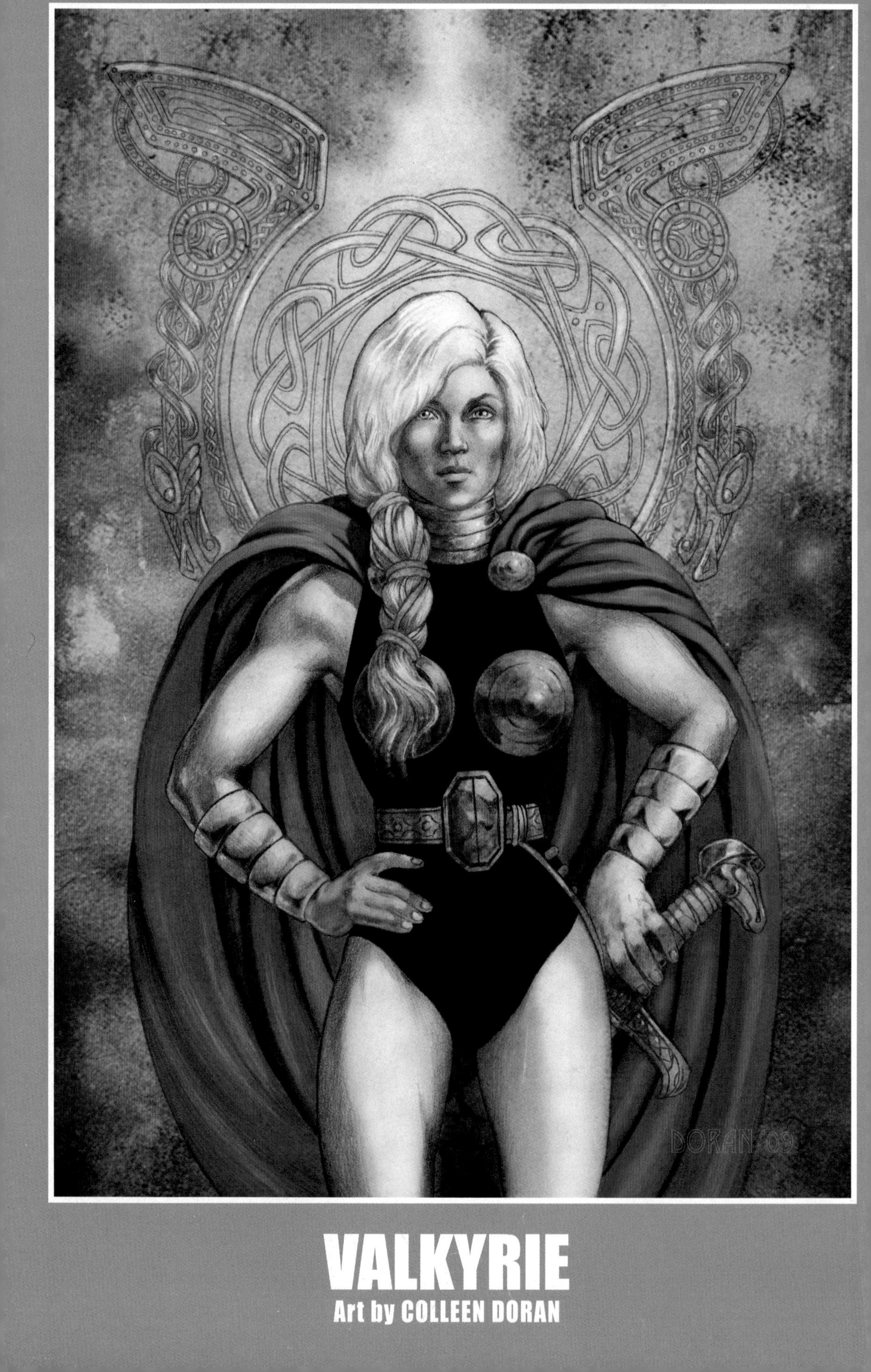
DORAN '09

VALKYRIE

Art by COLLEEN DORAN

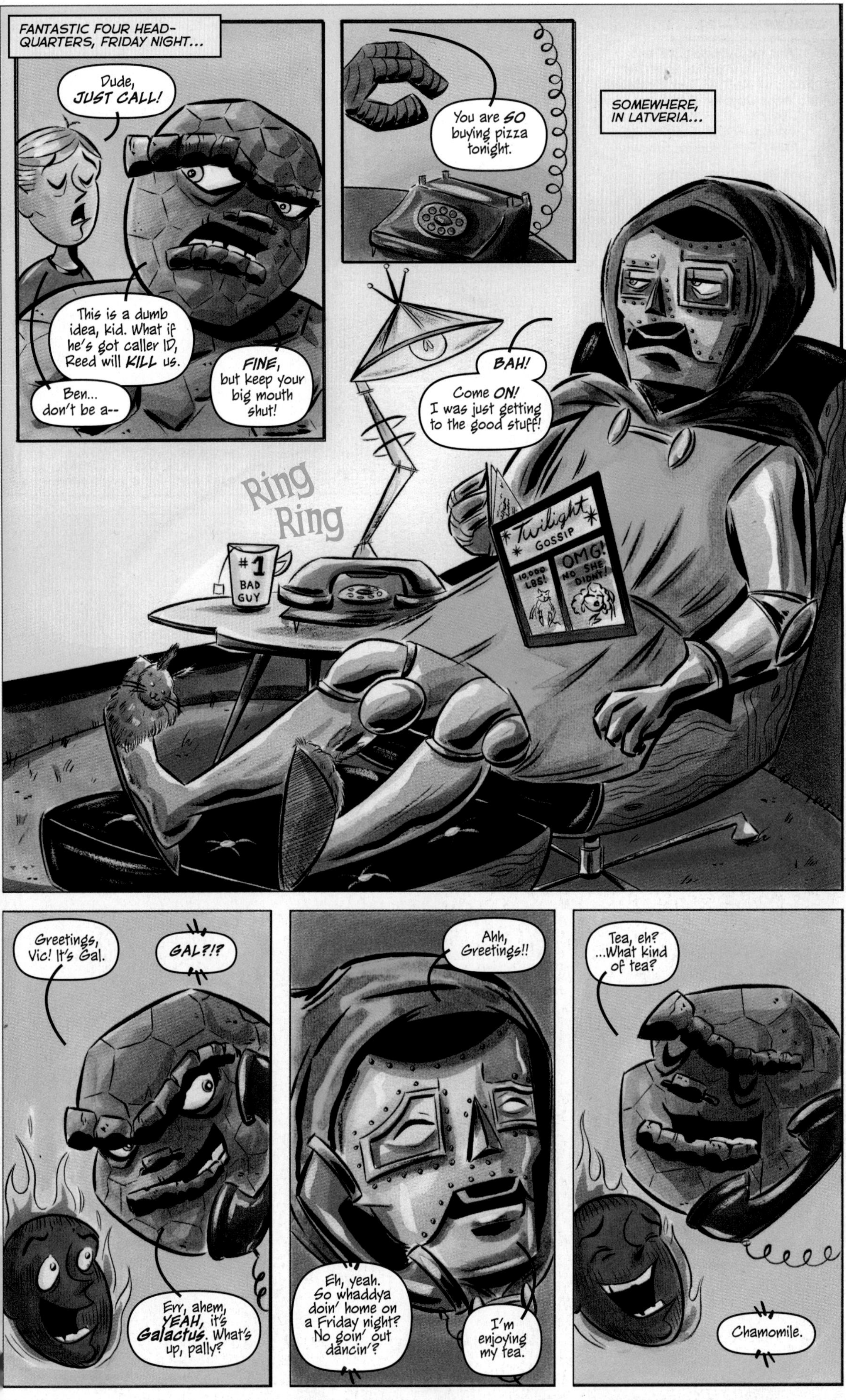
FANTASTIC FOUR HEAD-QUARTERS, FRIDAY NIGHT...
Dude, JUST CALL!
This is a dumb idea, kid. What if he's got caller ID, Reed will KILL us.
Ben... don't be a--
FINE, but keep your big mouth shut!
You are SO buying pizza tonight.
SOMEWHERE, IN LATVERIA...
BAH!
Come ON! I was just getting to the good stuff!
Ring Ring
#1 BAD GUY
Twilight GOSSIP
10,000 LBS!
OMG! NO SHE DIDN'T!
Greetings, Vic! It's Gal.
GAL?!?
Err, ahem, YEAH, it's Galactus. What's up, pally?
Ahh, Greetings!!
Eh, yeah. So whaddya doin' home on a Friday night? No goin' out dancin'?
I'm enjoying my tea.
Tea, eh? ...What kind of tea?
Chamomile.

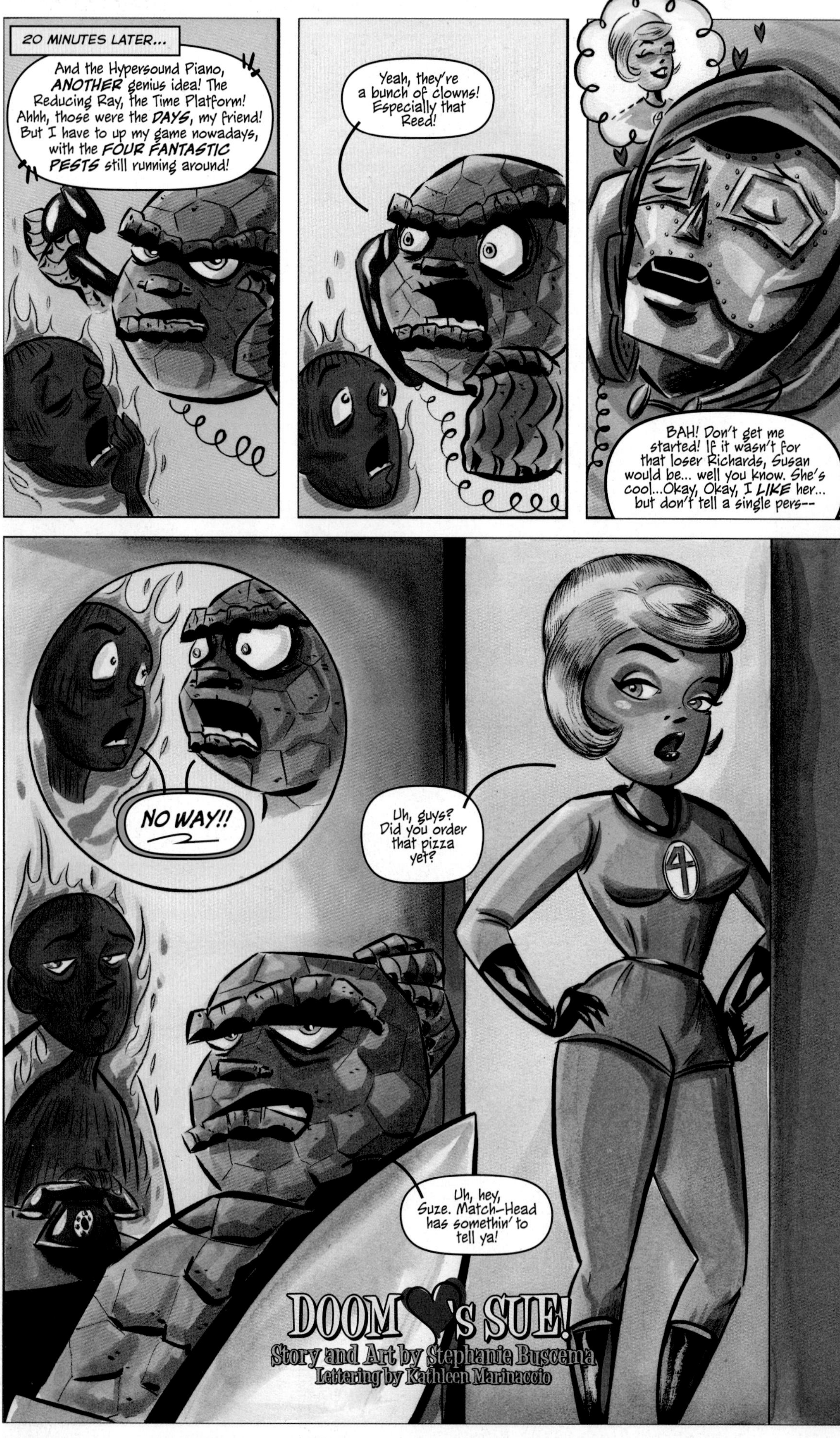
20 MINUTES LATER...
And the Hypersound Piano, ANOTHER genius idea! The Reducing Ray, the Time Platform! Ahhh, those were the DAYS, my friend! But I have to up my game nowadays, with the FOUR FANTASTIC PESTS still running around!
Yeah, they're a bunch of clowns! Especially that Reed!
BAH! Don't get me started! If it wasn't for that loser Richards, Susan would be... well you know. She's cool...Okay, Okay, I LIKE her... but don't tell a single pers--
NO WAY!!
Uh, guys? Did you order that pizza yet?
Uh, hey, Suze. Match-Head has somethin' to tell ya!
DOOM ♥'s SUE!
Story and Art by Stephanie Buscema
Lettering by Kathleen Marinaccio

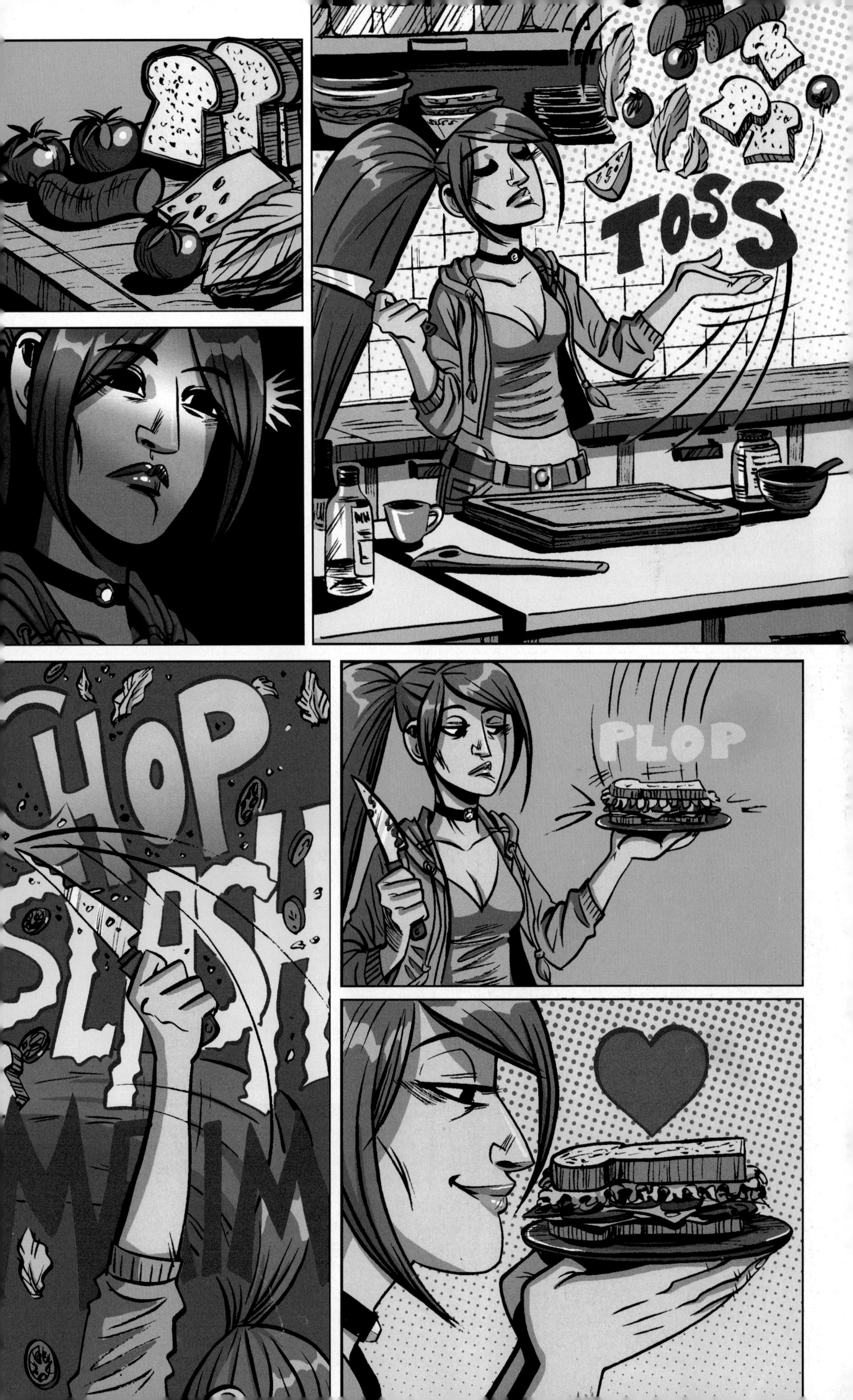
TOSS
PLOP

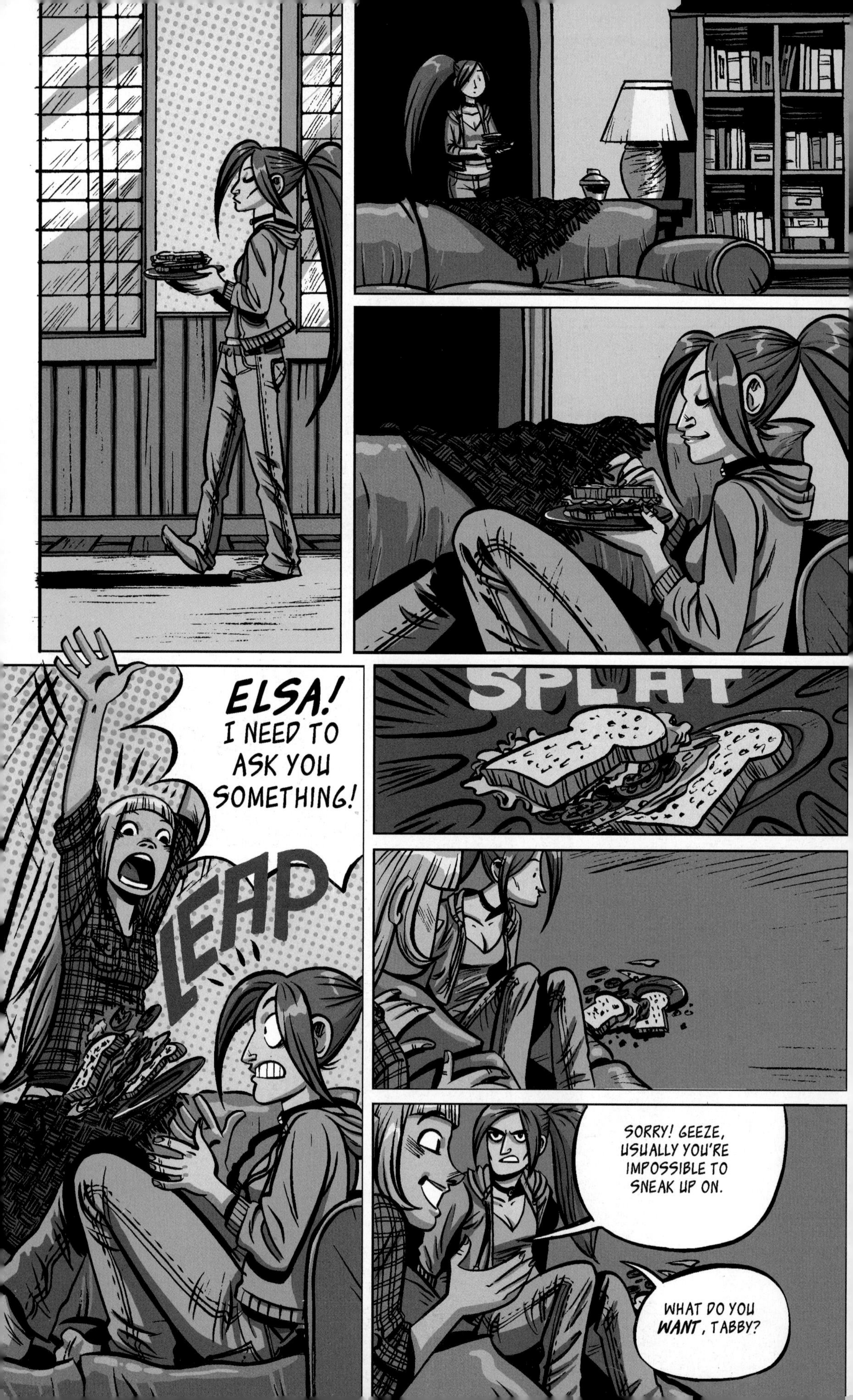
ELSA!
I NEED TO ASK YOU SOMETHING!
LEAP
SPLAT
SORRY! GEEZE, USUALLY YOU'RE IMPOSSIBLE TO SNEAK UP ON.
WHAT DO YOU WANT, TABBY?

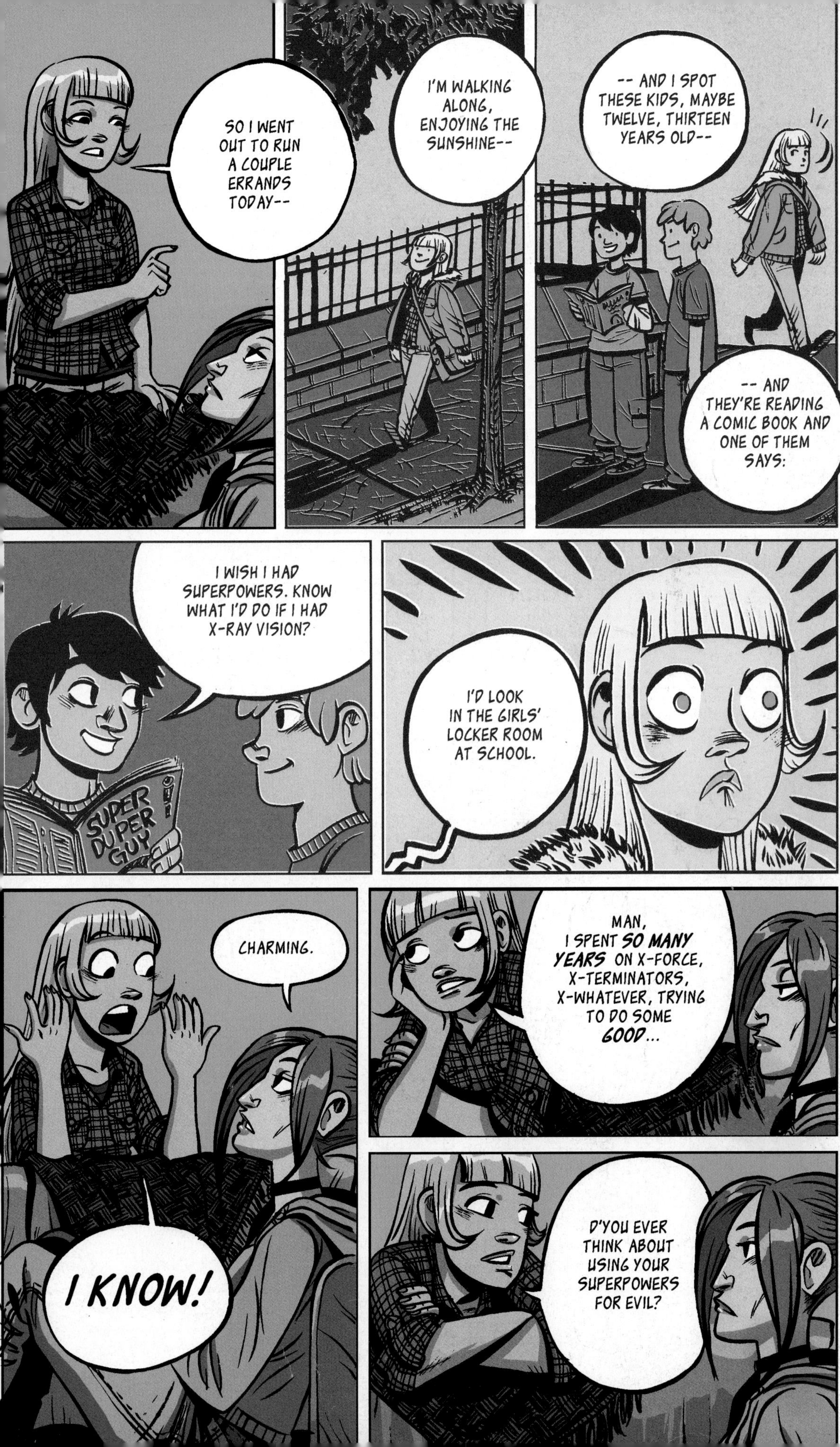
SO I WENT OUT TO RUN A COUPLE ERRANDS TODAY--
I'M WALKING ALONG, ENJOYING THE SUNSHINE--
-- AND I SPOT THESE KIDS, MAYBE TWELVE, THIRTEEN YEARS OLD--
-- AND THEY'RE READING A COMIC BOOK AND ONE OF THEM SAYS:
I WISH I HAD SUPERPOWERS. KNOW WHAT I'D DO IF I HAD X-RAY VISION?
SUPER DUPER GUY
I'D LOOK IN THE GIRLS' LOCKER ROOM AT SCHOOL.
CHARMING.
I KNOW!
MAN, I SPENT SO MANY YEARS ON X-FORCE, X-TERMINATORS, X-WHATEVER, TRYING TO DO SOME GOOD...
D'YOU EVER THINK ABOUT USING YOUR SUPERPOWERS FOR EVIL?

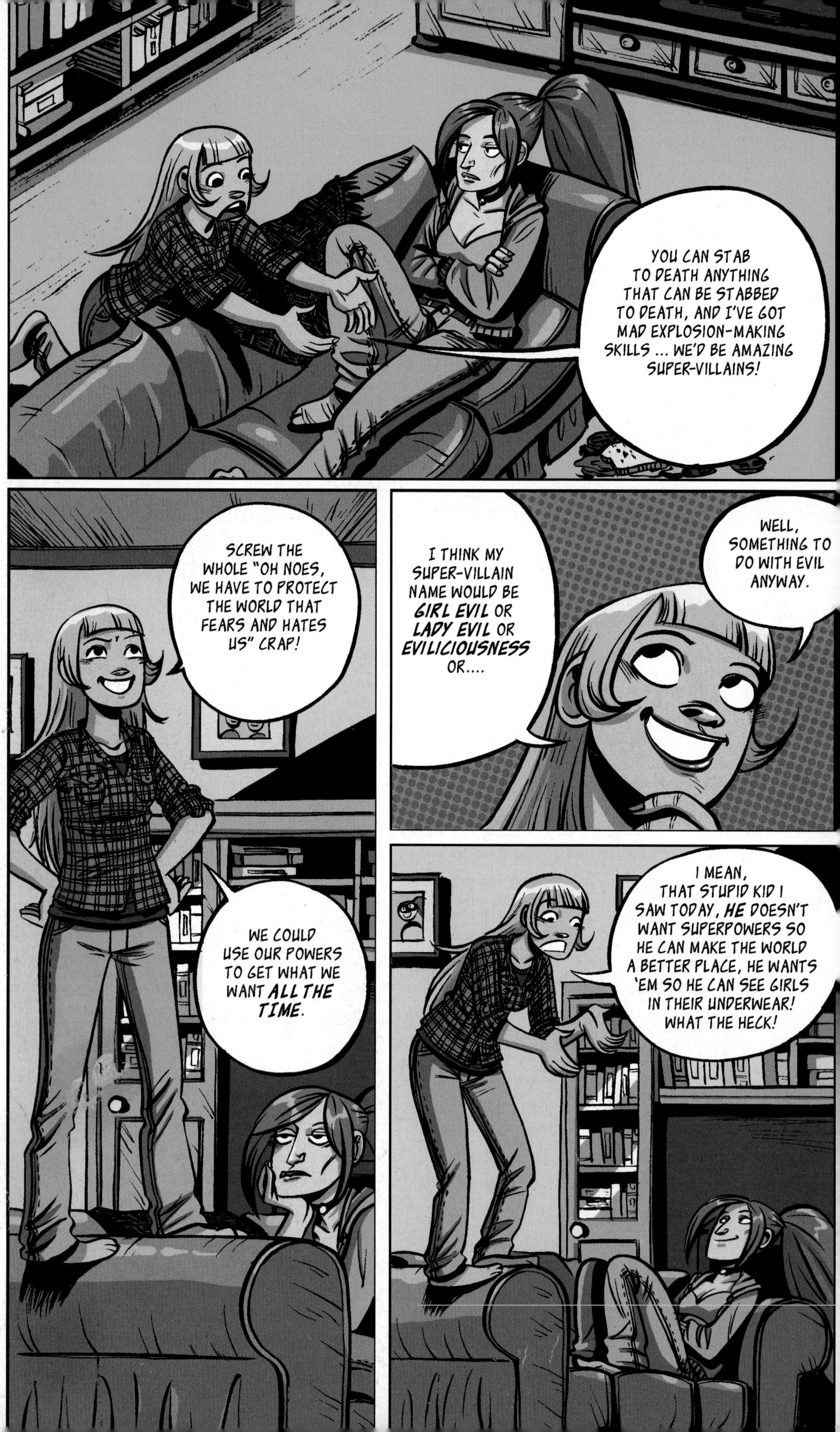
YOU CAN STAB TO DEATH ANYTHING THAT CAN BE STABBED TO DEATH, AND I'VE GOT MAD EXPLOSION-MAKING SKILLS ... WE'D BE AMAZING SUPER-VILLAINS!
SCREW THE WHOLE "OH NOES, WE HAVE TO PROTECT THE WORLD THAT FEARS AND HATES US" CRAP!
WE COULD USE OUR POWERS TO GET WHAT WE WANT ALL THE TIME.
I THINK MY SUPER-VILLAIN NAME WOULD BE GIRL EVIL OR LADY EVIL OR EVILICIOUSNESS OR....
WELL, SOMETHING TO DO WITH EVIL ANYWAY.
I MEAN, THAT STUPID KID I SAW TODAY, HE DOESN'T WANT SUPERPOWERS SO HE CAN MAKE THE WORLD A BETTER PLACE, HE WANTS 'EM SO HE CAN SEE GIRLS IN THEIR UNDERWEAR! WHAT THE HECK!

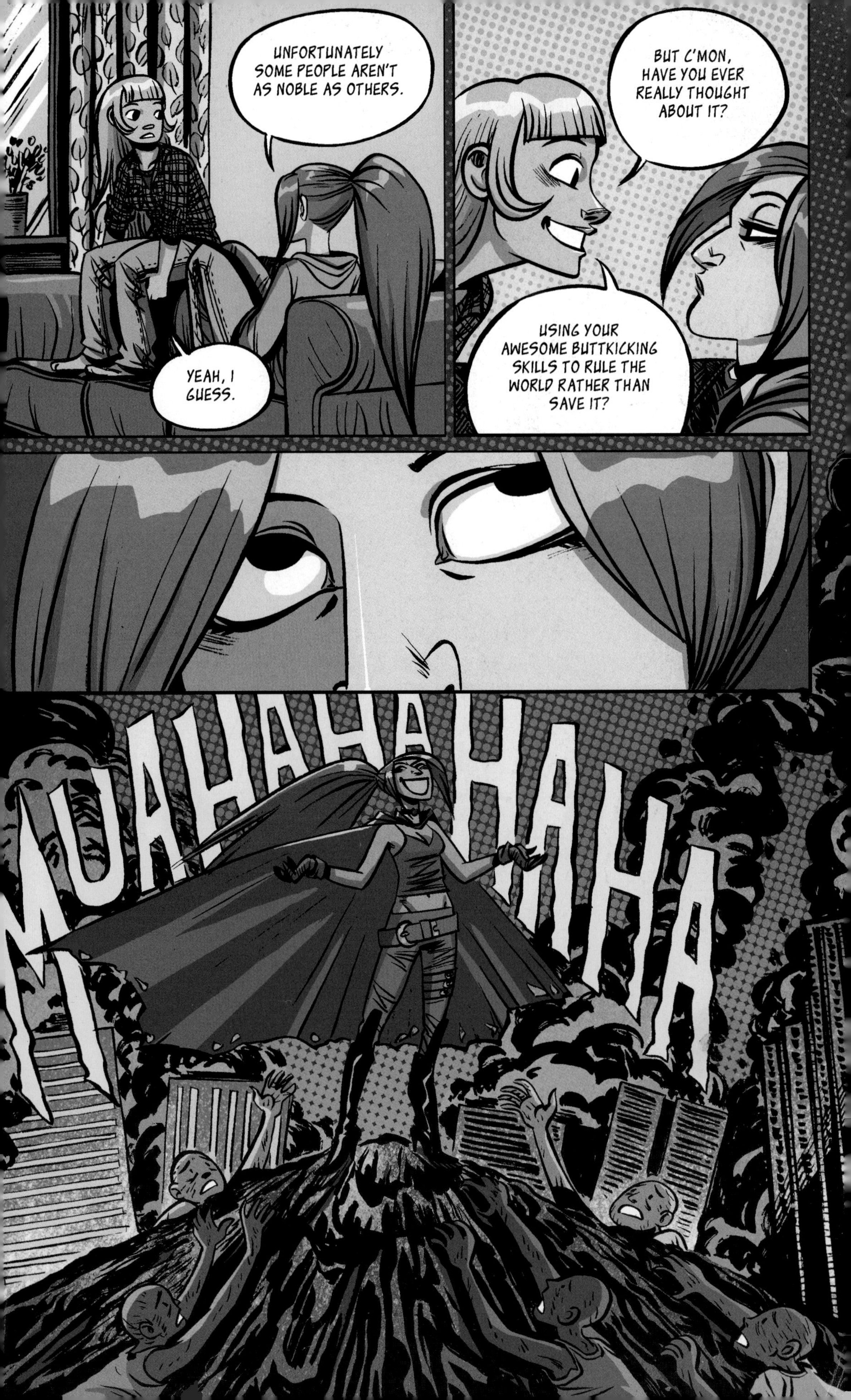
UNFORTUNATELY SOME PEOPLE AREN'T AS NOBLE AS OTHERS.
YEAH, I GUESS.
BUT C'MON, HAVE YOU EVER REALLY THOUGHT ABOUT IT?
USING YOUR AWESOME BUTTKICKING SKILLS TO RULE THE WORLD RATHER THAN SAVE IT?
MUAHAHAHAHAHAHA

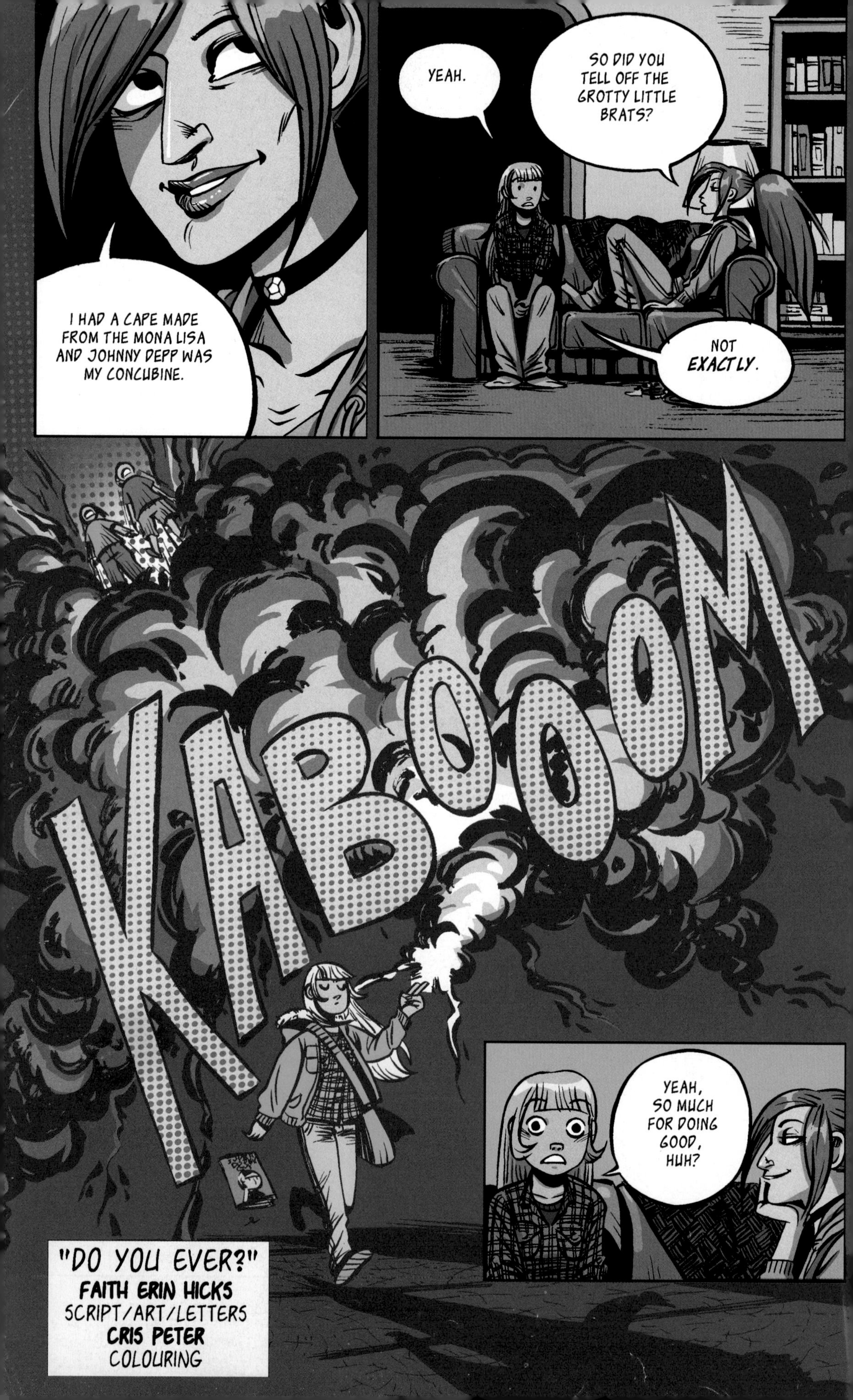
I HAD A CAPE MADE FROM THE MONA LISA AND JOHNNY DEPP WAS MY CONCUBINE.
YEAH.
SO DID YOU TELL OFF THE GROTTY LITTLE BRATS?
NOT EXACTLY.
KABOOOM
YEAH, SO MUCH FOR DOING GOOD, HUH?
"DO YOU EVER?"
FAITH ERIN HICKS
SCRIPT/ART/LETTERS
CRIS PETER
COLOURING

SPOTLIGHT

VALERIE BARCLAY

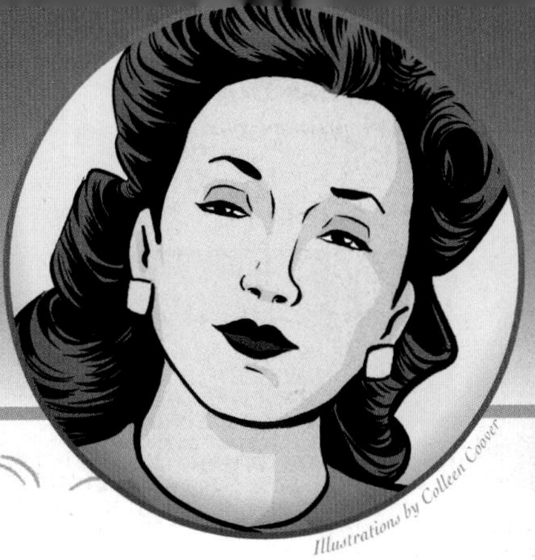

Illustrations by Colleen Coover

Stan Lee wrote the now-rare book called *Secrets Behind the Comics* in 1947. It imparted Lee's comics knowledge and is an entertaining and insightful read about the how-to of comic book publishing. But what caught our eye was a shout-out to one of Timely Comics inkers at the time: Ms. Violet Barclay. Stan called her their "glamorous girl inker," noting that, in fact, women did work alongside men in the comics business. At a time where credits for many of the Timely titles are unclear, this specific acknowledgment has particular importance. Not only was she one of the first women at the company, she was also one of the few female cartoonists working during the Golden Age.

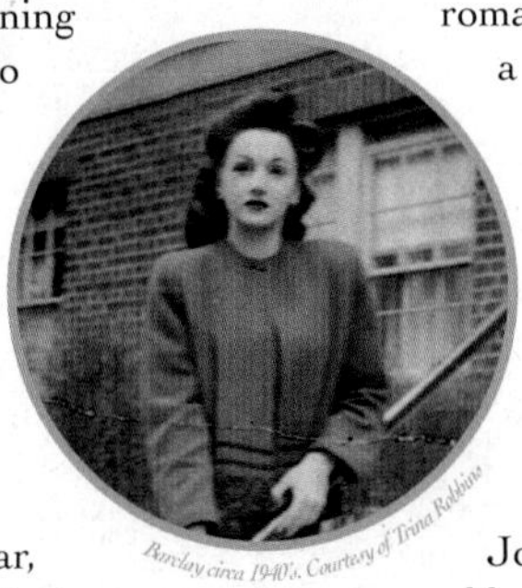

Barclay circa 1940's. Courtesy of Trina Robbins

Born in Manhattan in 1922, Valerie (she changed her name to Valerie as "Violet" was too feminine for her taste) honed her artistic skills at a young age. She enrolled in the School of Industrial Art high school (now known as the School of Art and Design), a notable educational institution that focuses on the creative arts. Unable to find decent work in the general art industry post graduation, Valerie worked as a hostess at the Café Rouge to help make ends meet, earning about $18 a month. At the very same restaurant in 1941, she ran into her old high school classmate, Mike Sekowsky. He encouraged her to join Timely Comics (later called Marvel Comics) where he worked as a penciler. By January of 1942 and at the age of 18, Valerie was working at Timely as an inker with a nice bump in salary to $35 a month.

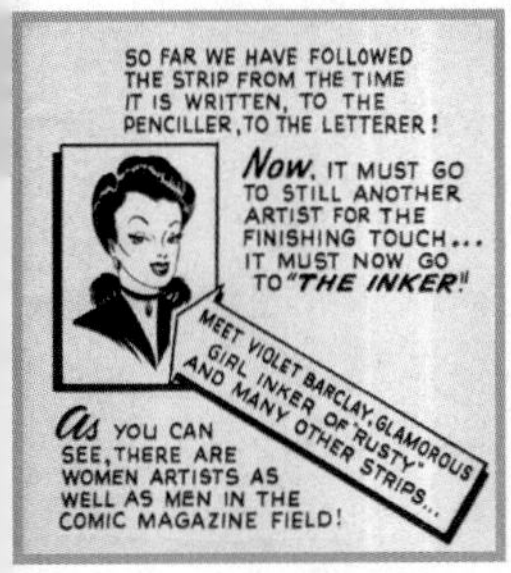
SO FAR WE HAVE FOLLOWED THE STRIP FROM THE TIME IT IS WRITTEN, TO THE PENCILLER, TO THE LETTERER!
NOW, IT MUST GO TO STILL ANOTHER ARTIST FOR THE FINISHING TOUCH... IT MUST NOW GO TO "THE INKER"!
MEET VIOLET BARCLAY, GLAMOROUS GIRL INKER OF "RUSTY" AND MANY OTHER STRIPS...
AS YOU CAN SEE, THERE ARE WOMEN ARTISTS AS WELL AS MEN IN THE COMIC MAGAZINE FIELD!

Valerie's shout-out in "Secrets Behind the Comics."
Courtesy of Trina Robbins

She didn't have any specific training in inking, but credits inker and penciler Dave Gantz for teaching her—although her lessons were mostly achieved by watching Gantz, a credit to her artistic talents. Valerie's inking contributions were mostly on romance and humor titles, the latter being a recent inclusion to Timely's editorial focus. They included such titles as *Super Rabbit, Ziggy Pig and Silly Seal, Rusty, and Nellie the Nurse.*

Valerie was at Timely for almost seven years, eventually leaving to freelance as a penciler and inker for DC Comics, Ace Periodicals, and St. Johns' Publications, to name a few. In an unlikely career shift and due to the industry slump, Valerie dabbled in modeling for awhile. But her calling as an artist was strong, and eventually she transitioned to fashion illustration working on catalogues for such retailers as Lane Bryant and Abraham & Straus. Though she retired in 2004, she continued to paint in her spare time, until her death on February 26, 2010.

Valerie's quiet contribution to Marvel Comics will always be remembered. At a time when men dominated the workforce, Valerie was able to achieve a prolific career in an even more male-centric industry. For this and for her artistic finesse, we salute the memory of Valerie Barclay, Marvel's "glamorous" and talented girl inker.

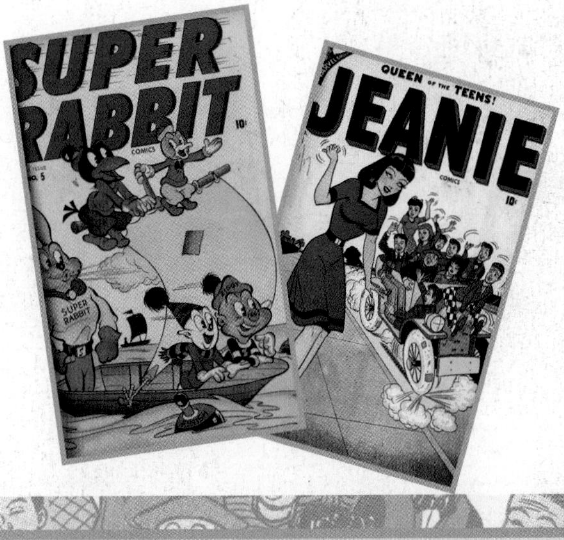
SUPER RABBIT
COMICS
10¢
QUEEN OF THE TEENS!
JEANIE
COMICS
10¢

Special thanks to Trina Robbins

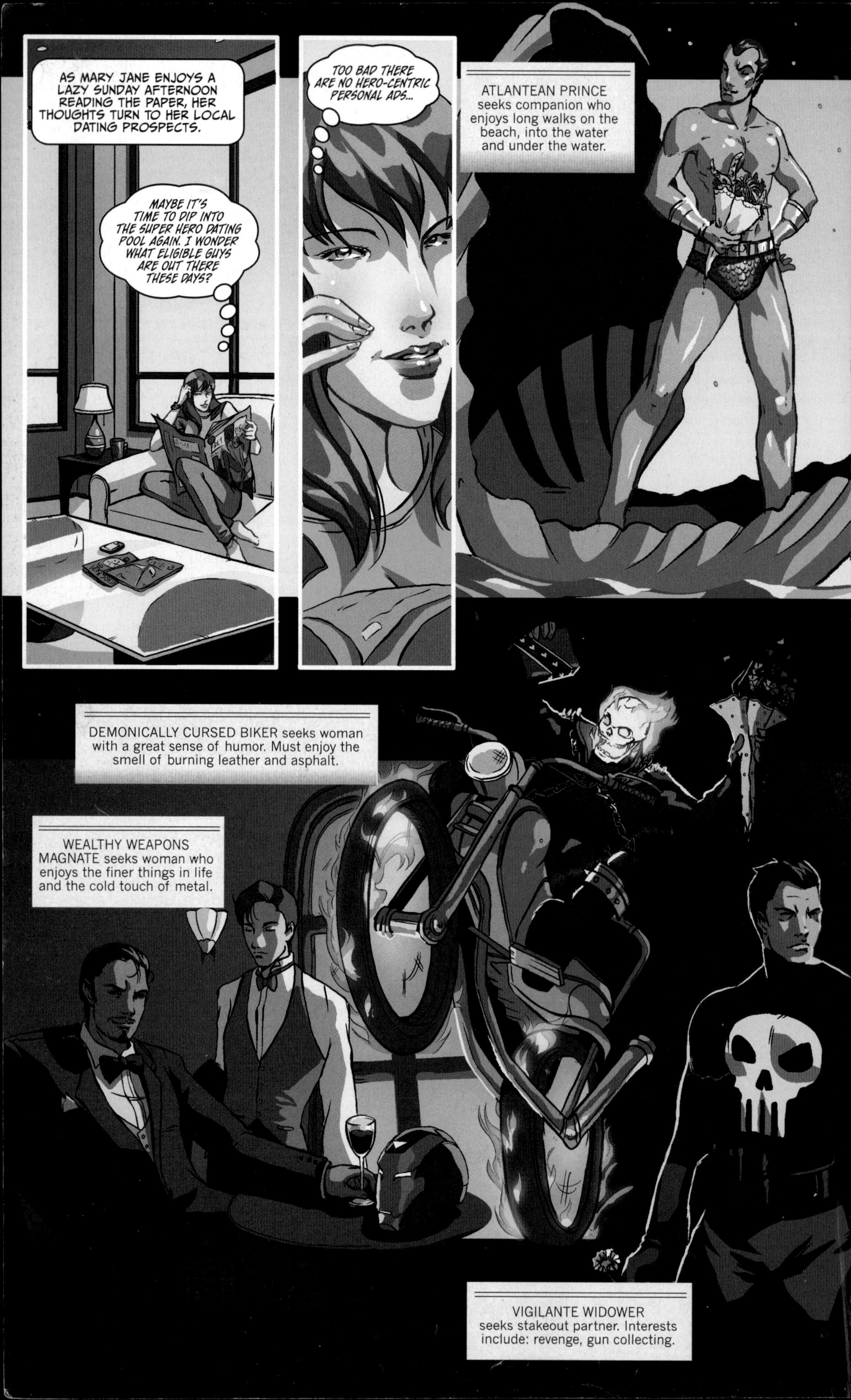

AS MARY JANE ENJOYS A LAZY SUNDAY AFTERNOON READING THE PAPER, HER THOUGHTS TURN TO HER LOCAL DATING PROSPECTS.
MAYBE IT'S TIME TO DIP INTO THE SUPER HERO DATING POOL AGAIN. I WONDER WHAT ELIGIBLE GUYS ARE OUT THERE THESE DAYS?
TOO BAD THERE ARE NO HERO-CENTRIC PERSONAL ADS...
ATLANTEAN PRINCE seeks companion who enjoys long walks on the beach, into the water and under the water.
DEMONICALLY CURSED BIKER seeks woman with a great sense of humor. Must enjoy the smell of burning leather and asphalt.
WEALTHY WEAPONS MAGNATE seeks woman who enjoys the finer things in life and the cold touch of metal.
VIGILANTE WIDOWER seeks stakeout partner. Interests include: revenge, gun collecting.

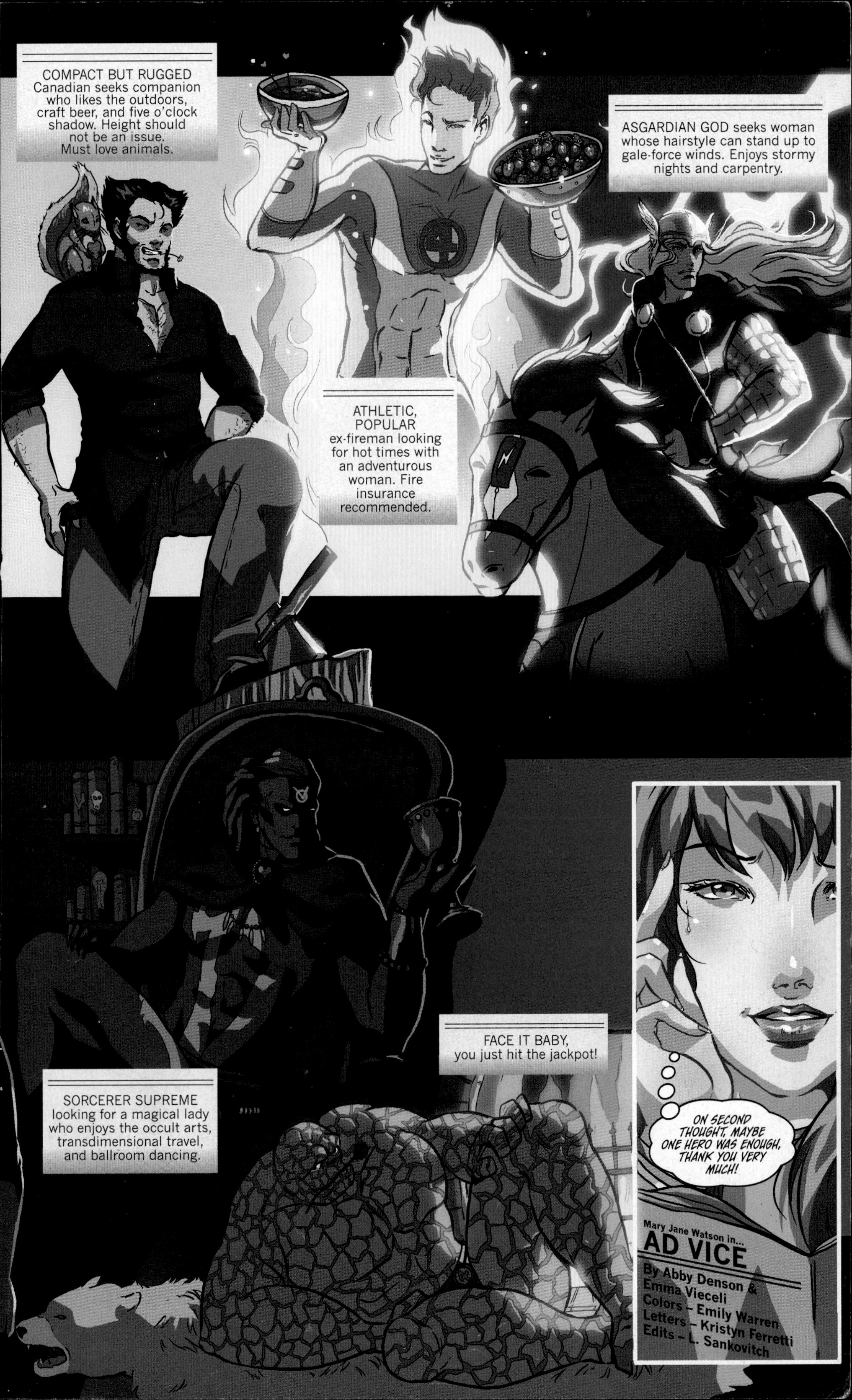
COMPACT BUT RUGGED
Canadian seeks companion who likes the outdoors, craft beer, and five o'clock shadow. Height should not be an issue. Must love animals.
ASGARDIAN GOD seeks woman whose hairstyle can stand up to gale-force winds. Enjoys stormy nights and carpentry.
ATHLETIC, POPULAR
ex-fireman looking for hot times with an adventurous woman. Fire insurance recommended.
FACE IT BABY,
you just hit the jackpot!
SORCERER SUPREME
looking for a magical lady who enjoys the occult arts, transdimensional travel, and ballroom dancing.
ON SECOND THOUGHT, MAYBE ONE HERO WAS ENOUGH, THANK YOU VERY MUCH!
Mary Jane Watson in...
AD VICE
By Abby Denson & Emma Vieceli
Colors – Emily Warren
Letters – Kristyn Ferretti
Edits – L. Sankovitch

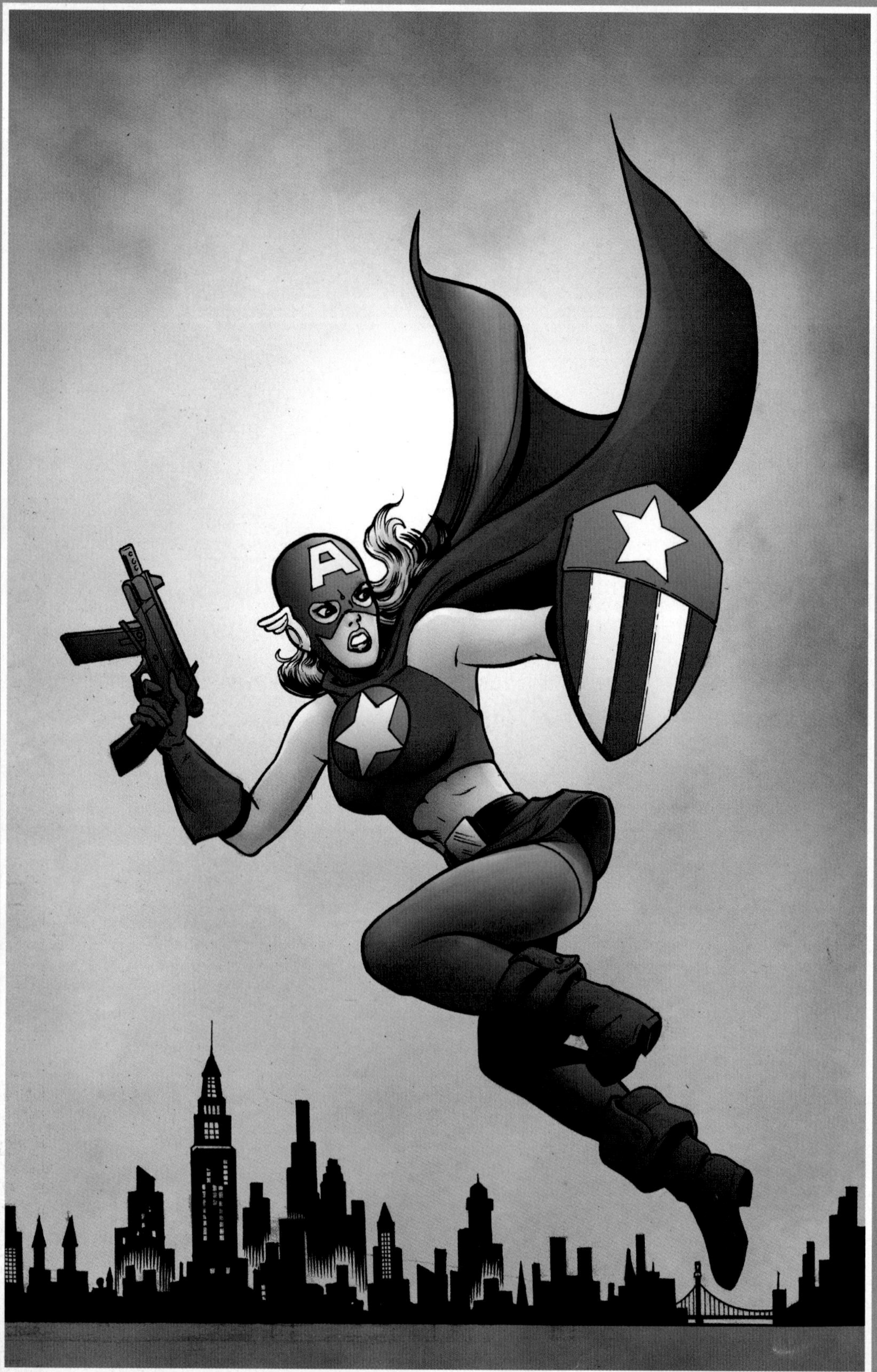
A

MISS AMERICA

Pencils by RAMONA FRADON   Inks by REBECCA BUCHMAN   Colors by JUNE CHUNG

SPOTLIGHT

LINDA FITE

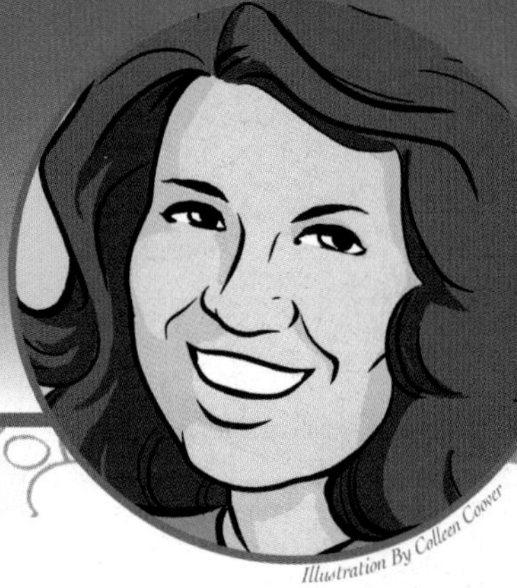

Illustration By Colleen Coover

What was fascinating about Marvel in the '60s was the potential the company inspired and cultivated. No one quite exemplifies that like Linda Fite, an editorial assistant to Stan Lee who worked under Flo Steinberg, Marvel's original Girl Friday. For her short time there, Linda managed to go from assistant to writer fairly quickly, which was quite a path for a girl who applied to Marvel on a whim. But if you've ever been acquainted with Linda, it's no surprise to see why.

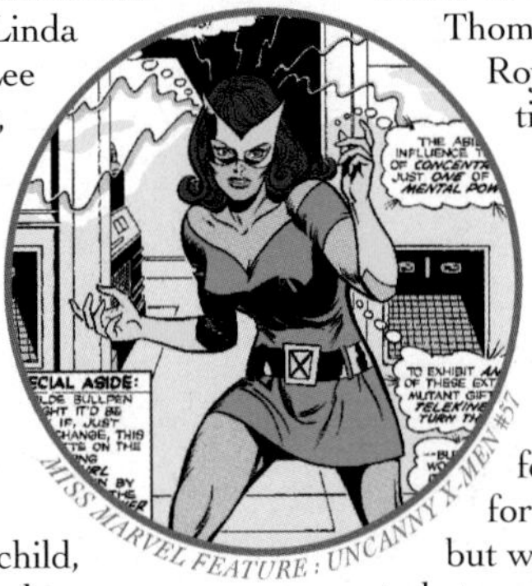

SPECIAL ASIDE:
MENTAL POW

MISS MARVEL FEATURE : UNCANNY X-MEN #57

Though she was a comics fan as a child, Linda discovered Marvel while she was in college in Lynchburg, Virginia. While she was applying for jobs post-graduation, she realized she could go one of two ways: "I could work for a big generic magazine, or I could work in comics. And I decided to go after the oddball option: Marvel!" As a tenacious and motivated post-grad, Linda moved to New York City and sent a letter of interest to Stan Lee. She enumerated upon her many skills as a public relations assistant, writer and typist, rounding it off with a wisecrack about not there not being enough "heifers in the Bullpen". Flo Steinberg and Stan Lee were so amused and impressed by the letter they asked her to come by the offices if she were ever in New York. "When I heard Flo's voice on the other end, I fell off my chair!" After their first meeting in 1967, Marvel offered Linda a summer position which eventually turned into an editorial assistant gig.

Linda worked for Flo and as Stan's assistant mostly, answering fan mail and doing production work. All the while she was amongst some of Marvel's biggest and brightest creators like John Romita, Marie Severin, Sol Brodsky, and Roy Thomas, to name a few. "All of the legends people hear are true. It really was a fun time. There was no bickering. Everyone just got along." History repeated itself when Linda responded to Barry Windsor Smith's letter to Marvel. She showed it to Stan, noting that he seemed talented and per Stan's request wrote back to Barry inviting him to stop by the offices if he were ever in New York. A few months later, Barry flew in from England and showed up at Marvel's door, a daring move which launched his career and a very long and fond friendship with Linda.

Meanwhile, Linda was getting the writing bug. A writer at heart, she began to nudge editor Roy Thomas to let her work on a title. Eventually Roy agreed and put her on a *Kid Colt Outlaw* title called "Dixie or Die" in 1968. After that was published, Linda remembers excitedly sending it to her old college professor with a note bragging: "Published at 23!" Thereafter she worked on *Night Nurse #4* and backup stories for *Uncanny X-Men*. In 1972 Stan and Roy had an idea to tap into the female market by creating a comic book for girls called *The Cat*. Linda, who had quit but was freelancing at the time, was given the task to write with Marie Severin on as penciler. The series followed Greer Grant, a model house wife turned super hero after a twist of fate. Though Linda mourns the title for its short shelf life, she loves that she was able to write an engaging tale about a strong and independent female super hero, of which at the time there were few. The Cat eventually evolved into the character Tigra and the Cat's costume was later donned by Patsy Walker when she became Hellcat.

Although Linda has moved on from comics as a profession (she's now a features writer for the *Times Herald-Record* in Middletown, NY) her friendships and memories from Marvel haven't left her. Linda truly embodied the Marvel spirit with her excitement and passion for the content, while her charm and tenacity made her beloved by all who met her—and that makes her a woman of Marvel for life.

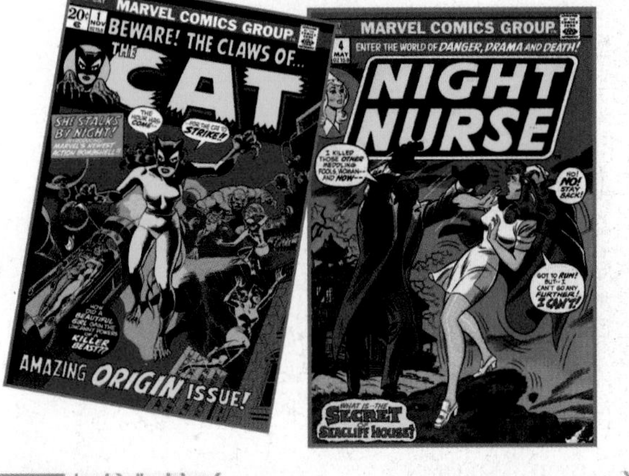

MARVEL COMICS GROUP
BEWARE! THE CLAWS OF...
THE CAT
SHE STALKS BY NIGHT!
STRIKE!!
AMAZING ORIGIN ISSUE!
MARVEL COMICS GROUP
ENTER THE WORLD OF DANGER, DRAMA AND DEATH!
NIGHT NURSE
I KILLED THOSE OTHER MEDDLING FOOLS WOMAN-- AND NOW--
NO! NO! STAY BACK!
GOT TO RUN! BUT-- I CAN'T GO ANY FURTHER! I CAN'T!
WHAT IS--THE SECRET OF SEACLIFF HOUSE?

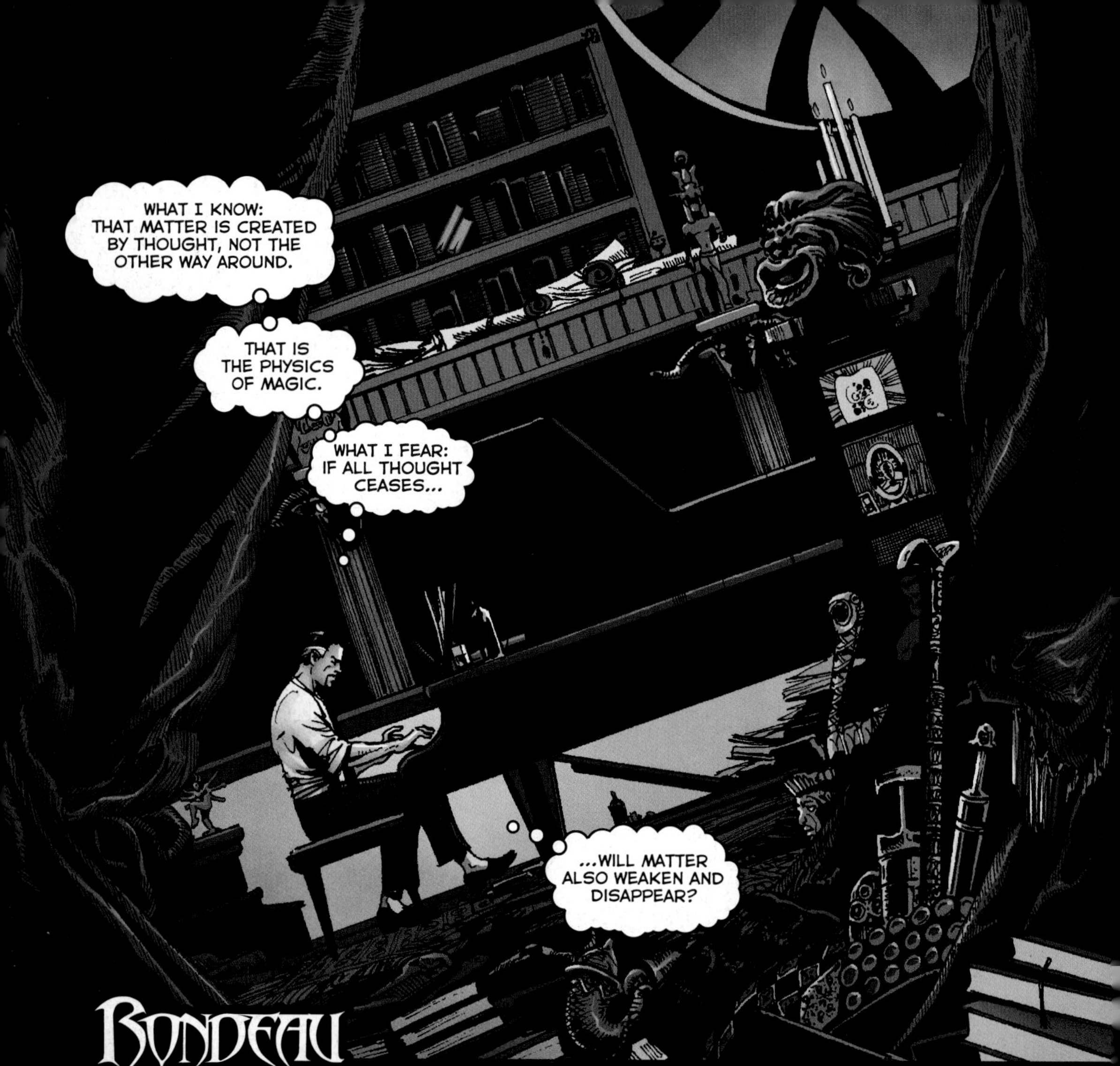
WHAT I KNOW: THAT MATTER IS CREATED BY THOUGHT, NOT THE OTHER WAY AROUND.
THAT IS THE PHYSICS OF MAGIC.
WHAT I FEAR: IF ALL THOUGHT CEASES...
...WILL MATTER ALSO WEAKEN AND DISAPPEAR?
RONDEAU

Script by Christine Boylan & Art by Cynthia Martin & Color Art by June Chung & Letters by Kathleen Marinaccio

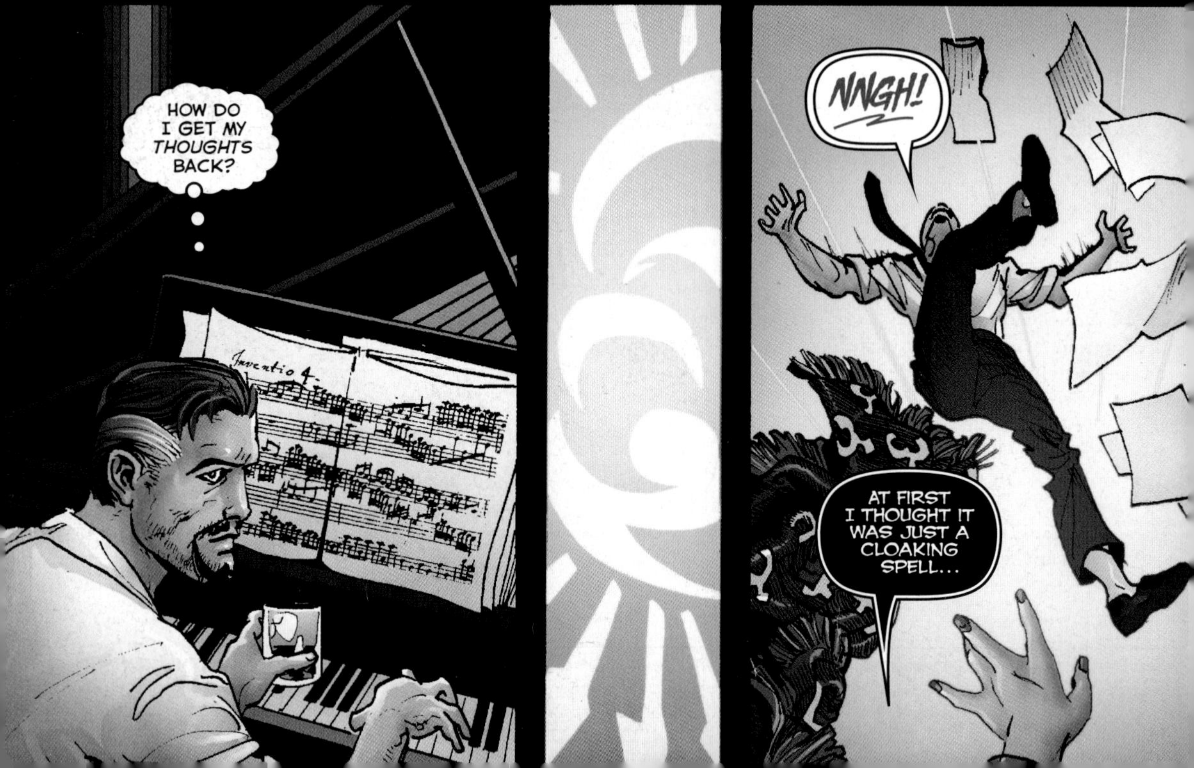
HOW DO I GET MY *THOUGHTS* BACK?
Inventio 4.
NNGH!
AT FIRST I THOUGHT IT WAS JUST A CLOAKING SPELL...

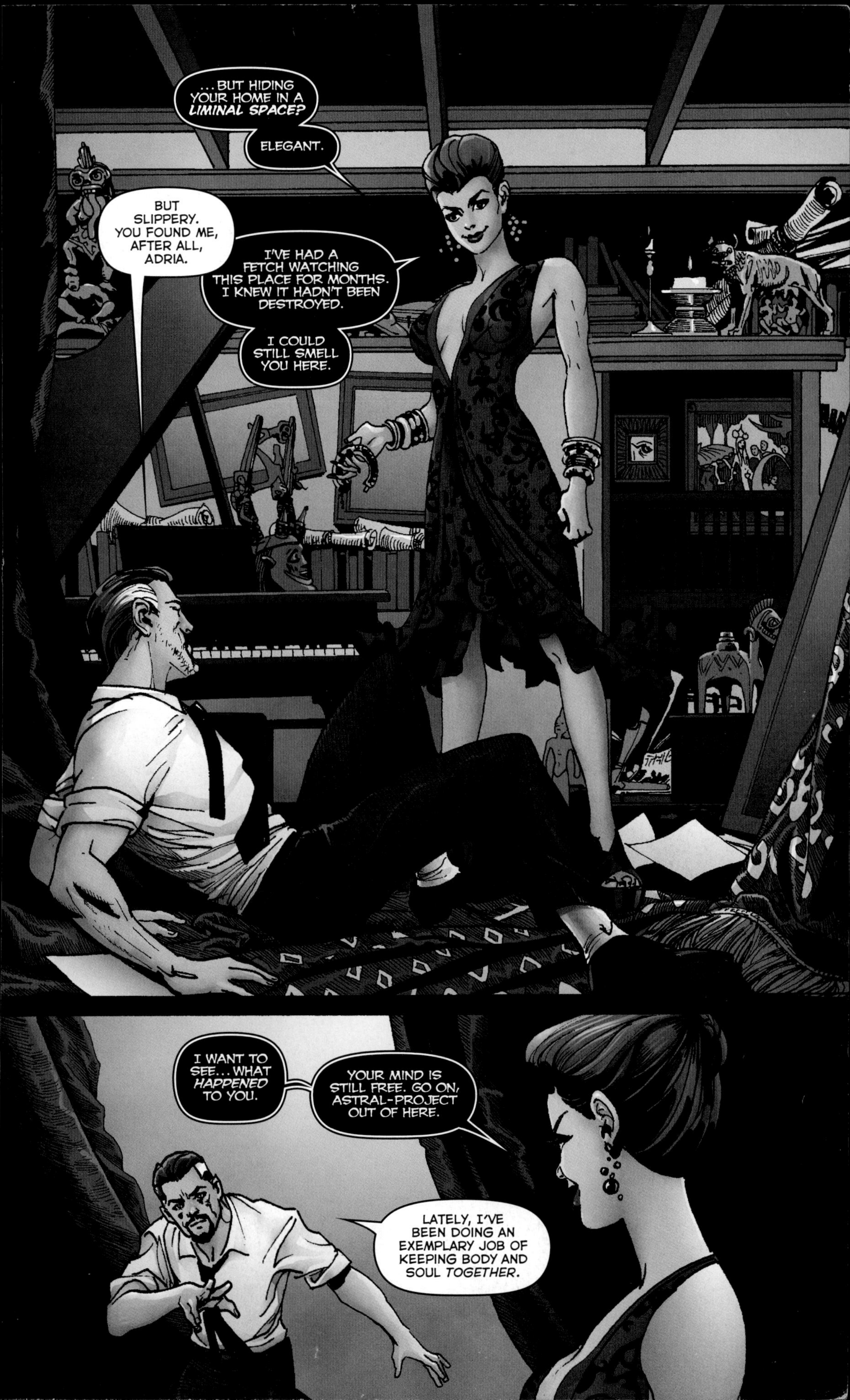
...BUT HIDING YOUR HOME IN A *LIMINAL SPACE?*
ELEGANT.
BUT SLIPPERY. YOU FOUND ME, AFTER ALL, ADRIA.
I'VE HAD A FETCH WATCHING THIS PLACE FOR MONTHS. I KNEW IT HADN'T BEEN DESTROYED.
I COULD STILL SMELL YOU HERE.
I WANT TO SEE... WHAT *HAPPENED* TO YOU.
YOUR MIND IS STILL FREE. GO ON, ASTRAL-PROJECT OUT OF HERE.
LATELY, I'VE BEEN DOING AN EXEMPLARY JOB OF KEEPING BODY AND SOUL *TOGETHER*.

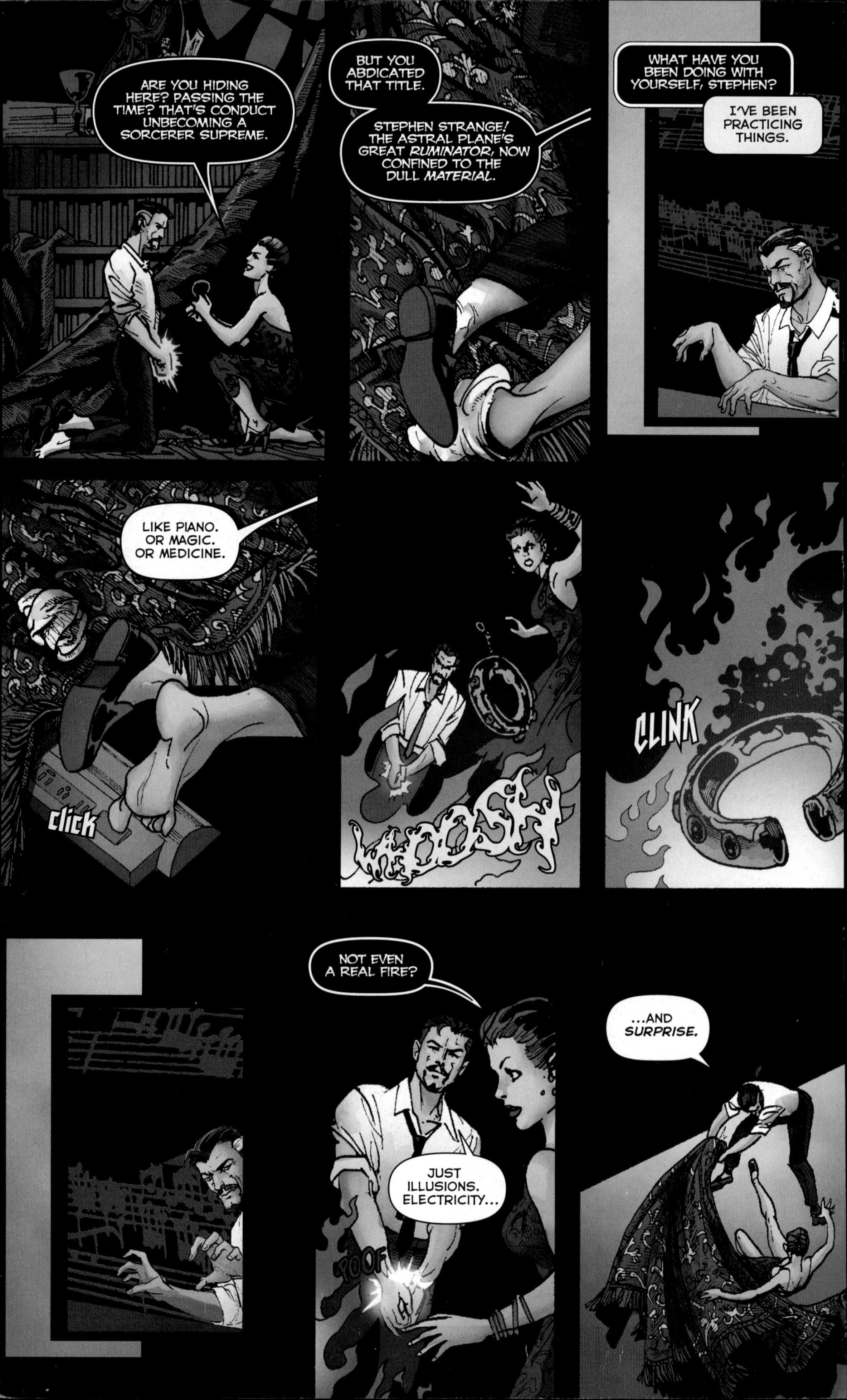
ARE YOU HIDING HERE? PASSING THE TIME? THAT'S CONDUCT UNBECOMING A SORCERER SUPREME.
BUT YOU ABDICATED THAT TITLE.
STEPHEN STRANGE! THE ASTRAL PLANE'S GREAT *RUMINATOR*, NOW CONFINED TO THE DULL *MATERIAL*.
WHAT HAVE YOU BEEN DOING WITH YOURSELF, STEPHEN?
I'VE BEEN PRACTICING THINGS.
LIKE PIANO. OR MAGIC. OR MEDICINE.
click
WHOOSH
CLINK
NOT EVEN A REAL FIRE?
JUST ILLUSIONS. ELECTRICITY...
POOF
...AND *SURPRISE.*

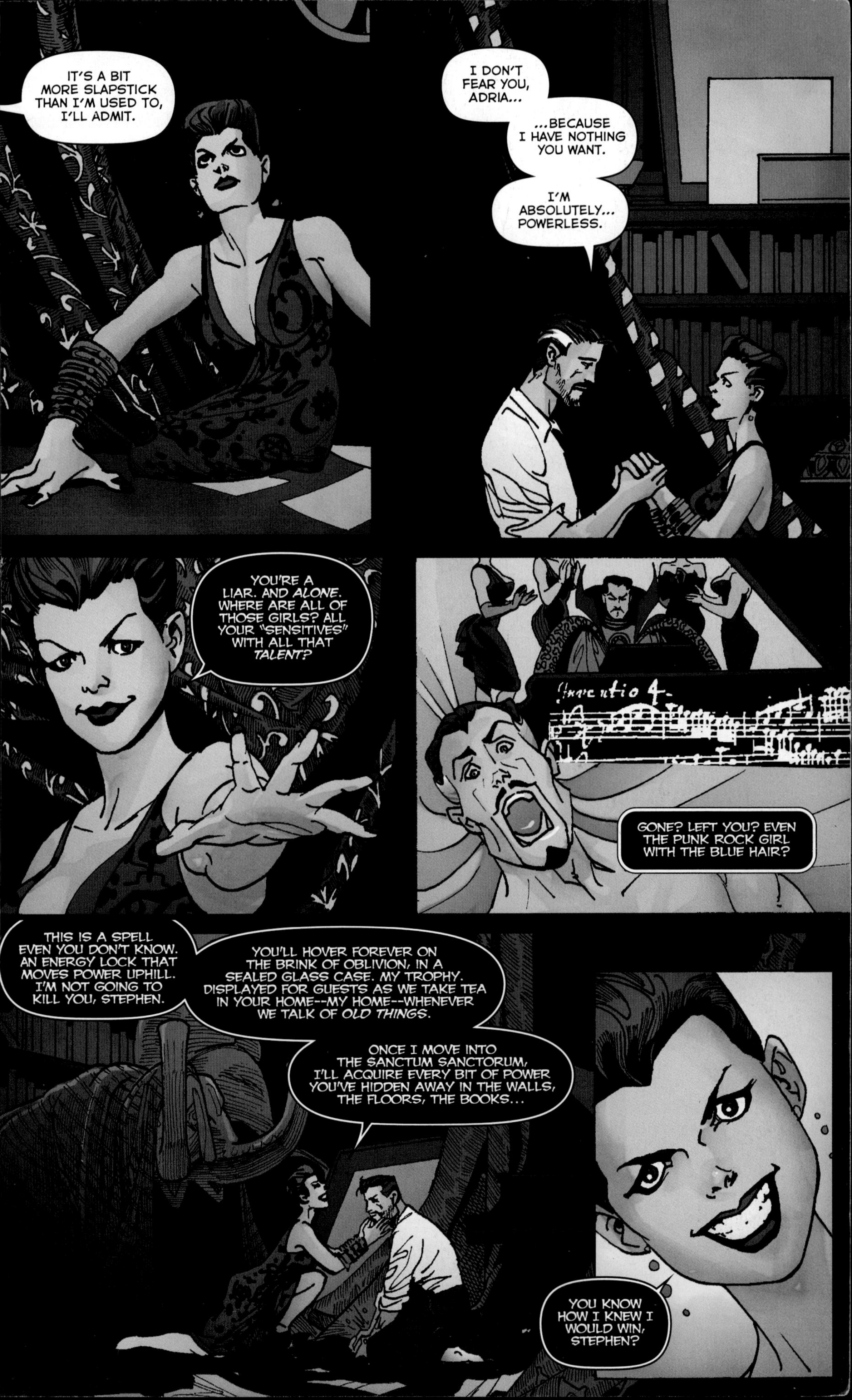
IT'S A BIT MORE SLAPSTICK THAN I'M USED TO, I'LL ADMIT.
I DON'T FEAR YOU, ADRIA...
...BECAUSE I HAVE NOTHING YOU WANT.
I'M ABSOLUTELY... POWERLESS.
YOU'RE A LIAR. AND *ALONE*. WHERE ARE ALL OF THOSE GIRLS? ALL YOUR "SENSITIVES" WITH ALL THAT *TALENT*?
Inventio 4.
GONE? LEFT YOU? EVEN THE PUNK ROCK GIRL WITH THE BLUE HAIR?
THIS IS A SPELL EVEN YOU DON'T KNOW. AN ENERGY LOCK THAT MOVES POWER UPHILL. I'M NOT GOING TO KILL YOU, STEPHEN.
YOU'LL HOVER FOREVER ON THE BRINK OF OBLIVION, IN A SEALED GLASS CASE. MY TROPHY. DISPLAYED FOR GUESTS AS WE TAKE TEA IN YOUR HOME--MY HOME--WHENEVER WE TALK OF *OLD THINGS*.
ONCE I MOVE INTO THE SANCTUM SANCTORUM, I'LL ACQUIRE EVERY BIT OF POWER YOU'VE HIDDEN AWAY IN THE WALLS, THE FLOORS, THE BOOKS...
YOU KNOW HOW I KNEW I WOULD WIN, STEPHEN?

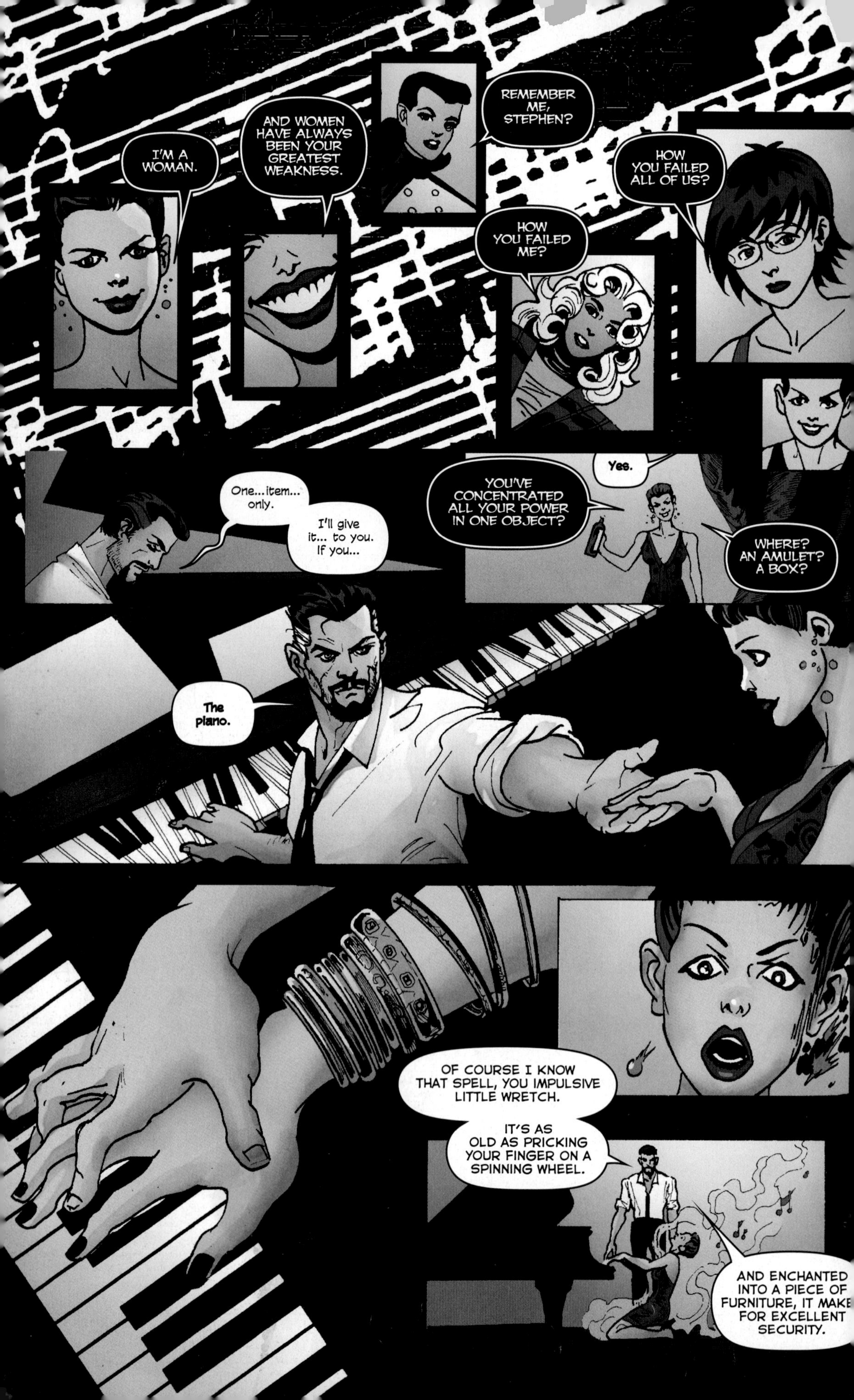
I'M A WOMAN.
AND WOMEN HAVE ALWAYS BEEN YOUR GREATEST WEAKNESS.
REMEMBER ME, STEPHEN?
HOW YOU FAILED ME?
HOW YOU FAILED ALL OF US?
One...item... only.
I'll give it... to you. If you...
Yes.
YOU'VE CONCENTRATED ALL YOUR POWER IN ONE OBJECT?
WHERE? AN AMULET? A BOX?
The piano.
OF COURSE I KNOW THAT SPELL, YOU IMPULSIVE LITTLE WRETCH.
IT'S AS OLD AS PRICKING YOUR FINGER ON A SPINNING WHEEL.
AND ENCHANTED INTO A PIECE OF FURNITURE, IT MAKE FOR EXCELLENT SECURITY.

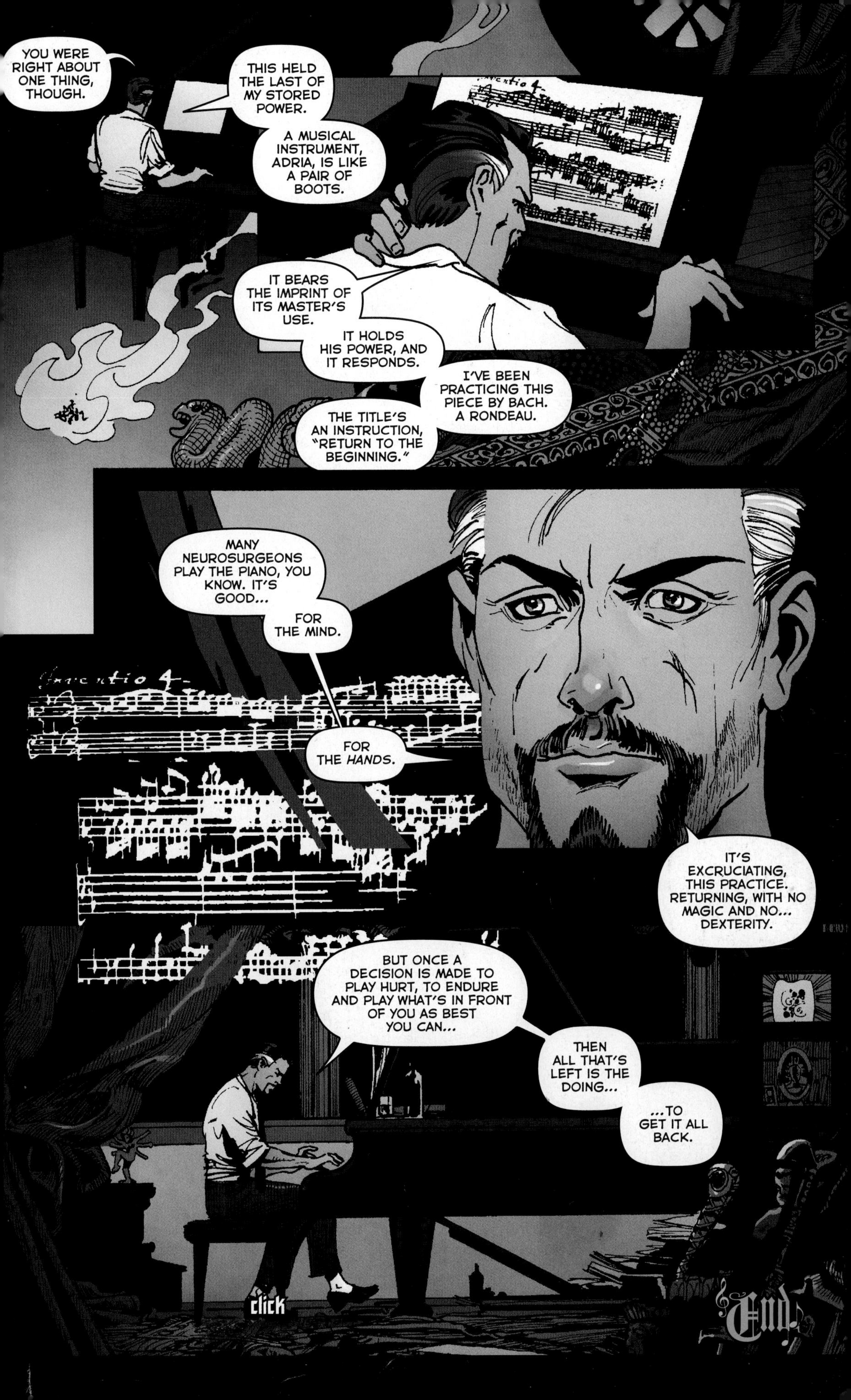

YOU WERE RIGHT ABOUT ONE THING, THOUGH.
THIS HELD THE LAST OF MY STORED POWER.
A MUSICAL INSTRUMENT, ADRIA, IS LIKE A PAIR OF BOOTS.
IT BEARS THE IMPRINT OF ITS MASTER'S USE.
IT HOLDS HIS POWER, AND IT RESPONDS.
I'VE BEEN PRACTICING THIS PIECE BY BACH. A RONDEAU.
THE TITLE'S AN INSTRUCTION, "RETURN TO THE BEGINNING."
MANY NEUROSURGEONS PLAY THE PIANO, YOU KNOW. IT'S GOOD...
FOR THE MIND.
FOR THE HANDS.
IT'S EXCRUCIATING, THIS PRACTICE. RETURNING, WITH NO MAGIC AND NO... DEXTERITY.
BUT ONCE A DECISION IS MADE TO PLAY HURT, TO ENDURE AND PLAY WHAT'S IN FRONT OF YOU AS BEST YOU CAN...
THEN ALL THAT'S LEFT IS THE DOING...
...TO GET IT ALL BACK.
click
End

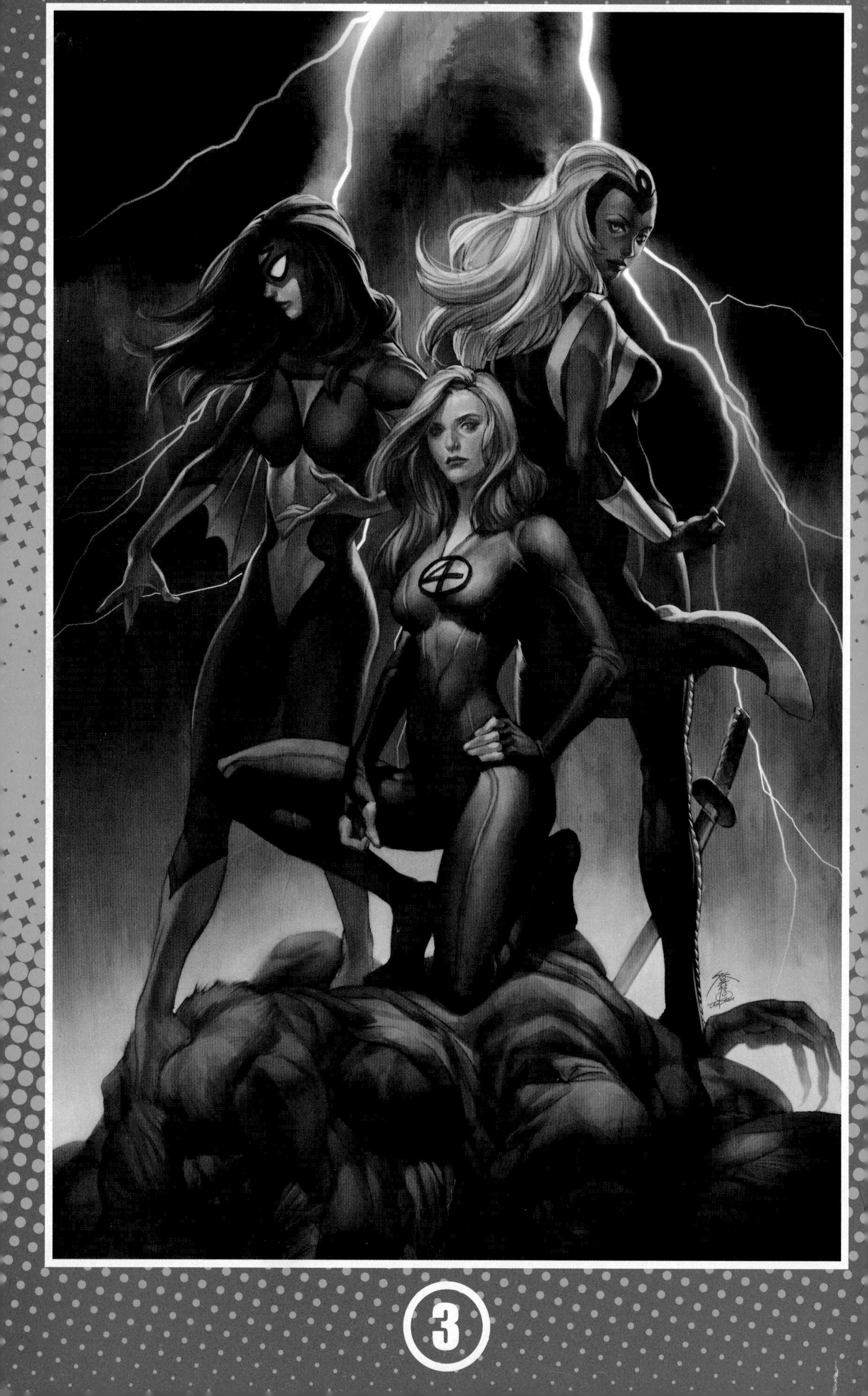

3

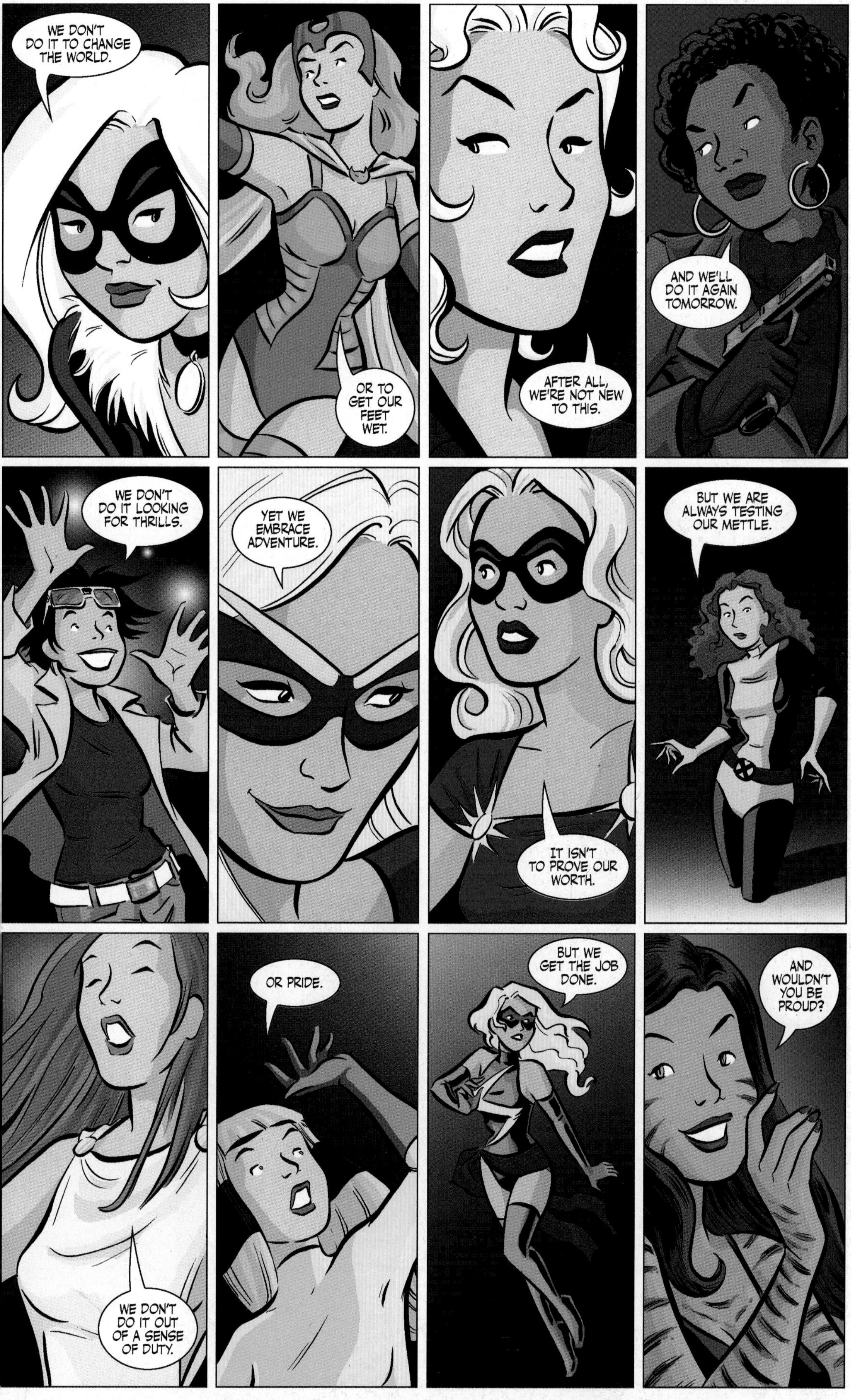
WE DON'T DO IT TO CHANGE THE WORLD.
OR TO GET OUR FEET WET.
AFTER ALL, WE'RE NOT NEW TO THIS.
AND WE'LL DO IT AGAIN TOMORROW.
WE DON'T DO IT LOOKING FOR THRILLS.
YET WE EMBRACE ADVENTURE.
IT ISN'T TO PROVE OUR WORTH.
BUT WE ARE ALWAYS TESTING OUR METTLE.
WE DON'T DO IT OUT OF A SENSE OF DUTY.
OR PRIDE.
BUT WE GET THE JOB DONE.
AND WOULDN'T YOU BE PROUD?

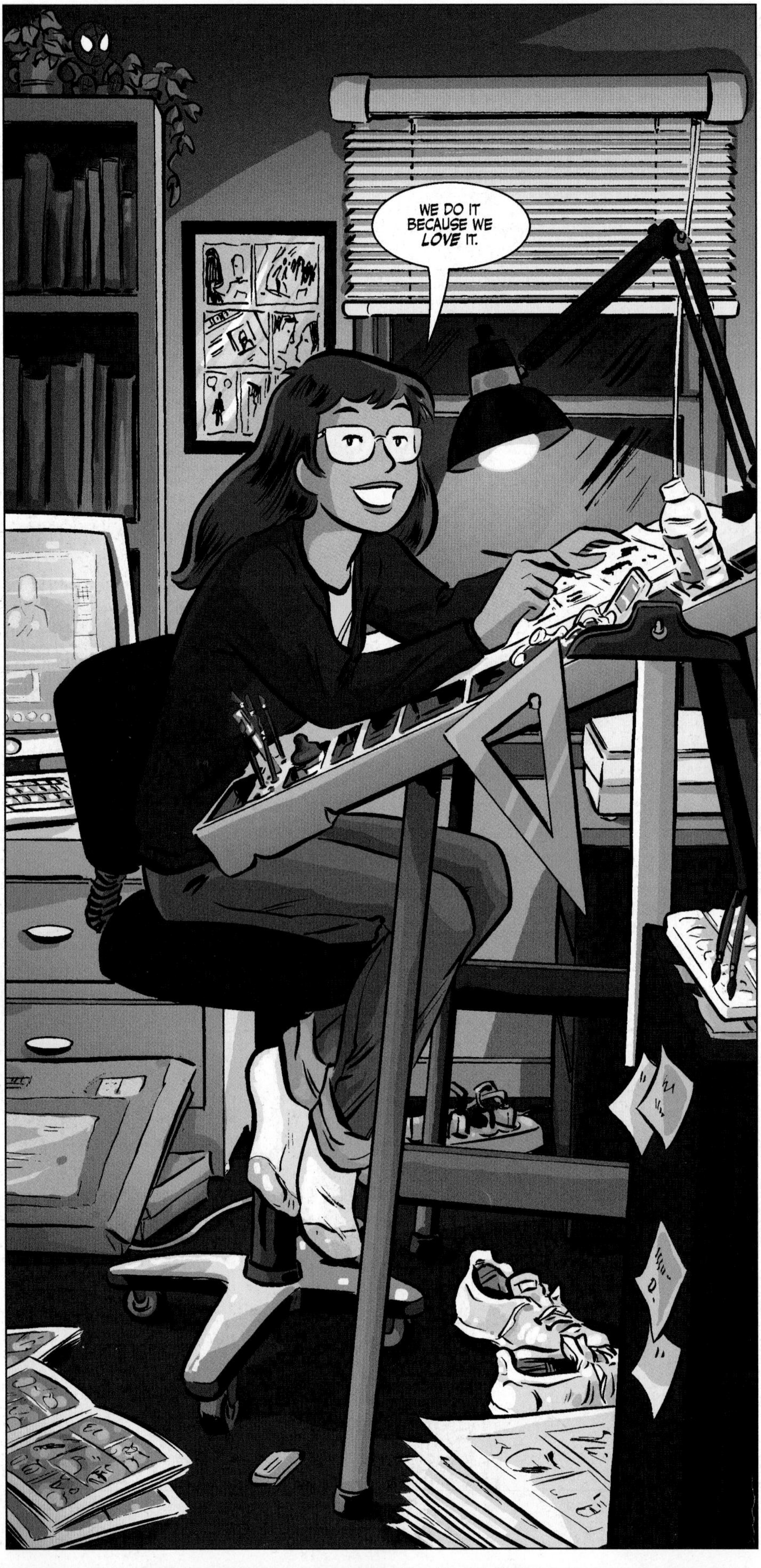
WE DO IT
BECAUSE WE
LOVE IT.

GIRL COMICS

Part Three of Three

INTRODUCTION:
COLLEEN COOVER

COVER ART:
JO CHEN

PRODUCTION:
IRENE LEE

ASSISTANT EDITORS:
SANA AMANAT
& RACHEL PINNELAS

ASSOCIATE EDITOR:
LAUREN SANKOVITCH

EDITOR:
JEANINE SCHAEFER

EDITOR IN CHIEF:
JOE QUESADA

PUBLISHER:
DAN BUCKLEY

EXEC. PRODUCER:
ALAN FINE

SPECIAL THANKS:
SPRING HOTELING

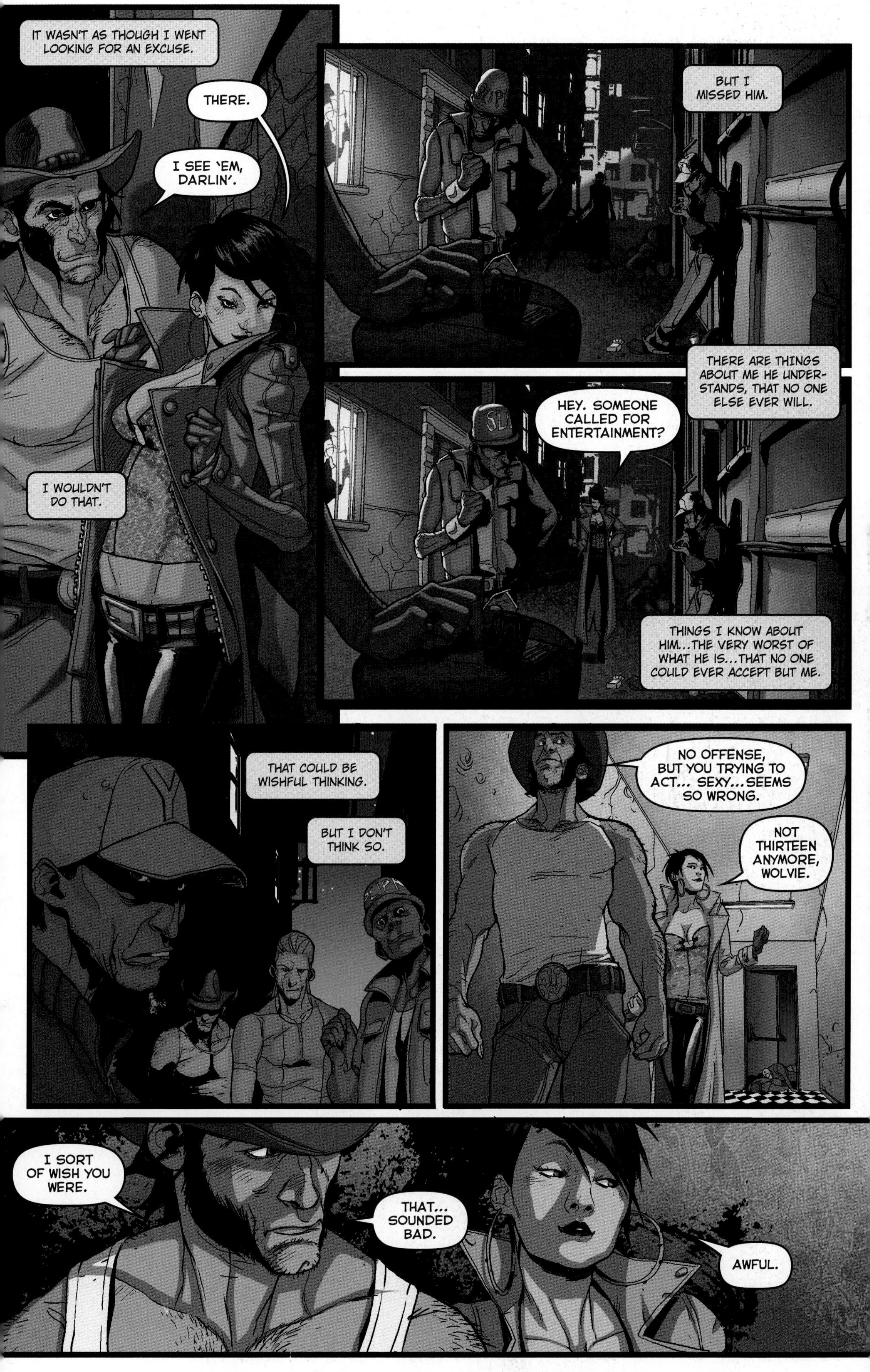
IT WASN'T AS THOUGH I WENT LOOKING FOR AN EXCUSE.
THERE.
I SEE 'EM, DARLIN'.
I WOULDN'T DO THAT.
BUT I MISSED HIM.
THERE ARE THINGS ABOUT ME HE UNDER-STANDS, THAT NO ONE ELSE EVER WILL.
HEY. SOMEONE CALLED FOR ENTERTAINMENT?
THINGS I KNOW ABOUT HIM...THE VERY WORST OF WHAT HE IS...THAT NO ONE COULD EVER ACCEPT BUT ME.
THAT COULD BE WISHFUL THINKING.
BUT I DON'T THINK SO.
NO OFFENSE, BUT YOU TRYING TO ACT... SEXY...SEEMS SO WRONG.
NOT THIRTEEN ANYMORE, WOLVIE.
I SORT OF WISH YOU WERE.
THAT... SOUNDED BAD.
AWFUL.

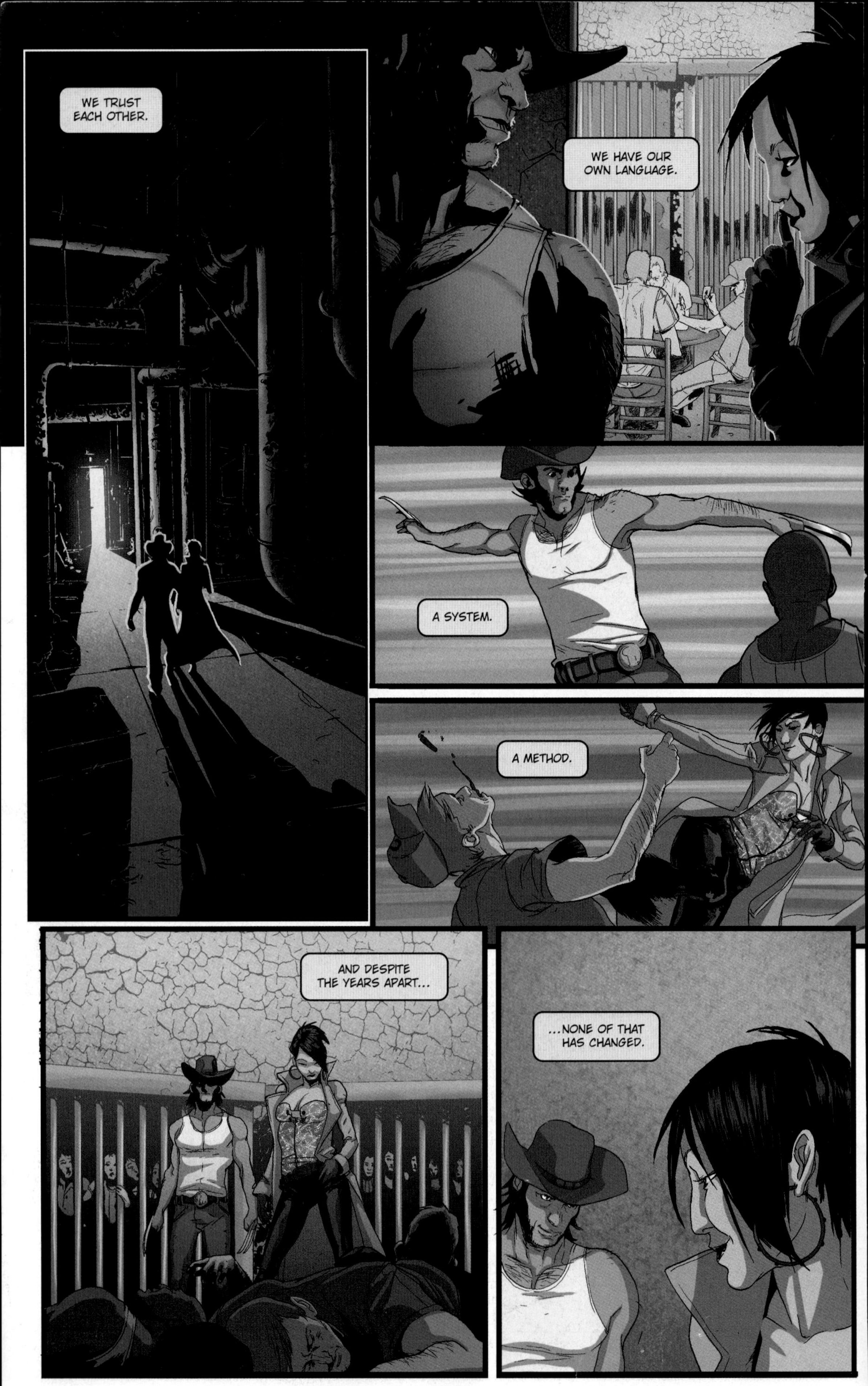
WE TRUST EACH OTHER.
WE HAVE OUR OWN LANGUAGE.
A SYSTEM.
A METHOD.
AND DESPITE THE YEARS APART...
...NONE OF THAT HAS CHANGED.

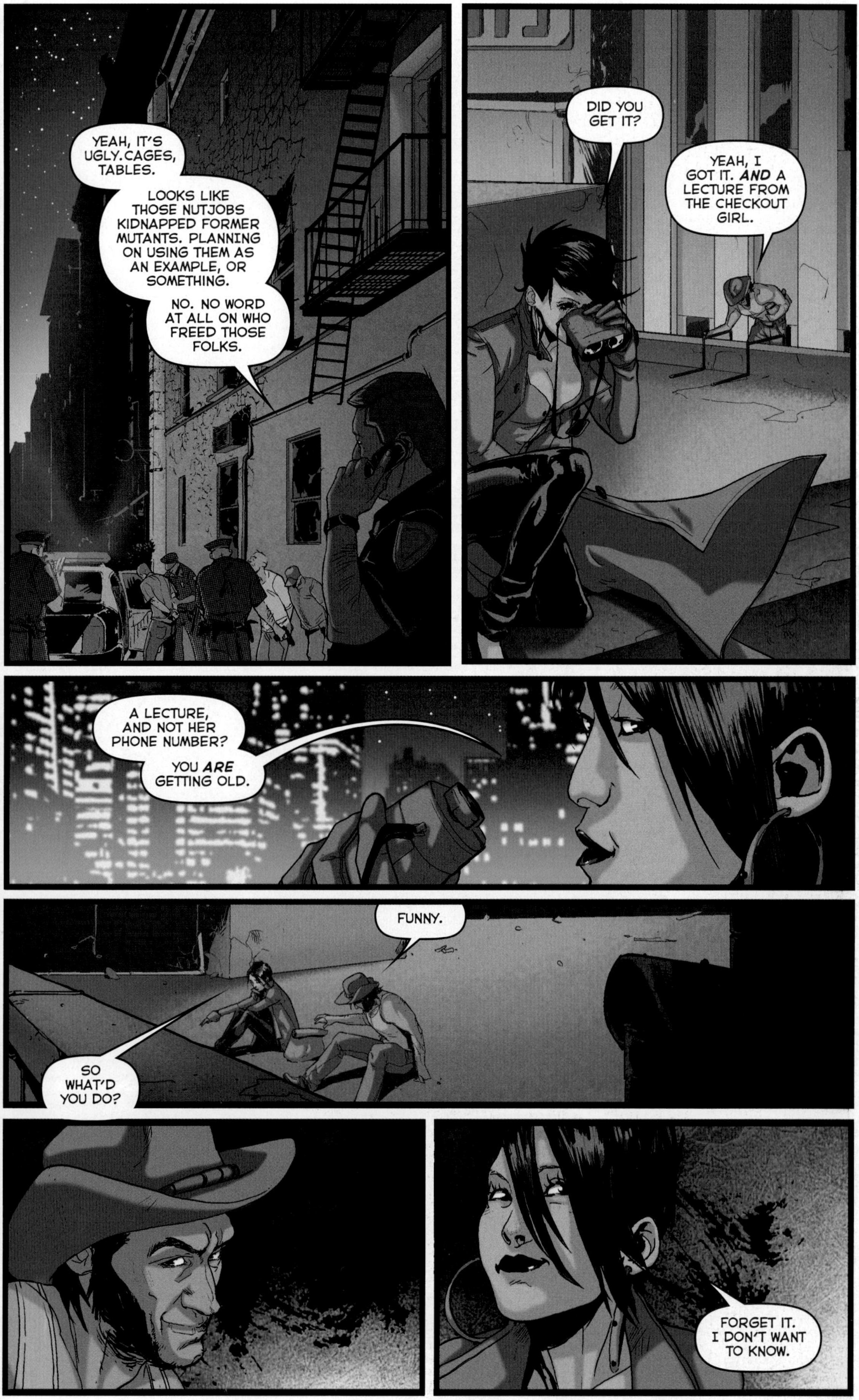
YEAH, IT'S UGLY.CAGES, TABLES.
LOOKS LIKE THOSE NUTJOBS KIDNAPPED FORMER MUTANTS. PLANNING ON USING THEM AS AN EXAMPLE, OR SOMETHING.
NO. NO WORD AT ALL ON WHO FREED THOSE FOLKS.
DID YOU GET IT?
YEAH, I GOT IT. **AND** A LECTURE FROM THE CHECKOUT GIRL.
A LECTURE, AND NOT HER PHONE NUMBER?
YOU **ARE** GETTING OLD.
FUNNY.
SO WHAT'D YOU DO?
FORGET IT. I DON'T WANT TO KNOW.

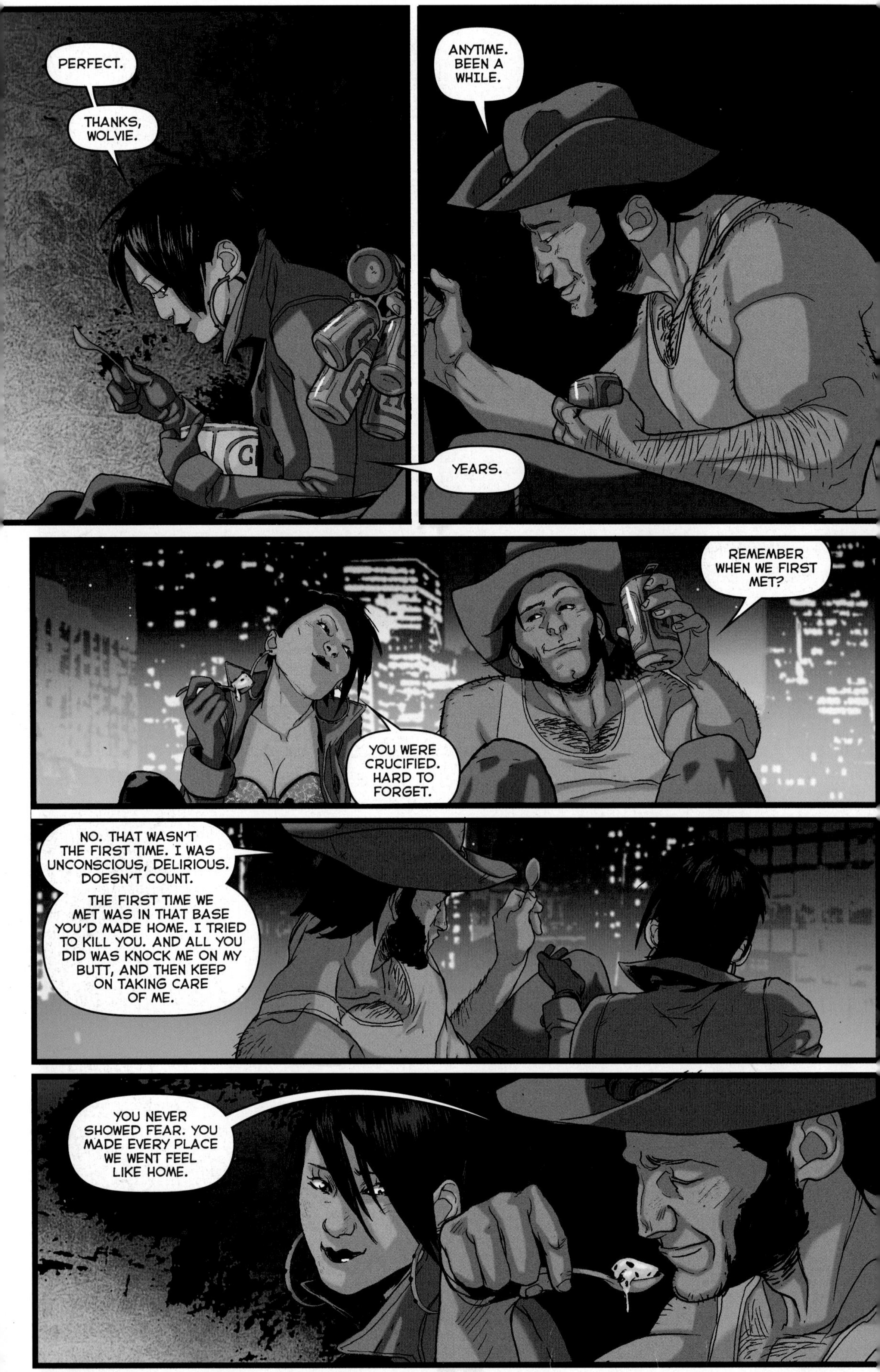
PERFECT.
THANKS, WOLVIE.
ANYTIME. BEEN A WHILE.
YEARS.
REMEMBER WHEN WE FIRST MET?
YOU WERE CRUCIFIED. HARD TO FORGET.
NO. THAT WASN'T THE FIRST TIME. I WAS UNCONSCIOUS, DELIRIOUS. DOESN'T COUNT.
THE FIRST TIME WE MET WAS IN THAT BASE YOU'D MADE HOME. I TRIED TO KILL YOU. AND ALL YOU DID WAS KNOCK ME ON MY BUTT, AND THEN KEEP ON TAKING CARE OF ME.
YOU NEVER SHOWED FEAR. YOU MADE EVERY PLACE WE WENT FEEL LIKE HOME.

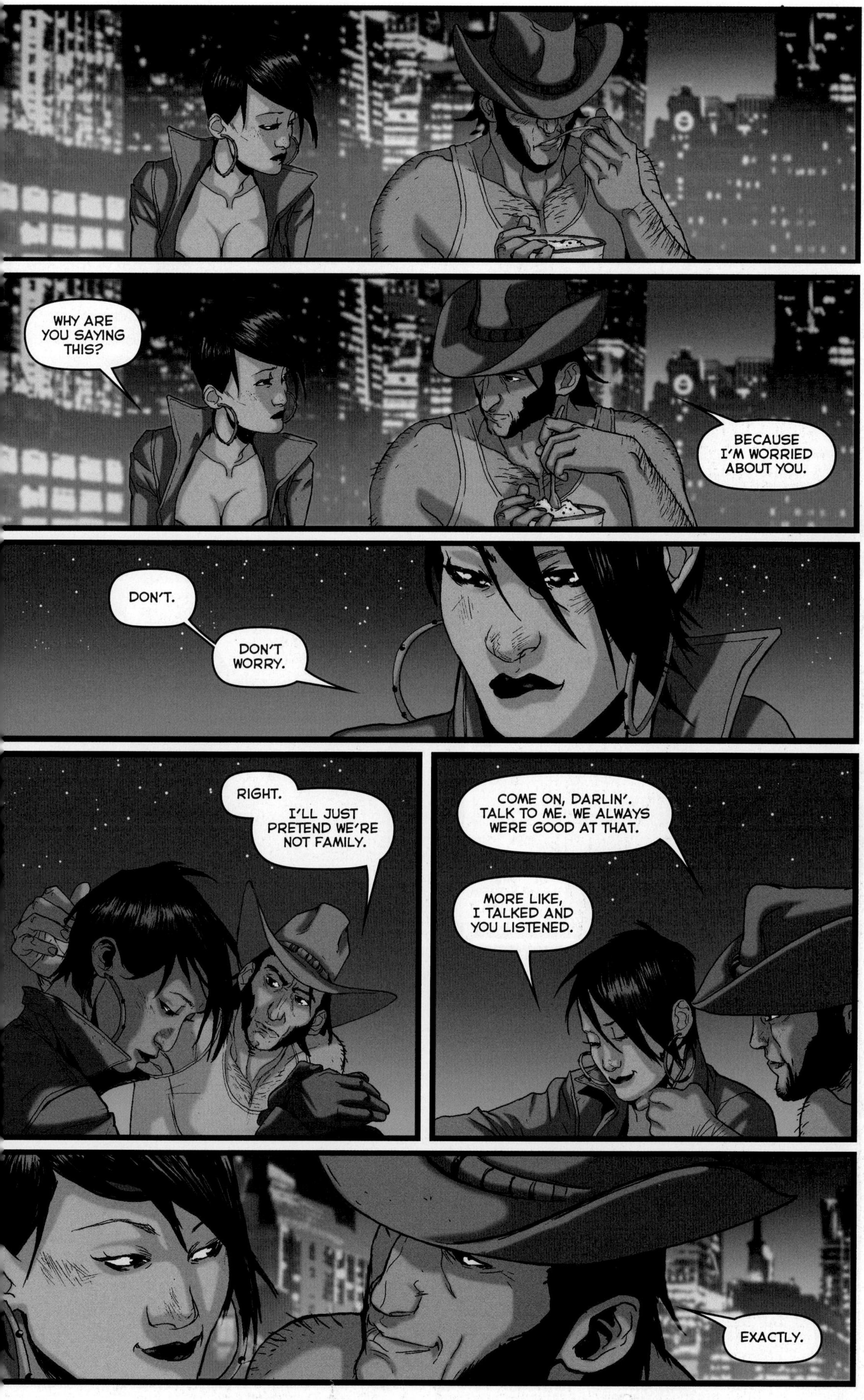
WHY ARE YOU SAYING THIS?
BECAUSE I'M WORRIED ABOUT YOU.
DON'T.
DON'T WORRY.
RIGHT. I'LL JUST PRETEND WE'RE NOT FAMILY.
COME ON, DARLIN'. TALK TO ME. WE ALWAYS WERE GOOD AT THAT.
MORE LIKE, I TALKED AND YOU LISTENED.
EXACTLY.

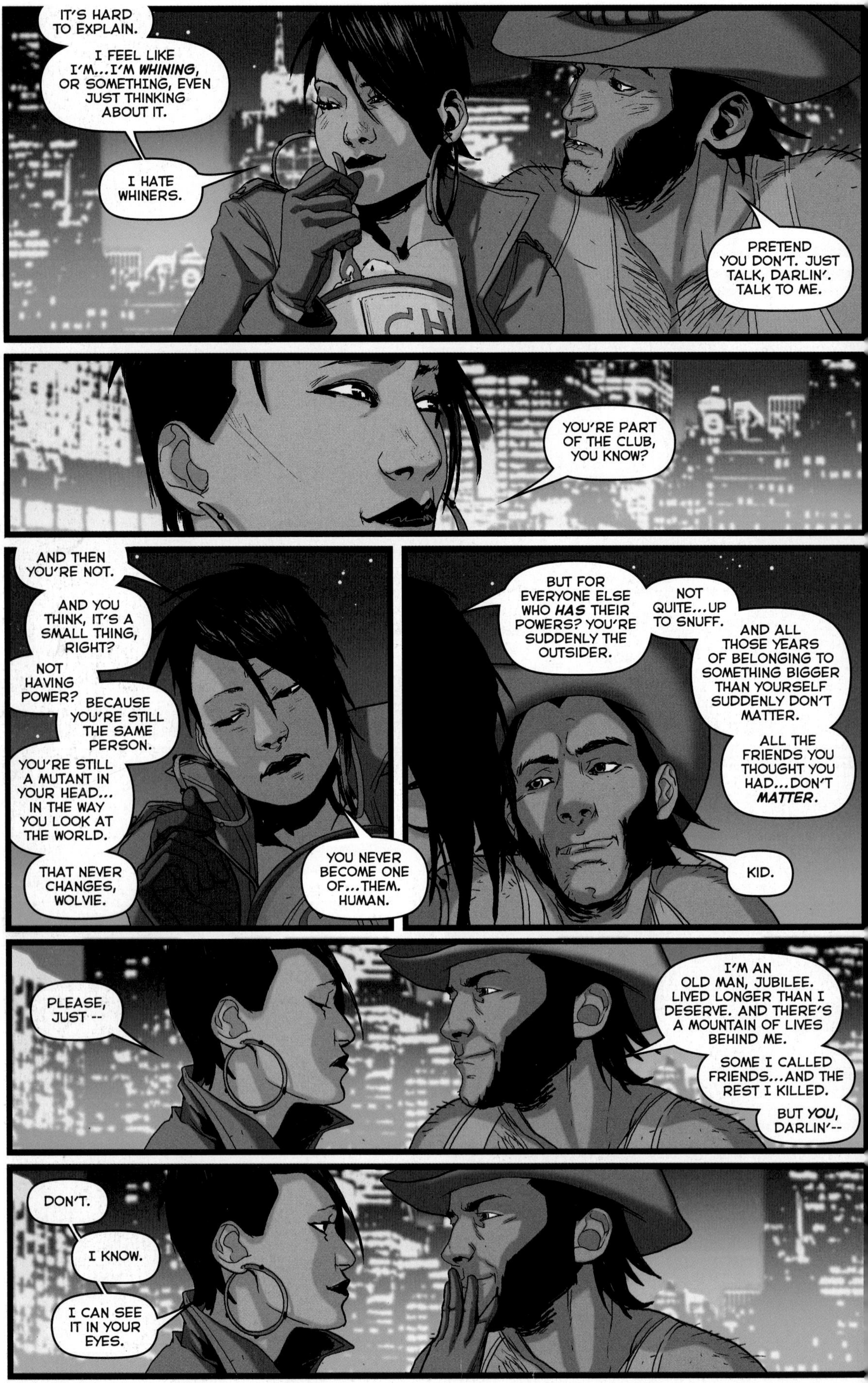
IT'S HARD TO EXPLAIN.
I FEEL LIKE I'M...I'M *WHINING*, OR SOMETHING, EVEN JUST THINKING ABOUT IT.
I HATE WHINERS.
PRETEND YOU DON'T. JUST TALK, DARLIN'. TALK TO ME.
YOU'RE PART OF THE CLUB, YOU KNOW?
AND THEN YOU'RE NOT.
AND YOU THINK, IT'S A SMALL THING, RIGHT?
NOT HAVING POWER?
BECAUSE YOU'RE STILL THE SAME PERSON.
YOU'RE STILL A MUTANT IN YOUR HEAD... IN THE WAY YOU LOOK AT THE WORLD.
THAT NEVER CHANGES, WOLVIE.
YOU NEVER BECOME ONE OF...THEM. HUMAN.
BUT FOR EVERYONE ELSE WHO **HAS** THEIR POWERS? YOU'RE SUDDENLY THE OUTSIDER.
NOT QUITE...UP TO SNUFF.
AND ALL THOSE YEARS OF BELONGING TO SOMETHING BIGGER THAN YOURSELF SUDDENLY DON'T MATTER.
ALL THE FRIENDS YOU THOUGHT YOU HAD...DON'T ***MATTER***.
KID.
PLEASE, JUST --
I'M AN OLD MAN, JUBILEE. LIVED LONGER THAN I DESERVE. AND THERE'S A MOUNTAIN OF LIVES BEHIND ME.
SOME I CALLED FRIENDS...AND THE REST I KILLED.
BUT *YOU*, DARLIN'--
DON'T.
I KNOW.
I CAN SEE IT IN YOUR EYES.

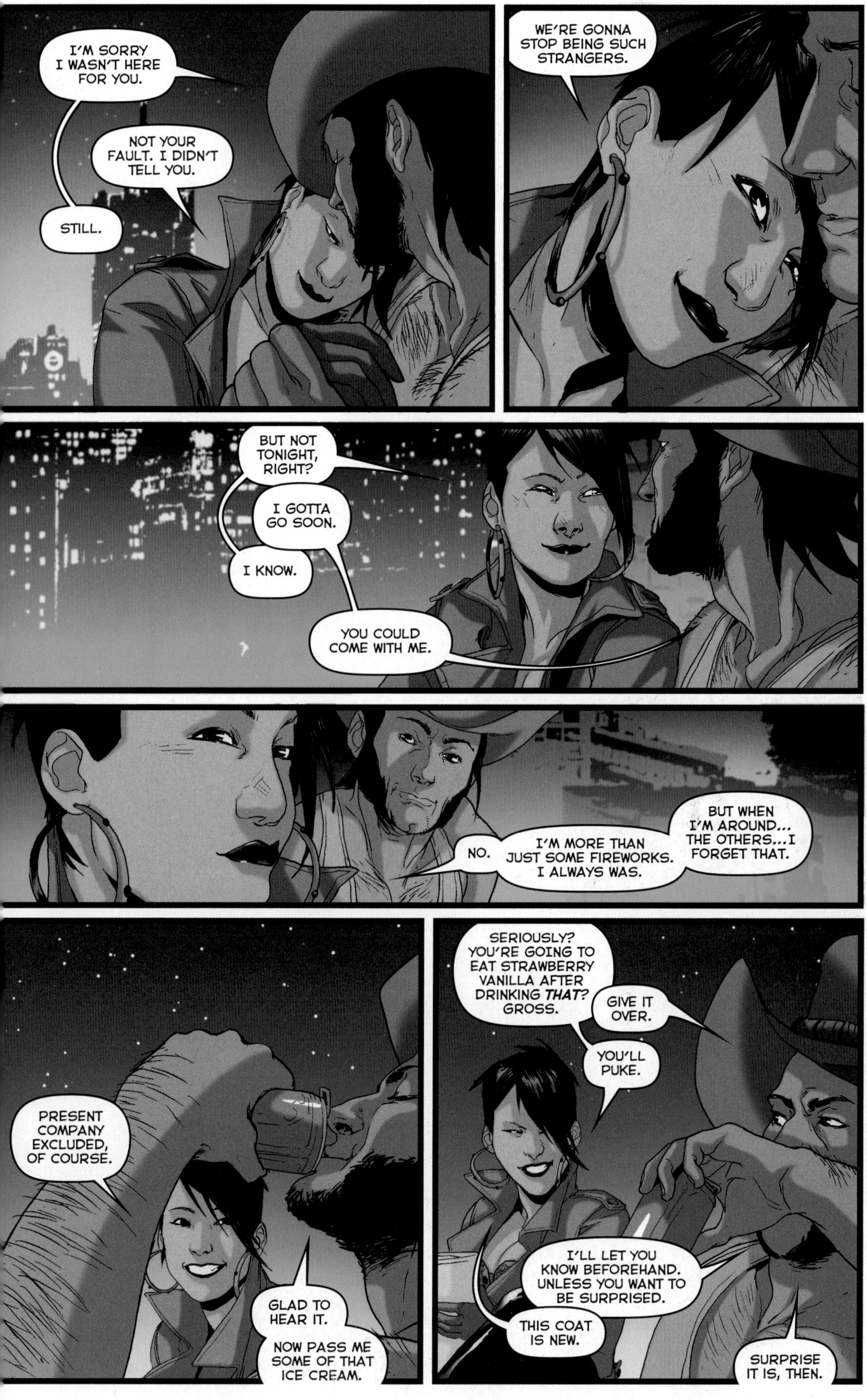
I'M SORRY I WASN'T HERE FOR YOU.
NOT YOUR FAULT. I DIDN'T TELL YOU.
STILL.
WE'RE GONNA STOP BEING SUCH STRANGERS.
BUT NOT TONIGHT, RIGHT?
I GOTTA GO SOON.
I KNOW.
YOU COULD COME WITH ME.
NO.
I'M MORE THAN JUST SOME FIREWORKS. I ALWAYS WAS.
BUT WHEN I'M AROUND... THE OTHERS...I FORGET THAT.
PRESENT COMPANY EXCLUDED, OF COURSE.
GLAD TO HEAR IT.
NOW PASS ME SOME OF THAT ICE CREAM.
SERIOUSLY? YOU'RE GOING TO EAT STRAWBERRY VANILLA AFTER DRINKING *THAT*? GROSS.
GIVE IT OVER.
YOU'LL PUKE.
I'LL LET YOU KNOW BEFOREHAND. UNLESS YOU WANT TO BE SURPRISED.
THIS COAT IS NEW.
SURPRISE IT IS, THEN.

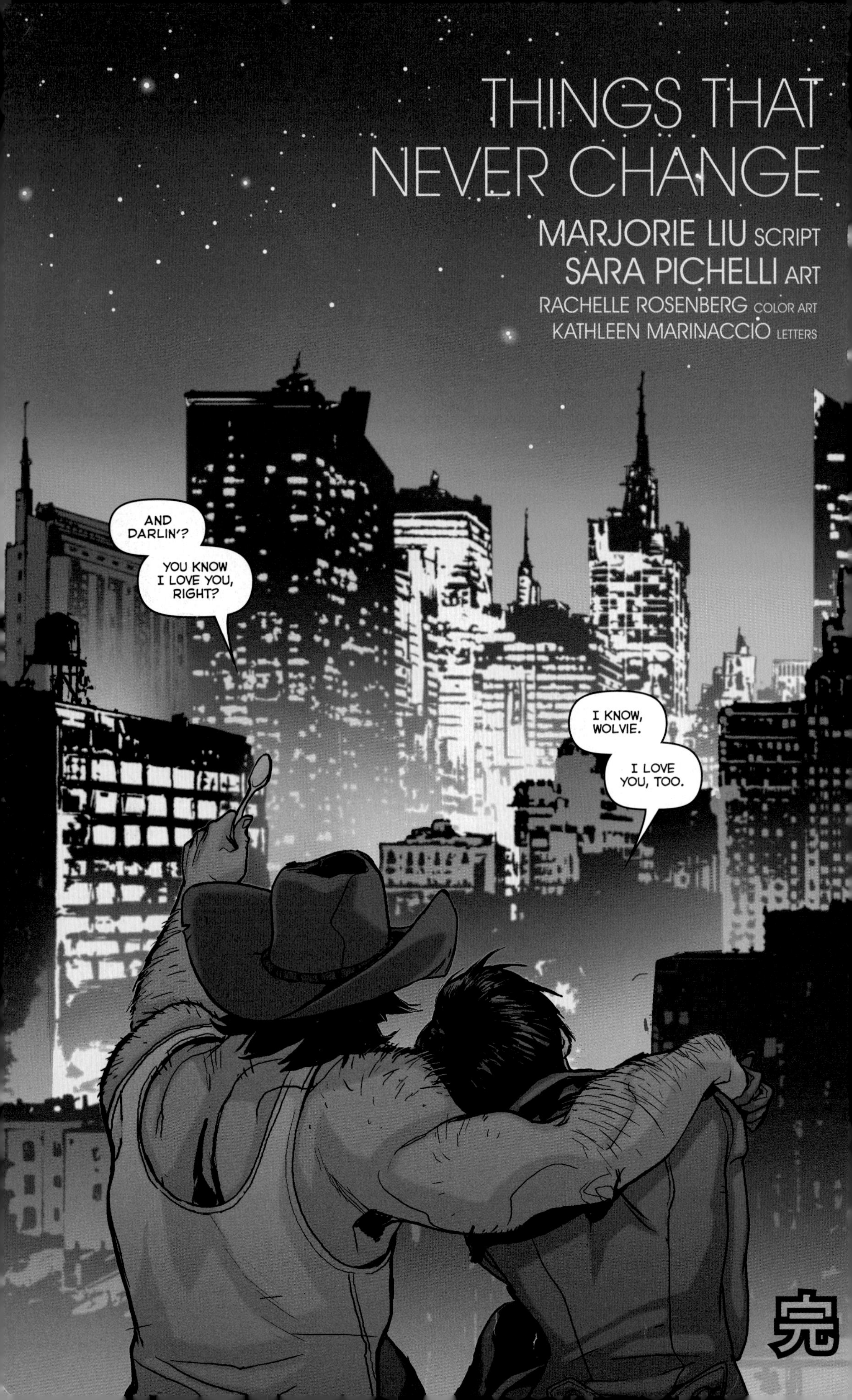
THINGS THAT NEVER CHANGE
MARJORIE LIU SCRIPT
SARA PICHELLI ART
RACHELLE ROSENBERG COLOR ART
KATHLEEN MARINACCIO LETTERS
AND DARLIN'?
YOU KNOW I LOVE YOU, RIGHT?
I KNOW, WOLVIE.
I LOVE YOU, TOO.
完

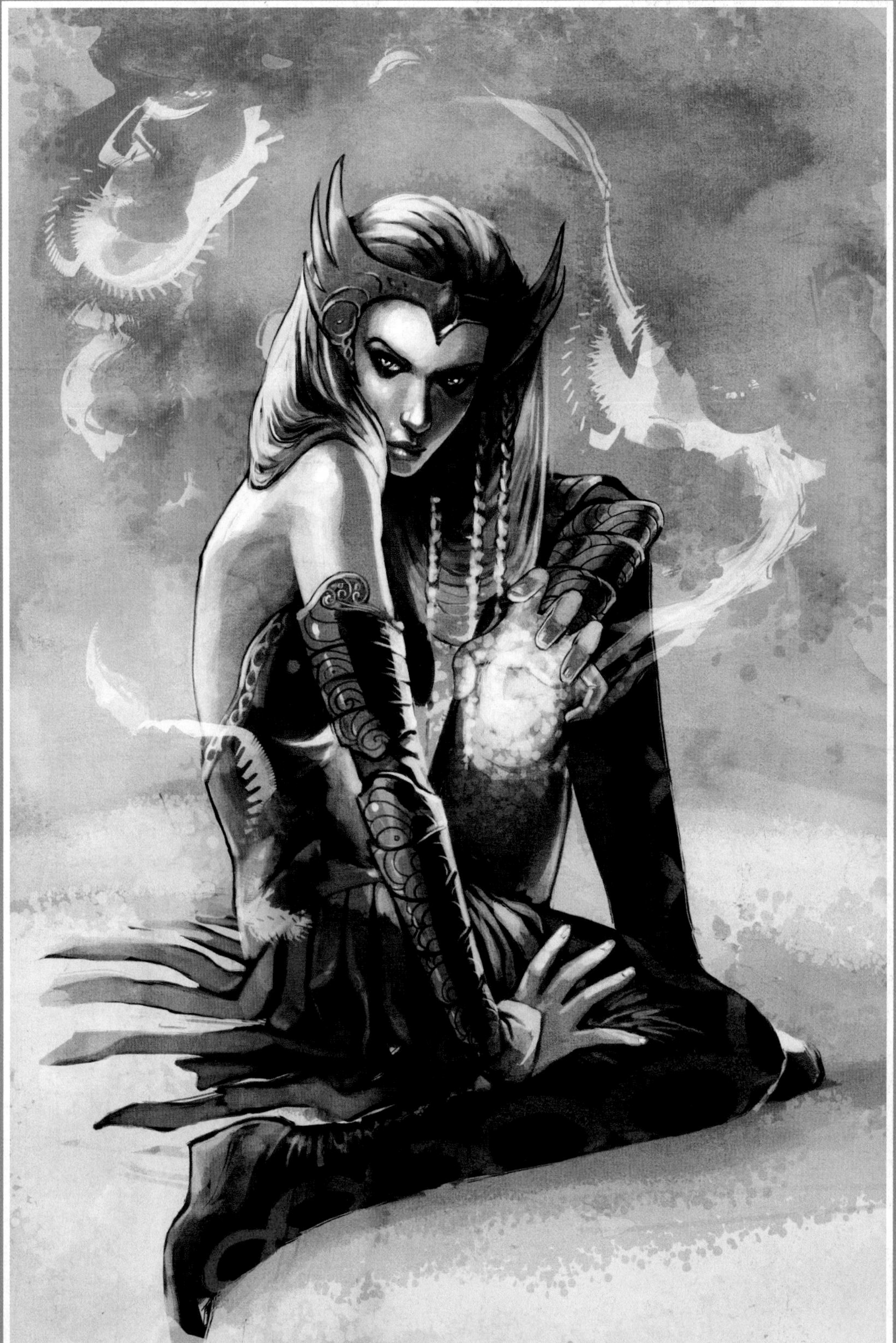

AMORA THE ENCHANTRESS

By STEPHANIE HANS

SPOTLIGHT

LOUISE SIMONSON

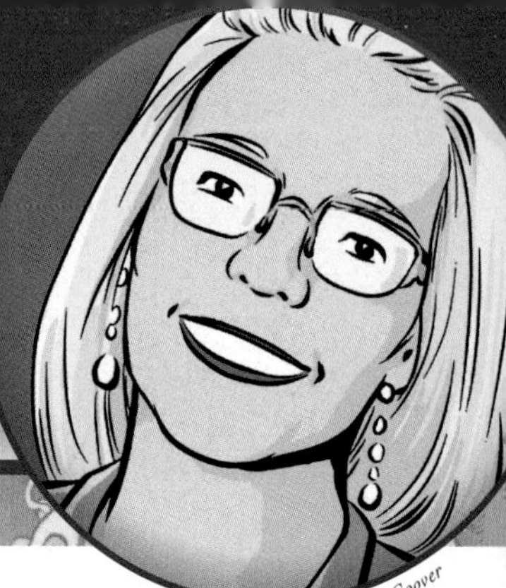

Illustration by Colleen Coover

You know when someone has the nickname Weezie, they're likely to be an interesting person to get to know. And you'd be right. Not only is Louise "Weezie" Simonson interesting, she's an accomplished, talented and beloved writer. What makes that a kick in the head is that she had no writing aspirations at all. In fact, her career in comics evolved through a series of happy accidents.

Raised in Atlanta, Georgia, Louise went to college at Georgia State, majoring in English and Illustration. She followed then husband, Jeff Jones, to New York and eventually applied for a production job at Warren Publishing. "They let me do anything: ad copy, letters columns and then eventually made me an assistant editor." While at Warren, Louise worked on the horror comics line with titles like *Creepy, Eerie* and *Vampirella*, and went on to become Senior Editor.

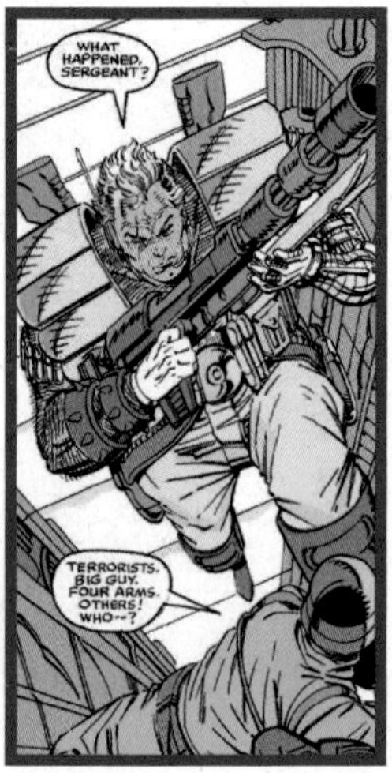
WHAT HAPPENED, SERGEANT?
TERRORISTS. BIG GUY. FOUR ARMS. OTHERS! WHO--?

Cable's debut in "New Mutants #87"

At the time, Louise, like most people who worked in comics back then, played in a volleyball league in Central Park. There she met Jim Shooter who asked her to join Marvel as an editor. By then Louise had already met current husband and celebrated artist, Walt Simonson. Newly married, she tackled the task of editing Marvel titles, much of them licensed properties like *Star Trek, Battlestar Galactica,* and *Micronauts*. She also worked on *Uncanny X-Men* and *New Mutants* for the bulk of her time at Marvel.

Louise's opportunity to write happened by chance. Jim Shooter had asked a few editors to try their hand at freelancing and see what it was like on the other side of the desk. "I had always loved to write, but I never thought of it as a career. My whole career was based on me bumbling along, finding things I'm good at—but I always knew if I ever wrote, I'd write kids books." It was around this time that the beginnings of *Power Pack* began to transpire. Louise asked Marvel artist June Brigman to help her out with some character sketches. She then drafted a plot and took the sketches to Shooter. When Louise had brought up the idea initially to Shooter, he was skeptical, but upon seeing the sketches and full plot, he quickly jumped on board.

Power Pack followed the lives of the Power children—Alex, Jack, Julie and Katie—pre-teen super heroes who battled evil while hiding their powers from their parents. It was the first series of its kind, eventually earning an Eagle Award and establishing Louise as a sought-after writer. By the end of 1983 she had quit her job as an editor and began to freelance full time. Louise went on to write *Red Sonja, X-Factor* (where she and Butch Guice introduced the character Apocalypse) and *New Mutants* (where she and Rob Liefeld introduced the adult Cable). In 1988-89 she and Walt wrote *Havoc and Wolverine: Meltdown*, a critical success.

Louise continues her prolific career as a writer today. She still writes for DC and Marvel (currently on *X-Factor Forever*), while working on a new middle-reader novel which is slated to come out next year. All in all, Louise has been very grateful for the opportunities she's been given: "I love comics and love the people I'm working with—and I'm lucky to be in a field where I can speak the best way I know how: through my fingers!" And we think her fans feel lucky, too.

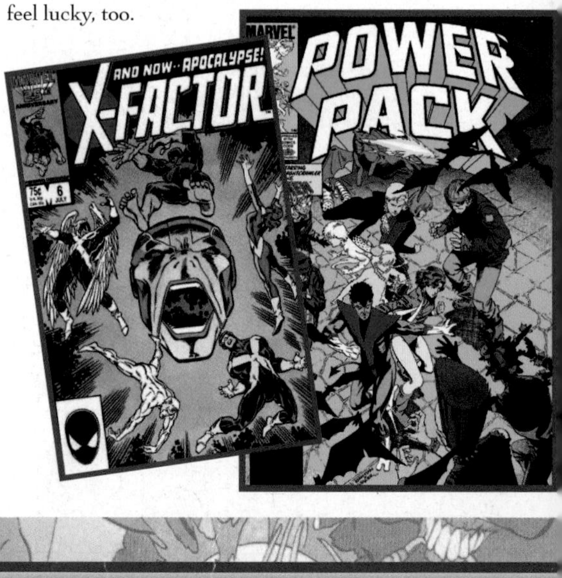
AND NOW.. APOCALYPSE!
X-FACTOR
MARVEL
POWER PACK

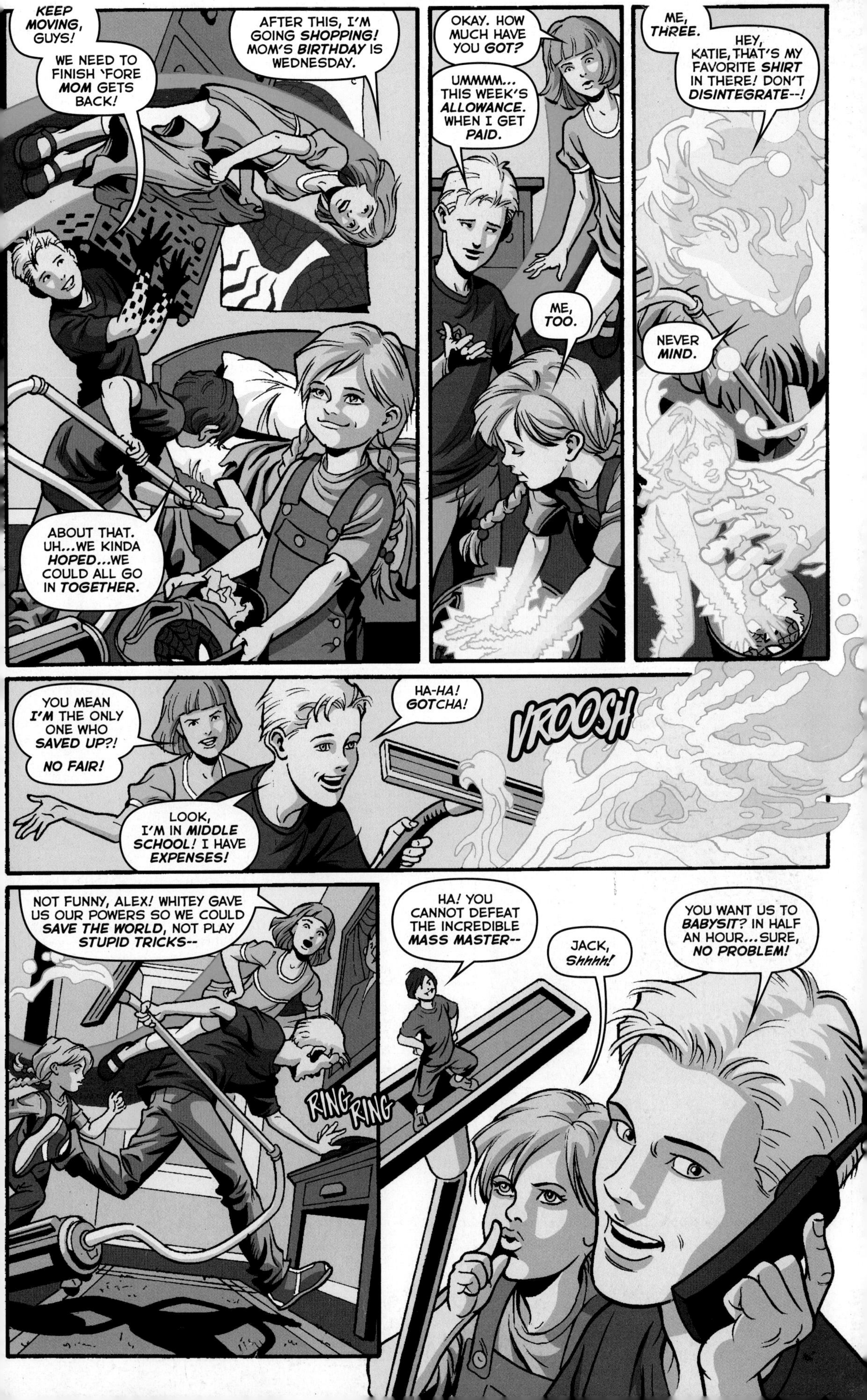
KEEP MOVING, GUYS!
WE NEED TO FINISH 'FORE MOM GETS BACK!
AFTER THIS, I'M GOING SHOPPING! MOM'S BIRTHDAY IS WEDNESDAY.
ABOUT THAT. UH...WE KINDA HOPED...WE COULD ALL GO IN TOGETHER.
OKAY. HOW MUCH HAVE YOU GOT?
UMMMM... THIS WEEK'S ALLOWANCE. WHEN I GET PAID.
ME, TOO.
ME, THREE.
HEY, KATIE, THAT'S MY FAVORITE SHIRT IN THERE! DON'T DISINTEGRATE--!
NEVER MIND.
YOU MEAN I'M THE ONLY ONE WHO SAVED UP?!
NO FAIR!
HA-HA! GOTCHA!
VROOSH
LOOK, I'M IN MIDDLE SCHOOL! I HAVE EXPENSES!
NOT FUNNY, ALEX! WHITEY GAVE US OUR POWERS SO WE COULD SAVE THE WORLD, NOT PLAY STUPID TRICKS--
RING RING
HA! YOU CANNOT DEFEAT THE INCREDIBLE MASS MASTER--
JACK, Shhhh!
YOU WANT US TO BABYSIT? IN HALF AN HOUR...SURE, NO PROBLEM!

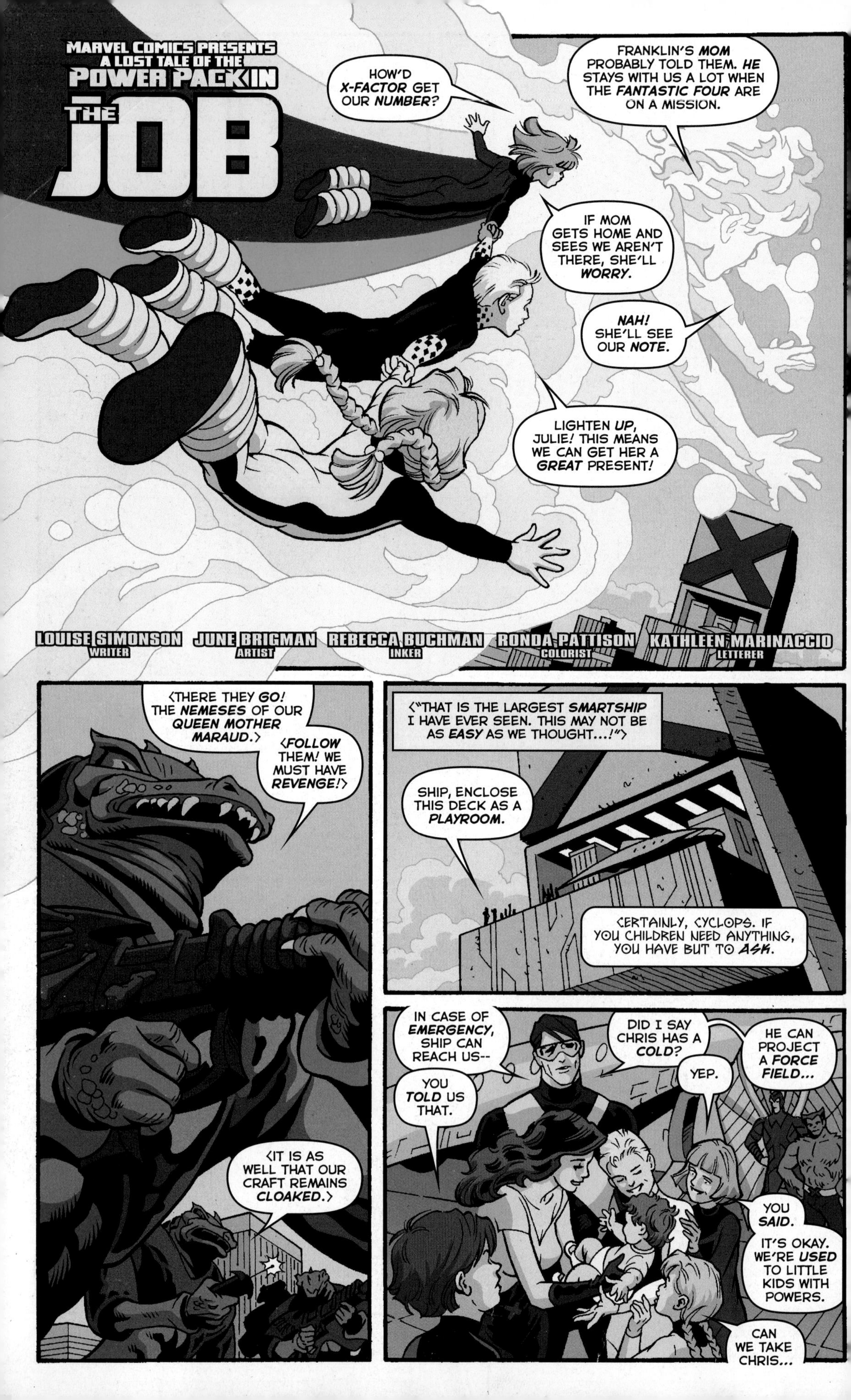
MARVEL COMICS PRESENTS
A LOST TALE OF THE
POWER PACK IN
THE JOB
HOW'D X-FACTOR GET OUR NUMBER?
FRANKLIN'S MOM PROBABLY TOLD THEM. HE STAYS WITH US A LOT WHEN THE FANTASTIC FOUR ARE ON A MISSION.
IF MOM GETS HOME AND SEES WE AREN'T THERE, SHE'LL WORRY.
NAH! SHE'LL SEE OUR NOTE.
LIGHTEN UP, JULIE! THIS MEANS WE CAN GET HER A GREAT PRESENT!
LOUISE SIMONSON WRITER
JUNE BRIGMAN ARTIST
REBECCA BUCHMAN INKER
RONDA PATTISON COLORIST
KATHLEEN MARINACCIO LETTERER
<THERE THEY GO! THE NEMESES OF OUR QUEEN MOTHER MARAUD.>
<FOLLOW THEM! WE MUST HAVE REVENGE!>
<IT IS AS WELL THAT OUR CRAFT REMAINS CLOAKED.>
<"THAT IS THE LARGEST SMARTSHIP I HAVE EVER SEEN. THIS MAY NOT BE AS EASY AS WE THOUGHT...!">
SHIP, ENCLOSE THIS DECK AS A PLAYROOM.
CERTAINLY, CYCLOPS. IF YOU CHILDREN NEED ANYTHING, YOU HAVE BUT TO ASK.
IN CASE OF EMERGENCY, SHIP CAN REACH US--
YOU TOLD US THAT.
DID I SAY CHRIS HAS A COLD?
YEP.
HE CAN PROJECT A FORCE FIELD...
YOU SAID.
IT'S OKAY. WE'RE USED TO LITTLE KIDS WITH POWERS.
CAN WE TAKE CHRIS...

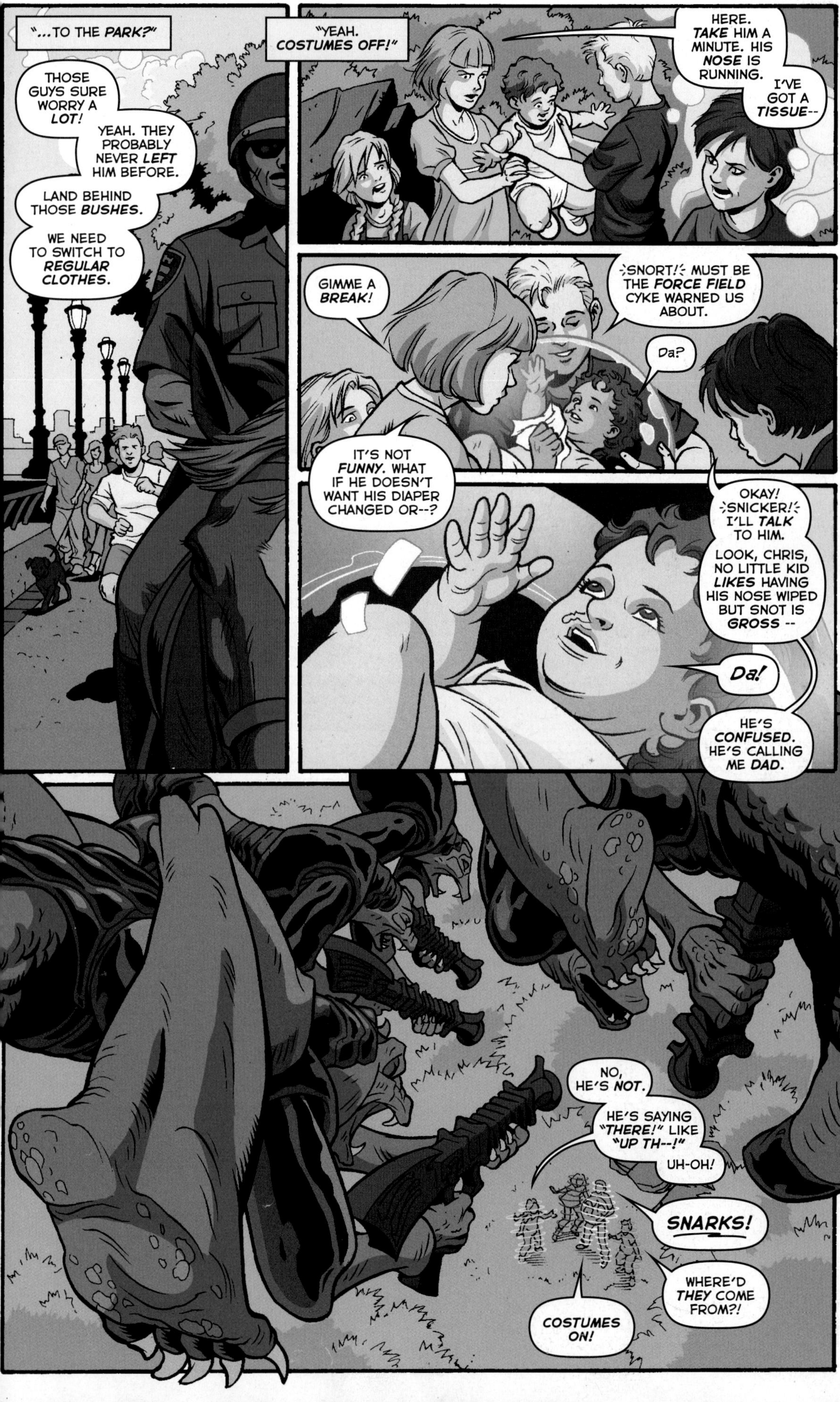
"...TO THE PARK?"
THOSE GUYS SURE WORRY A LOT!
YEAH. THEY PROBABLY NEVER LEFT HIM BEFORE.
LAND BEHIND THOSE BUSHES.
WE NEED TO SWITCH TO REGULAR CLOTHES.
"YEAH. COSTUMES OFF!"
HERE. TAKE HIM A MINUTE. HIS NOSE IS RUNNING.
I'VE GOT A TISSUE--
GIMME A BREAK!
SNORT! MUST BE THE FORCE FIELD CYKE WARNED US ABOUT.
Da?
IT'S NOT FUNNY. WHAT IF HE DOESN'T WANT HIS DIAPER CHANGED OR--?
OKAY! SNICKER! I'LL TALK TO HIM.
LOOK, CHRIS, NO LITTLE KID LIKES HAVING HIS NOSE WIPED BUT SNOT IS GROSS --
Da!
HE'S CONFUSED. HE'S CALLING ME DAD.
NO, HE'S NOT.
HE'S SAYING "THERE!" LIKE "UP TH--!"
UH-OH!
SNARKS!
WHERE'D THEY COME FROM?!
COSTUMES ON!

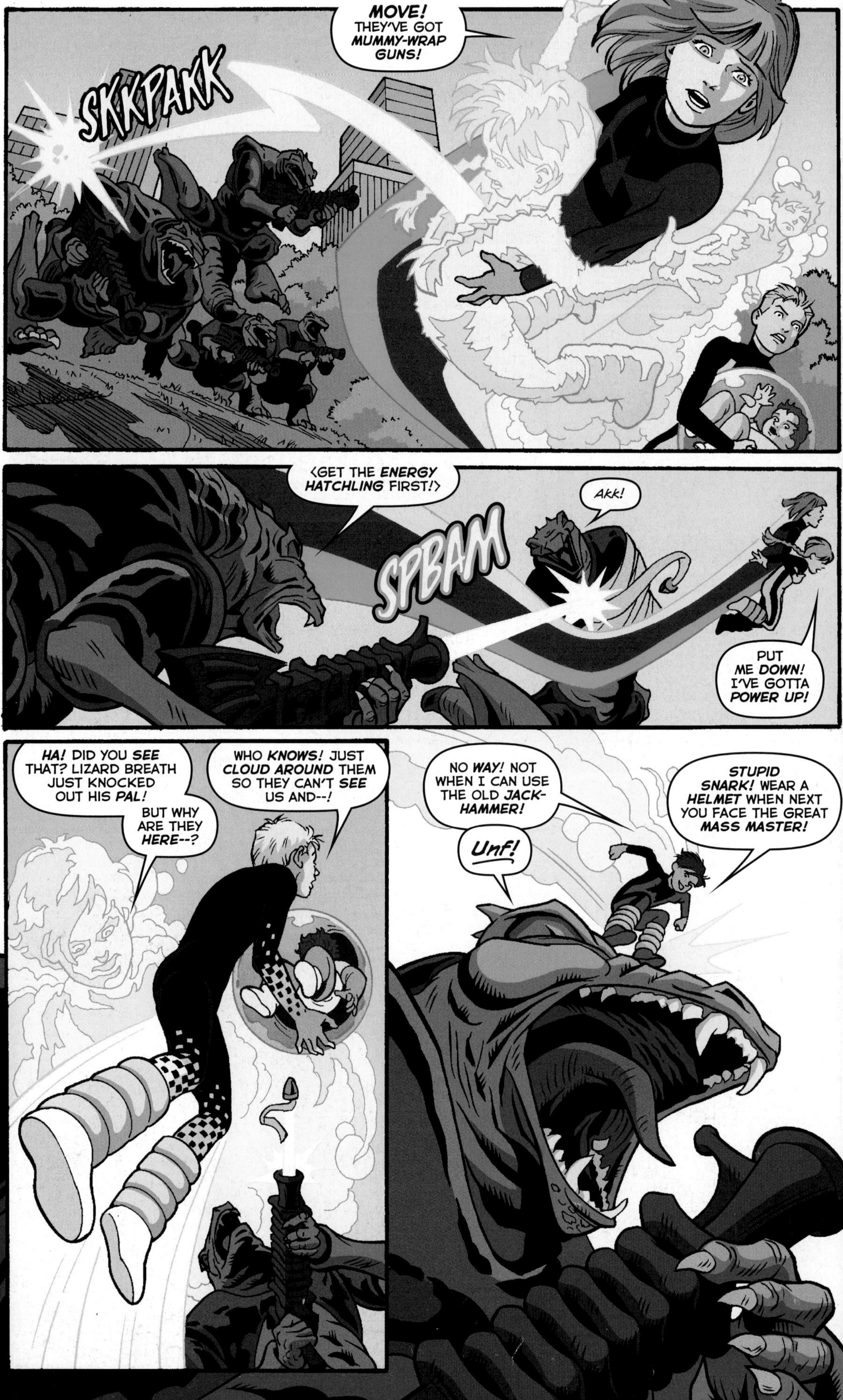
MOVE! THEY'VE GOT MUMMY-WRAP GUNS!
SKKPAKK
<GET THE ENERGY HATCHLING FIRST!>
Akk!
SPBAM
PUT ME DOWN! I'VE GOTTA POWER UP!
HA! DID YOU SEE THAT? LIZARD BREATH JUST KNOCKED OUT HIS PAL!
BUT WHY ARE THEY HERE--?
WHO KNOWS! JUST CLOUD AROUND THEM SO THEY CAN'T SEE US AND--!
NO WAY! NOT WHEN I CAN USE THE OLD JACK-HAMMER!
Unf!
STUPID SNARK! WEAR A HELMET WHEN NEXT YOU FACE THE GREAT MASS MASTER!

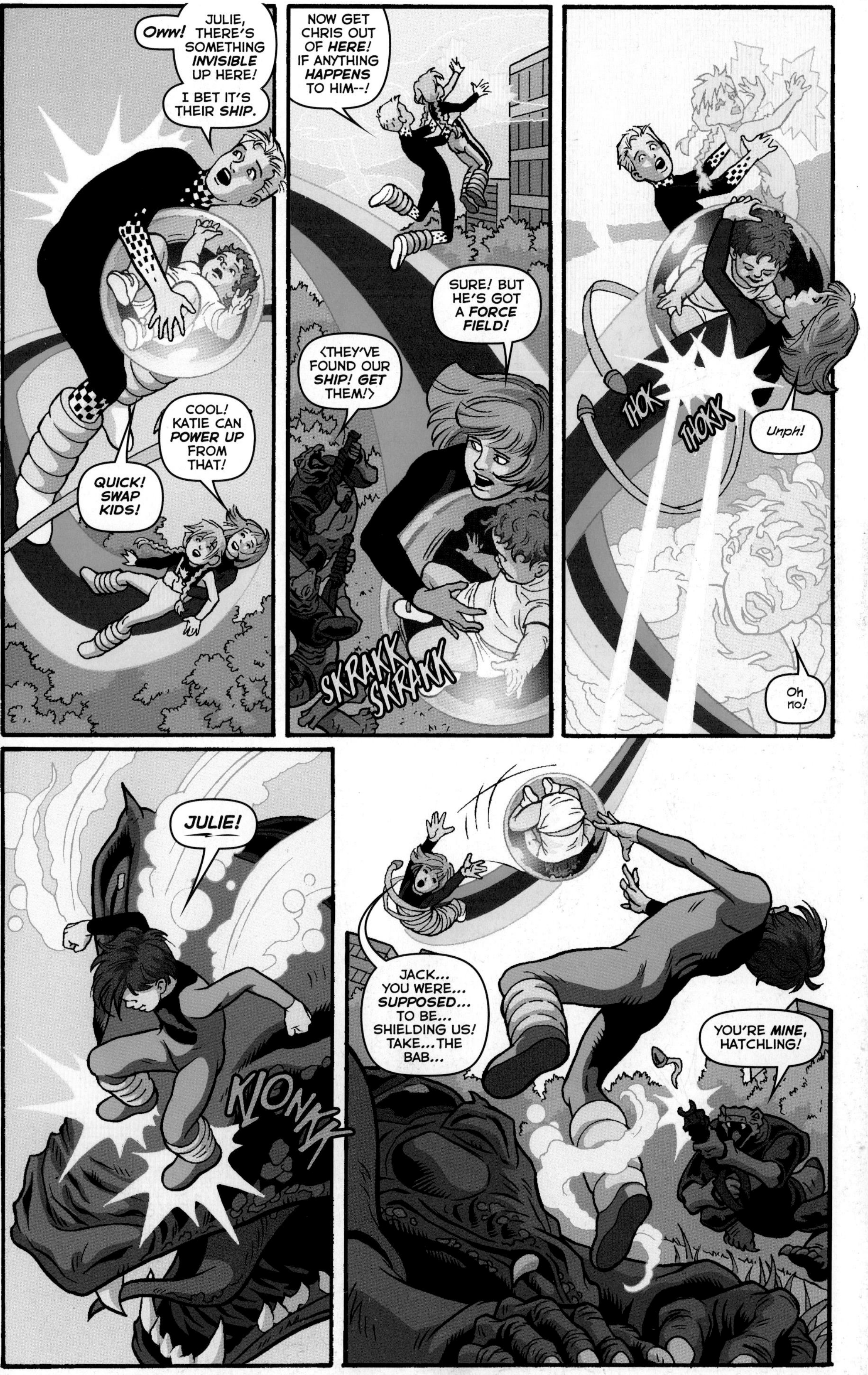
Oww!
JULIE, THERE'S SOMETHING INVISIBLE UP HERE!
I BET IT'S THEIR SHIP.
COOL! KATIE CAN POWER UP FROM THAT!
QUICK! SWAP KIDS!
NOW GET CHRIS OUT OF HERE! IF ANYTHING HAPPENS TO HIM--!
SURE! BUT HE'S GOT A FORCE FIELD!
<THEY'VE FOUND OUR SHIP! GET THEM!>
SKRAKK SKRAKK
THOK
THOKK
Unph!
Oh no!
JULIE!
KLONKK
JACK... YOU WERE... SUPPOSED... TO BE... SHIELDING US! TAKE... THE BAB...
YOU'RE MINE, HATCHLING!

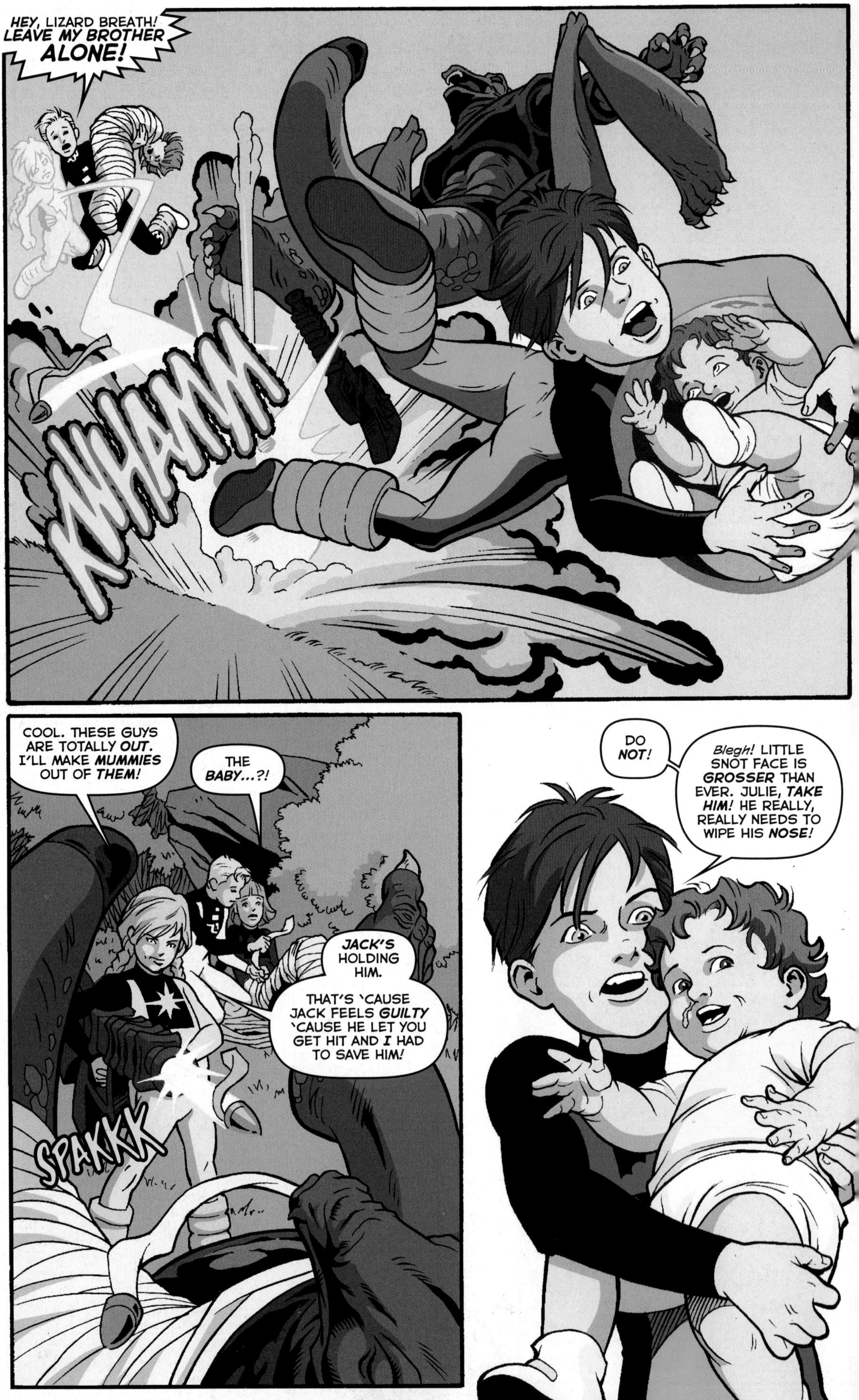

HEY, LIZARD BREATH! LEAVE MY BROTHER ALONE!
KWHAMM
COOL. THESE GUYS ARE TOTALLY OUT. I'LL MAKE MUMMIES OUT OF THEM!
THE BABY...?!
JACK'S HOLDING HIM.
THAT'S 'CAUSE JACK FEELS GUILTY 'CAUSE HE LET YOU GET HIT AND I HAD TO SAVE HIM!
SPAKKK
DO NOT!
Blegh! LITTLE SNOT FACE IS GROSSER THAN EVER. JULIE, TAKE HIM! HE REALLY, REALLY NEEDS TO WIPE HIS NOSE!

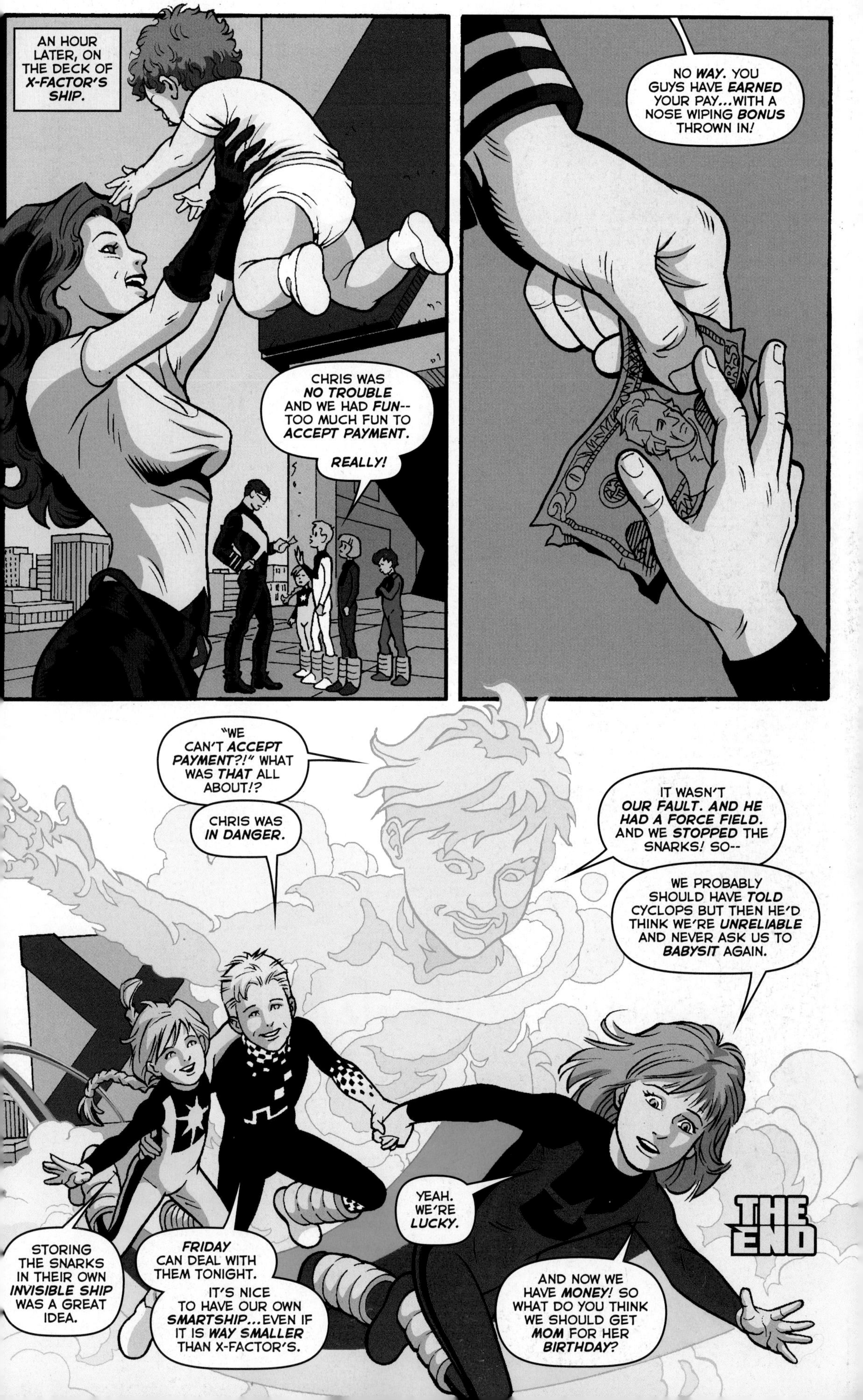
AN HOUR LATER, ON THE DECK OF X-FACTOR'S SHIP.
CHRIS WAS NO TROUBLE AND WE HAD FUN-- TOO MUCH FUN TO ACCEPT PAYMENT.
REALLY!
NO WAY. YOU GUYS HAVE EARNED YOUR PAY...WITH A NOSE WIPING BONUS THROWN IN!
"WE CAN'T ACCEPT PAYMENT?!" WHAT WAS THAT ALL ABOUT!?
CHRIS WAS IN DANGER.
IT WASN'T OUR FAULT. AND HE HAD A FORCE FIELD. AND WE STOPPED THE SNARKS! SO--
WE PROBABLY SHOULD HAVE TOLD CYCLOPS BUT THEN HE'D THINK WE'RE UNRELIABLE AND NEVER ASK US TO BABYSIT AGAIN.
STORING THE SNARKS IN THEIR OWN INVISIBLE SHIP WAS A GREAT IDEA.
FRIDAY CAN DEAL WITH THEM TONIGHT.
IT'S NICE TO HAVE OUR OWN SMARTSHIP...EVEN IF IT IS WAY SMALLER THAN X-FACTOR'S.
YEAH. WE'RE LUCKY.
AND NOW WE HAVE MONEY! SO WHAT DO YOU THINK WE SHOULD GET MOM FOR HER BIRTHDAY?
THE END

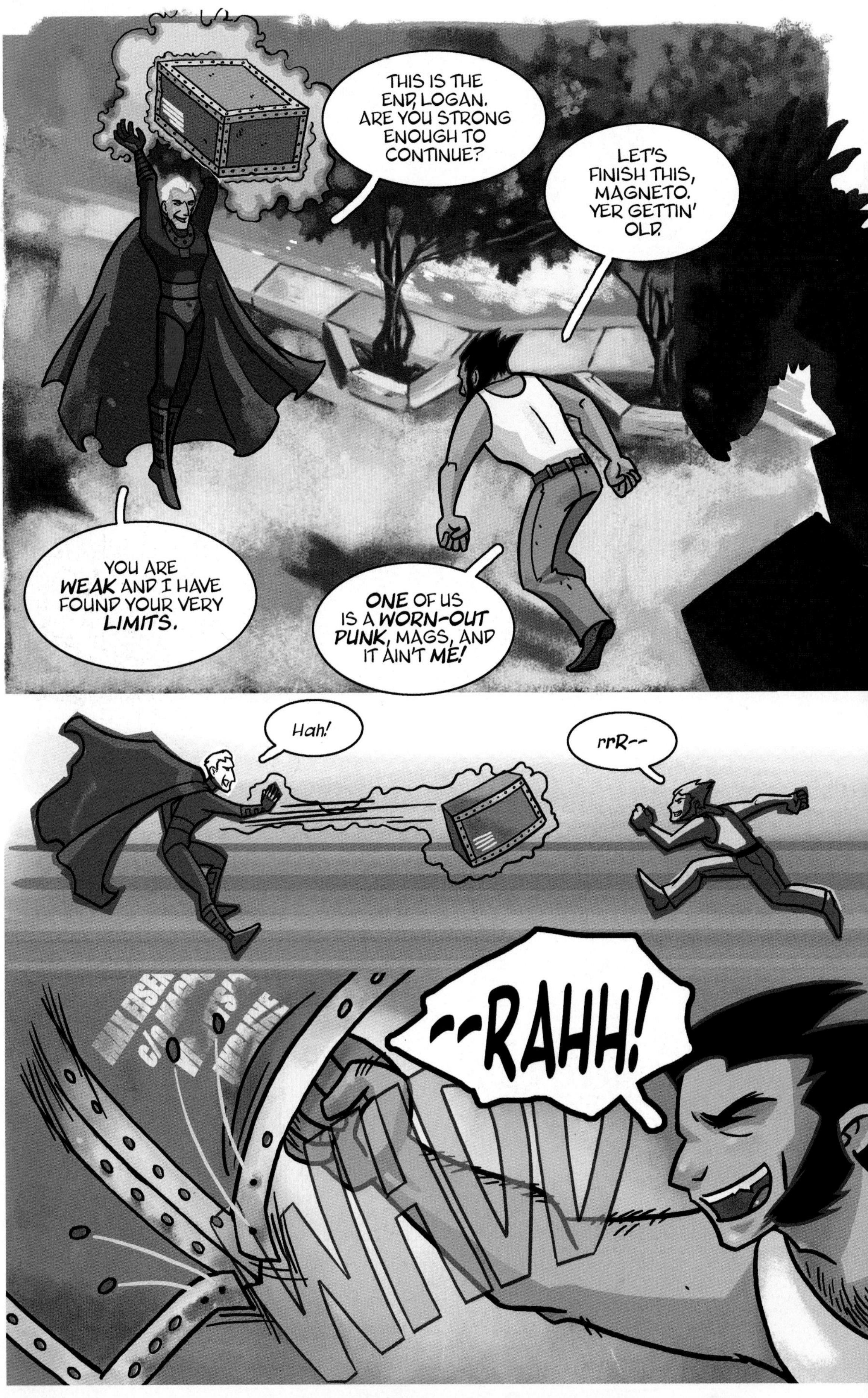
THIS IS THE END, LOGAN. ARE YOU STRONG ENOUGH TO CONTINUE?
LET'S FINISH THIS, MAGNETO. YER GETTIN' OLD.
YOU ARE **WEAK** AND I HAVE FOUND YOUR VERY **LIMITS.**
ONE OF US IS A **WORN-OUT PUNK,** MAGS, AND IT AIN'T **ME!**
Hah!
rrR--
--RAHH!

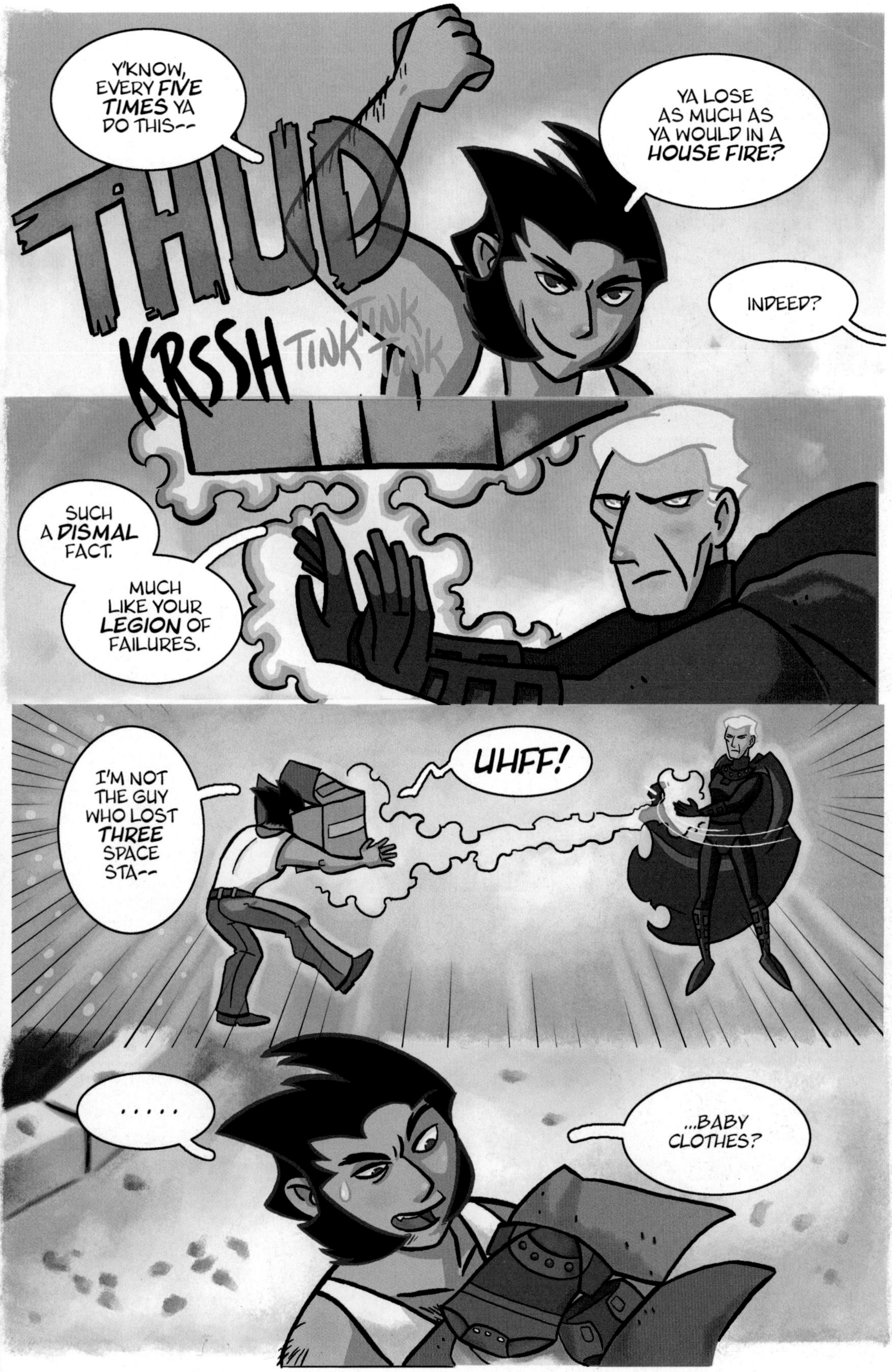

Y'KNOW, EVERY FIVE TIMES YA DO THIS--
THUD
YA LOSE AS MUCH AS YA WOULD IN A HOUSE FIRE?
KRSSH TINK TINK TINK
INDEED?
SUCH A DISMAL FACT.
MUCH LIKE YOUR LEGION OF FAILURES.
I'M NOT THE GUY WHO LOST THREE SPACE STA--
UHFF!
.....
...BABY CLOTHES?

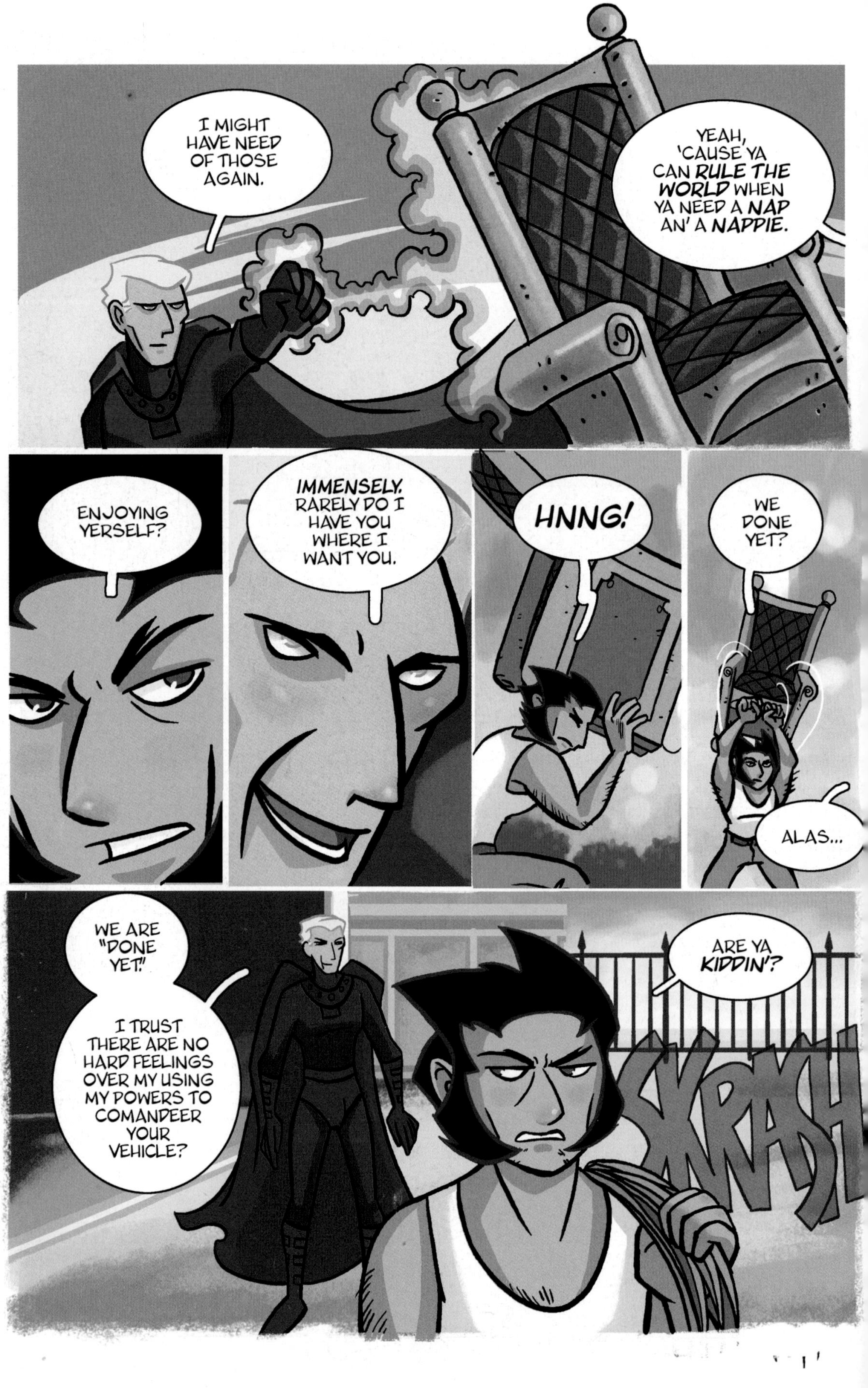
I MIGHT HAVE NEED OF THOSE AGAIN.
YEAH, 'CAUSE YA CAN RULE THE WORLD WHEN YA NEED A NAP AN' A NAPPIE.
ENJOYING YERSELF?
IMMENSELY. RARELY DO I HAVE YOU WHERE I WANT YOU.
HNNG!
WE DONE YET?
ALAS...
WE ARE "DONE YET."
I TRUST THERE ARE NO HARD FEELINGS OVER MY USING MY POWERS TO COMANDEER YOUR VEHICLE?
ARE YA KIDDIN'?
SKRASH

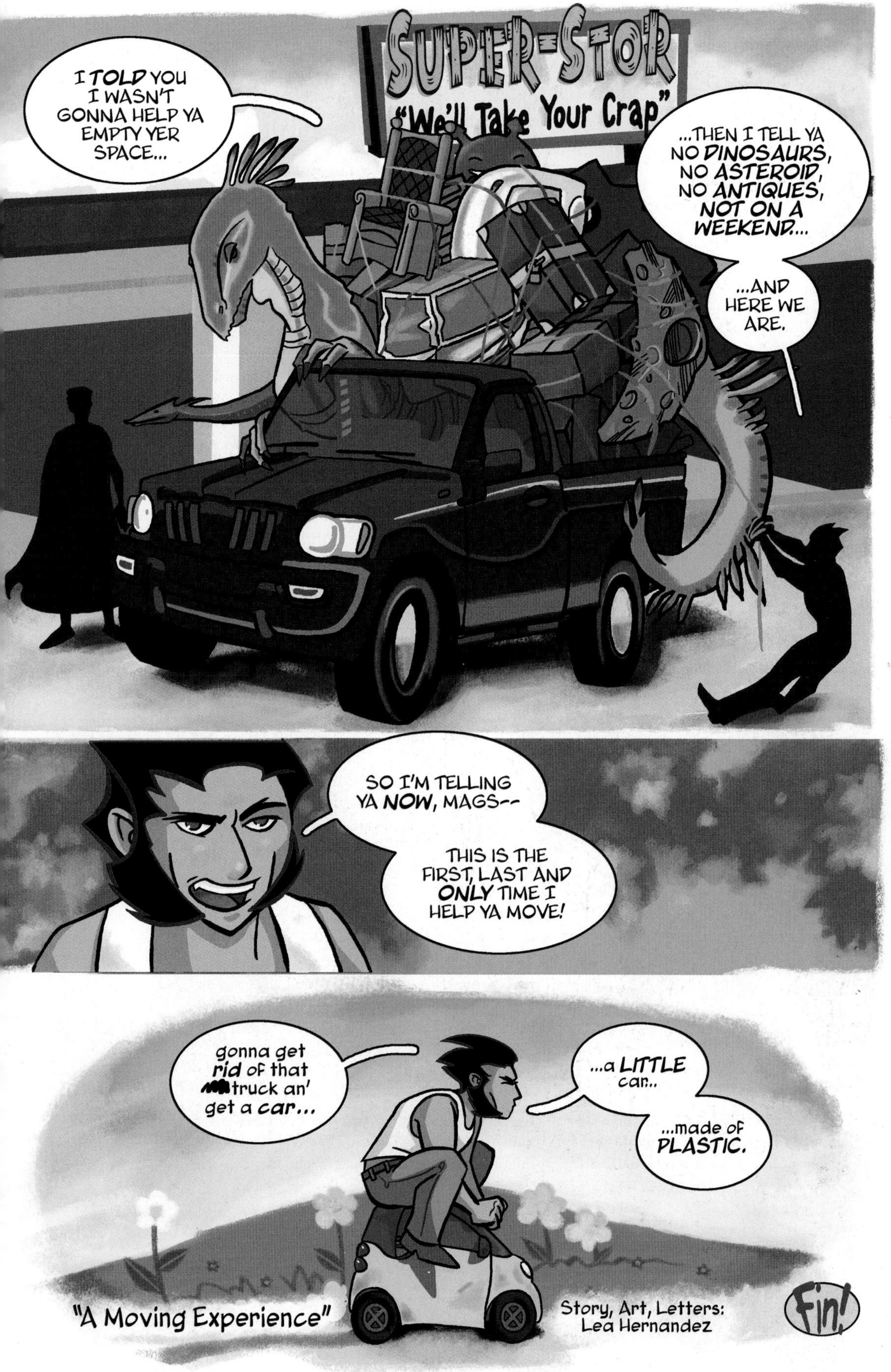
SUPER-STOR
"We'll Take Your Crap"
I TOLD YOU I WASN'T GONNA HELP YA EMPTY YER SPACE...
...THEN I TELL YA NO DINOSAURS, NO ASTEROID, NO ANTIQUES, NOT ON A WEEKEND....
...AND HERE WE ARE.
SO I'M TELLING YA NOW, MAGS--
THIS IS THE FIRST, LAST AND ONLY TIME I HELP YA MOVE!
gonna get rid of that [redacted] truck an' get a car...
...a LITTLE car..
...made of PLASTIC.
"A Moving Experience"
Story, Art, Letters: Lea Hernandez
Fin!

SPOTLIGHT

ANN NOCENTI

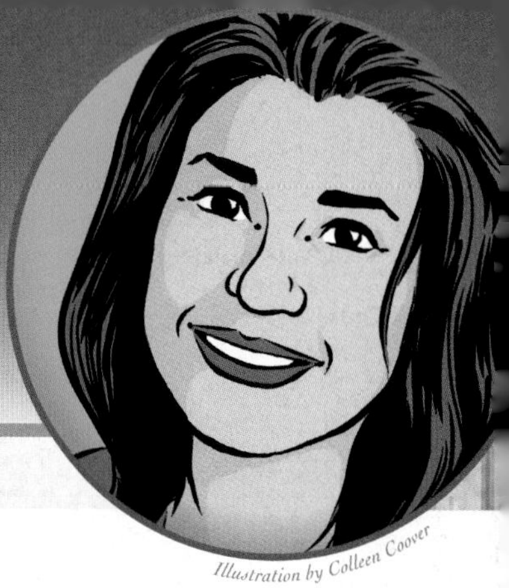

Illustration by Colleen Coover

It's particularly fascinating when one comes across a Marvel creator whose strengths aren't limited to the comic book world. They offer a perspective on storytelling that has a universal appeal, which in turn opens up comics to a new type of reader. Ann Nocenti is exactly that kind of creator. As a fiction and nonfiction writer, filmmaker, editor and fine artist, the stories Ann wrote for Marvel encompass a unique creative sensibility.

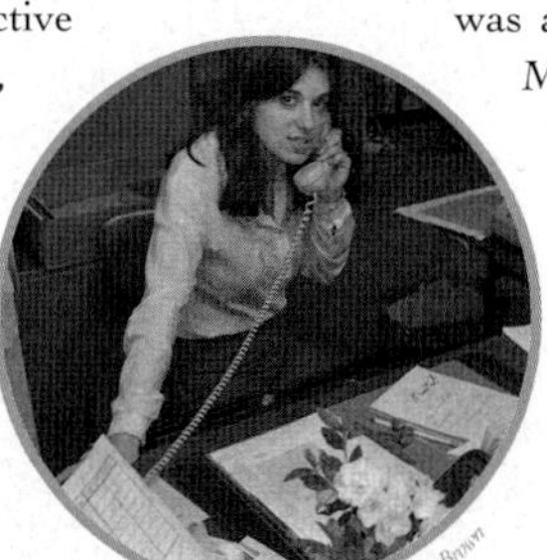

Ann in the office. Courtesy of Eliot R. Brown

It's no surprise then that Ann's entrance to the comics business was unconventional. She was a "voracious cineaste," interested more in painting and etching than writing. Her introduction to comics was scant as a child, mainly a few issues of *Jughead*, *Pogo* and *Dick Tracy*. Ann entered the mainstream comics world only after graduating college at SUNY New Paltz. Upon answering a "cryptic ad in the Village Voice for editorial and writing work," Ann was whisked away into the world of Marvel.

Although her familiarity with comics was limited, her love of film and art allowed her to quickly acclimate to the medium, which later evolved into a strong affinity for it. Initially, Ann was an assistant editor to Carl Potts and worked on *The Incredible Hulk*, *The Defenders* and *The Thing*. In 1982, former Marvel editor/writer Denny O'Neil got Ann her first writing gig with *Bizarre Adventures* #32, a mythological story about a man who runs out of so much luck that it destroys him. She went on to write issues of *Spider-Woman*, *Star Wars* and *Doctor Strange*, among others. As she proved her writing capabilities, Ann and artist Arthur Adams co-created the X-Men character Longshot in a six-issue miniseries of the same name in 1985.

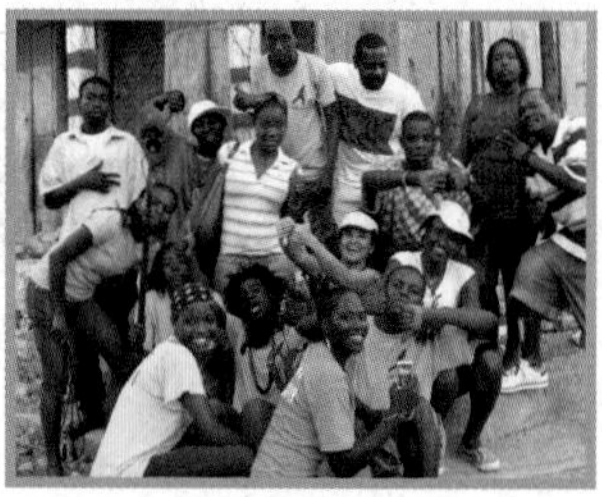

Ann with film students in Haiti.

After partnering with Barry Windsor-Smith on *Daredevil* #236, Ann was offered a momentous opportunity: to take over *Daredevil* writing duties post Frank Miller's run. It was a bold editorial decision, but it's one that Marvel Senior Editor Ralph Macchio has never regretted. "Unlike many writers at the time, Ann wasn't intimidated by having Miller as a predecessor. Her relatively recent exposure to comics at the time made her a comics bohemian of sorts, but gave her a fresh perspective on the content which truly reinvigorated the character like never before. She created a run that was—in my opinion—just as great as Miller's."

Ann wrote *Daredevil* for a little over four years, during which she and John Romita Jr. introduced the very popular twisted antagonist, Typhoid Mary. She successfully wove action and intrigue while integrating Ann's political and social beliefs—a controversial combination, but one that added depth and dimension to her stories.

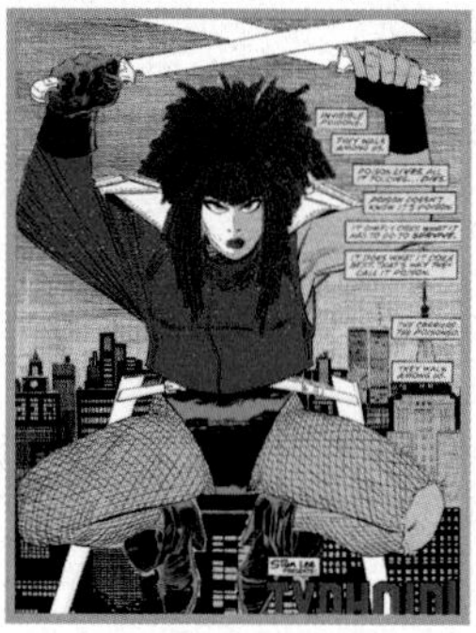

Typhoid Mary in Daredevil #254

Ann continued to write for Marvel and then Vertigo until the '90s. Today she maintains her love for writing and storytelling working as a journalist and filmmaker, also teaching film in Haiti. Her love of comics, though, hasn't gone anywhere. She's written for *Daredevil* and *Spider-Man*, and uses Marvel pages to teach storytelling through art to her Haitian students. The comics rebel has turned comics advocate—and we couldn't ask for a better ally.

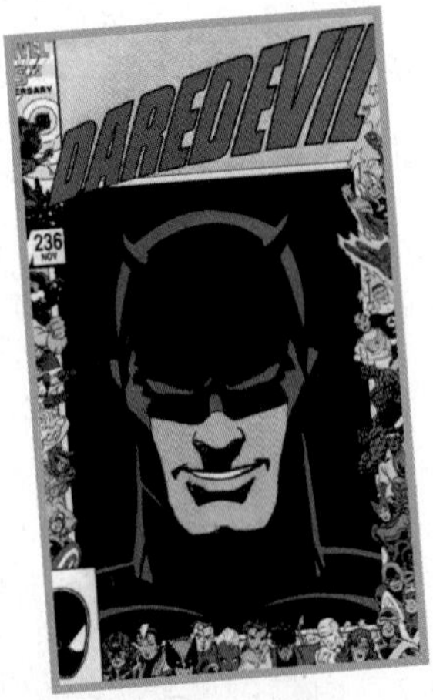
DAREDEVIL
236

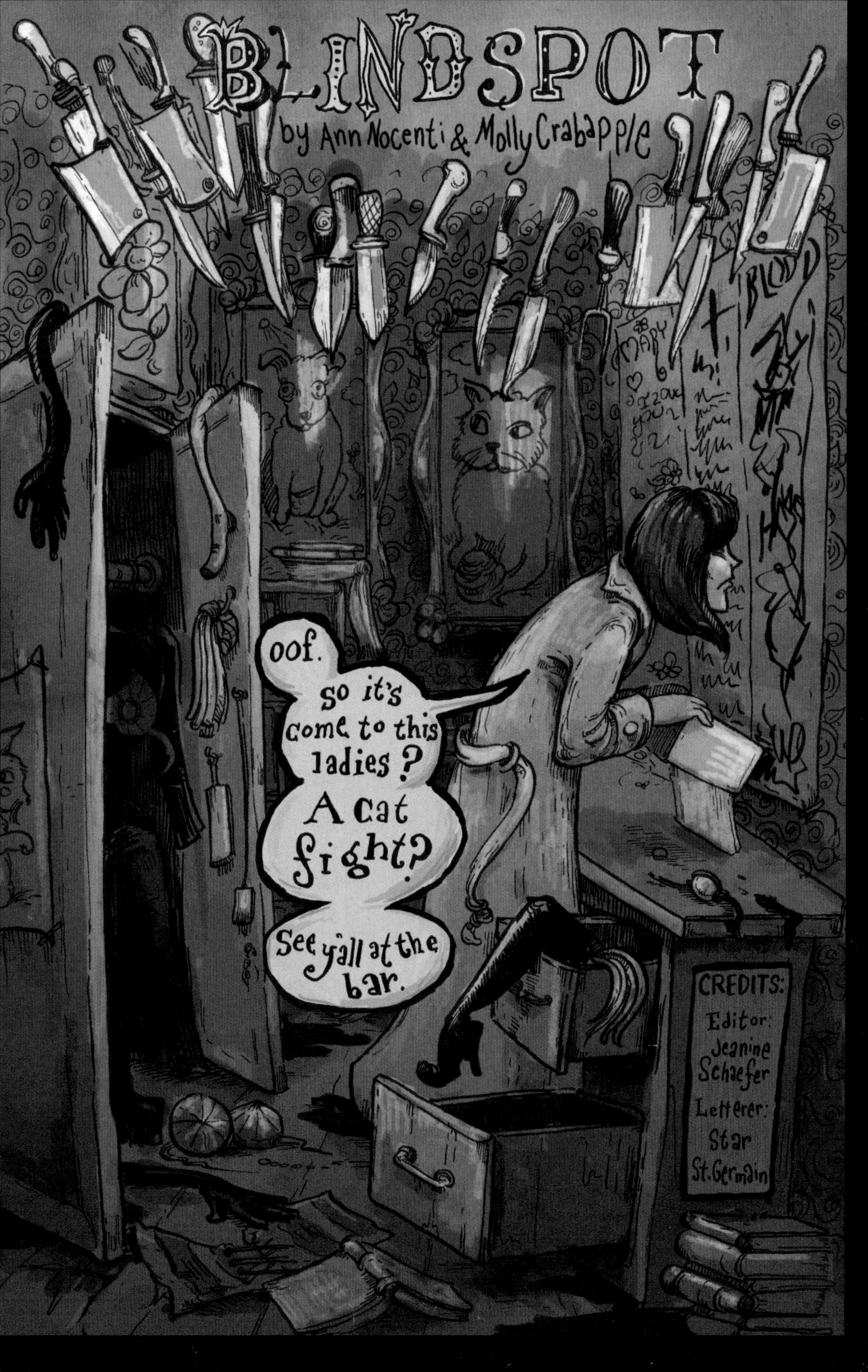
BLINDSPOT
by Ann Nocenti & Molly Crabapple
oof.
so it's come to this ladies? A cat fight?
See y'all at the bar.
CREDITS:
Editor: Jeanine Schaefer
Letterer: Star St.Germain

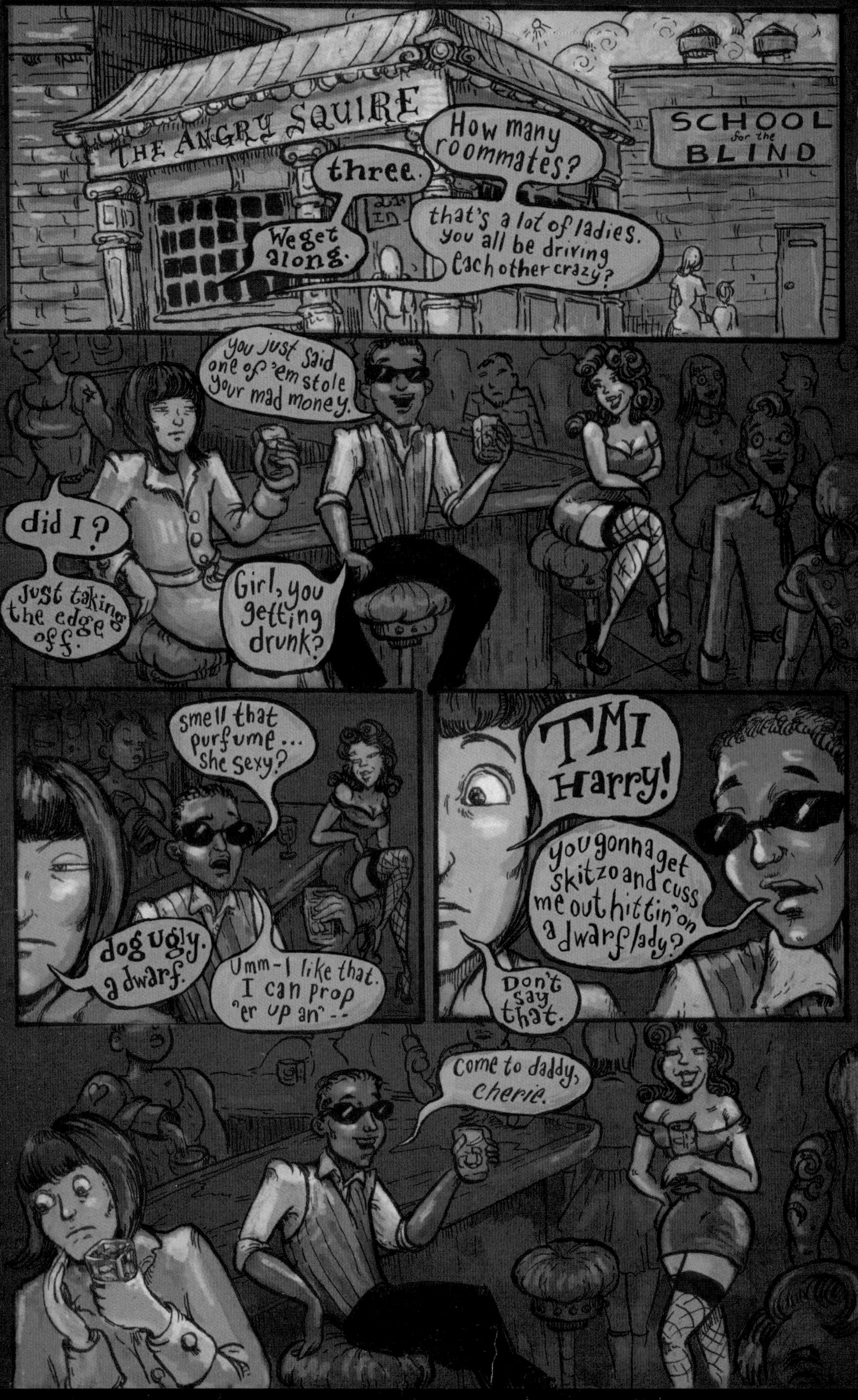
THE ANGRY SQUIRE
SCHOOL for the BLIND
How many roommates?
three.
We get along.
that's a lot of ladies. you all be driving each other crazy?
you just said one of 'em stole your mad money.
did I?
just taking the edge off.
Girl, you getting drunk?
smell that purfume... she sexy?
dog ugly. a dwarf.
Umm-I like that. I can prop 'er up an'--
TMI Harry!
you gonna get skitzo and cuss me out hittin' on a dwarf lady?
Don't say that.
Come to daddy, cherie.

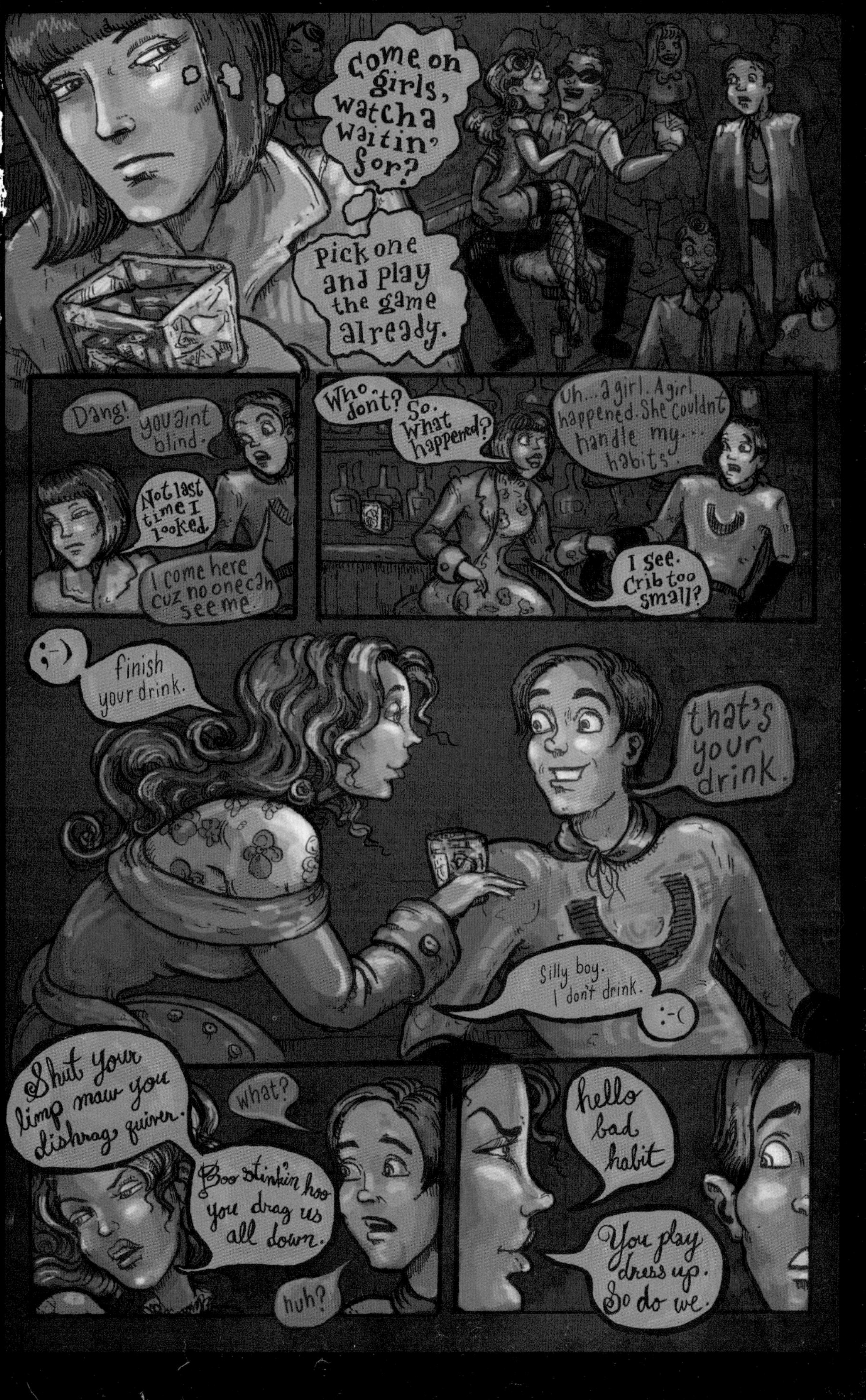
come on girls, watcha waitin' for?
Pick one and play the game already.
Dang!
you aint blind.
Not last time I looked.
I come here cuz no one can see me.
Who don't? So. What happened?
Uh...a girl. A girl happened. She couldnt handle my... habits.
I see. Crib too small?
:-)
finish your drink.
that's your drink.
Silly boy. I don't drink.
:-(
Shut your limp maw you dishrag quiver.
what?
Boo stinkin hoo you drag us all down.
huh?
hello bad habit
You play dress up. So do we.

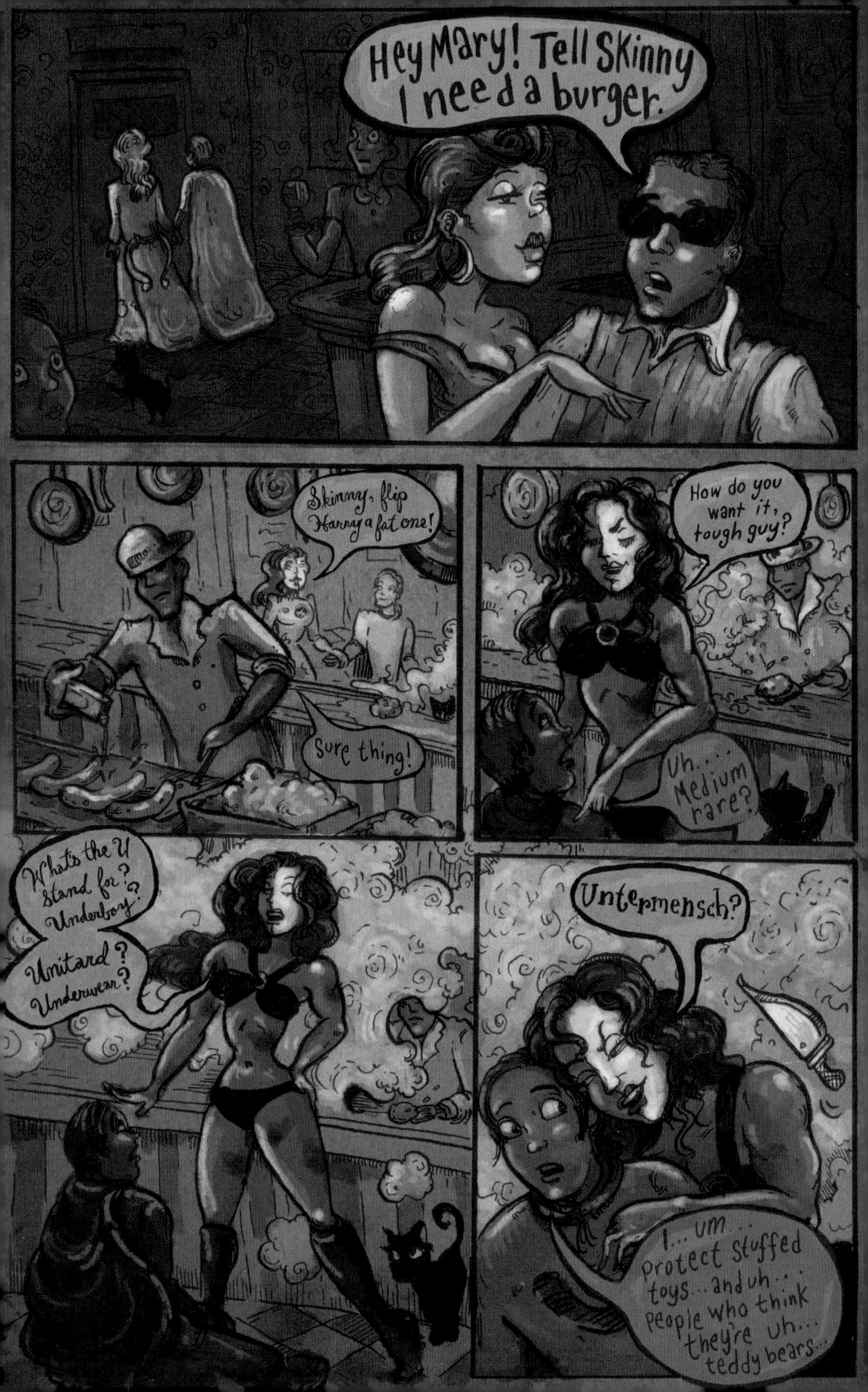
Hey Mary! Tell Skinny I need a burger.
Skinny, flip Harry a fat one!
Sure thing!
How do you want it, tough guy?
Uh.... Medium rare?
What's the U stand for? Underboy?
Unitard? Underwear?
Untermensch?
I... um... protect stuffed toys... and uh... people who think they're uh... teddy bears...

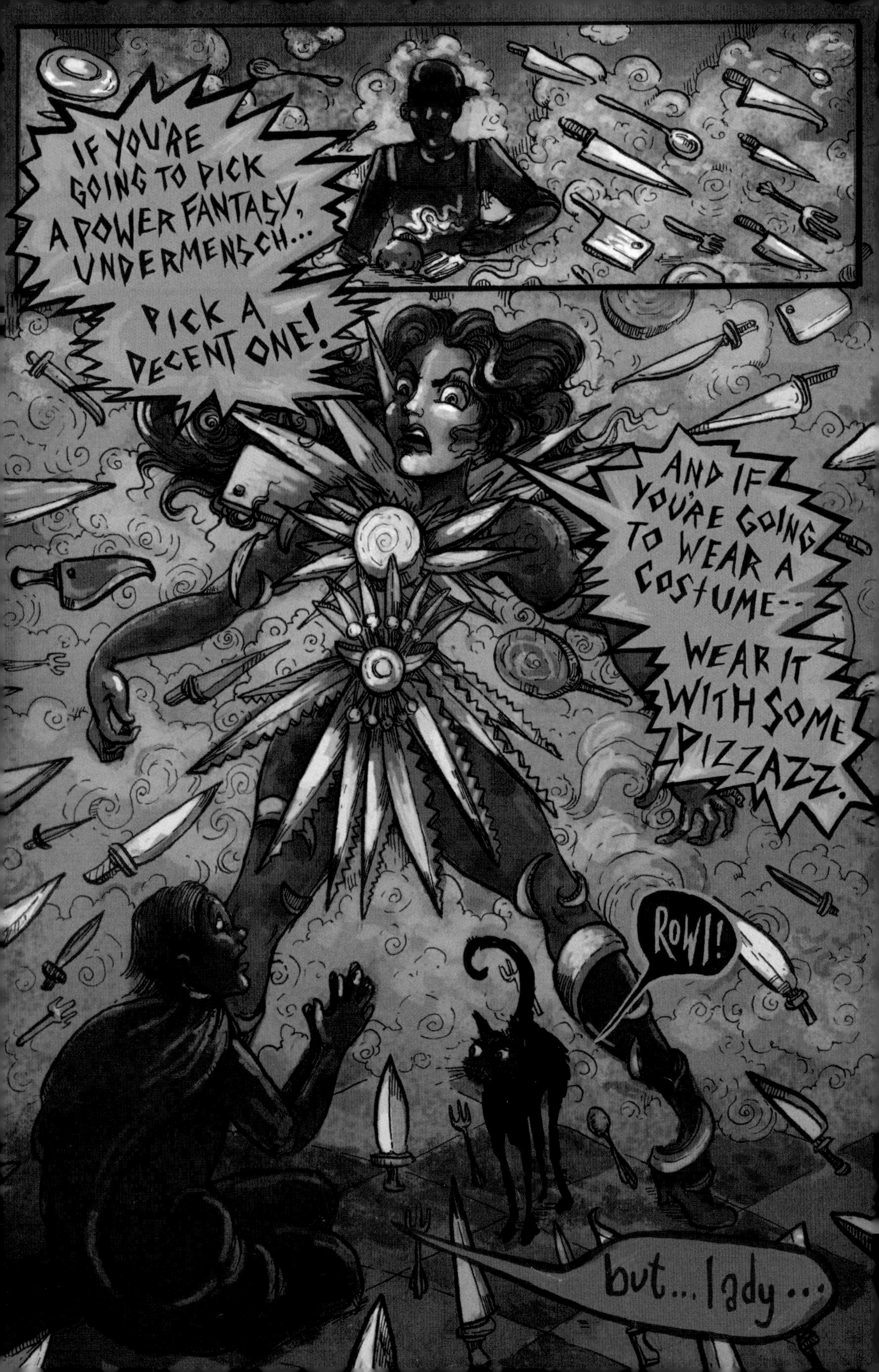
IF YOU'RE GOING TO PICK A POWER FANTASY, UNDERMENSCH...
PICK A DECENT ONE!
AND IF YOU'RE GOING TO WEAR A COSTUME--
WEAR IT WITH SOME PIZZAZZ.
ROWL!
but... lady...

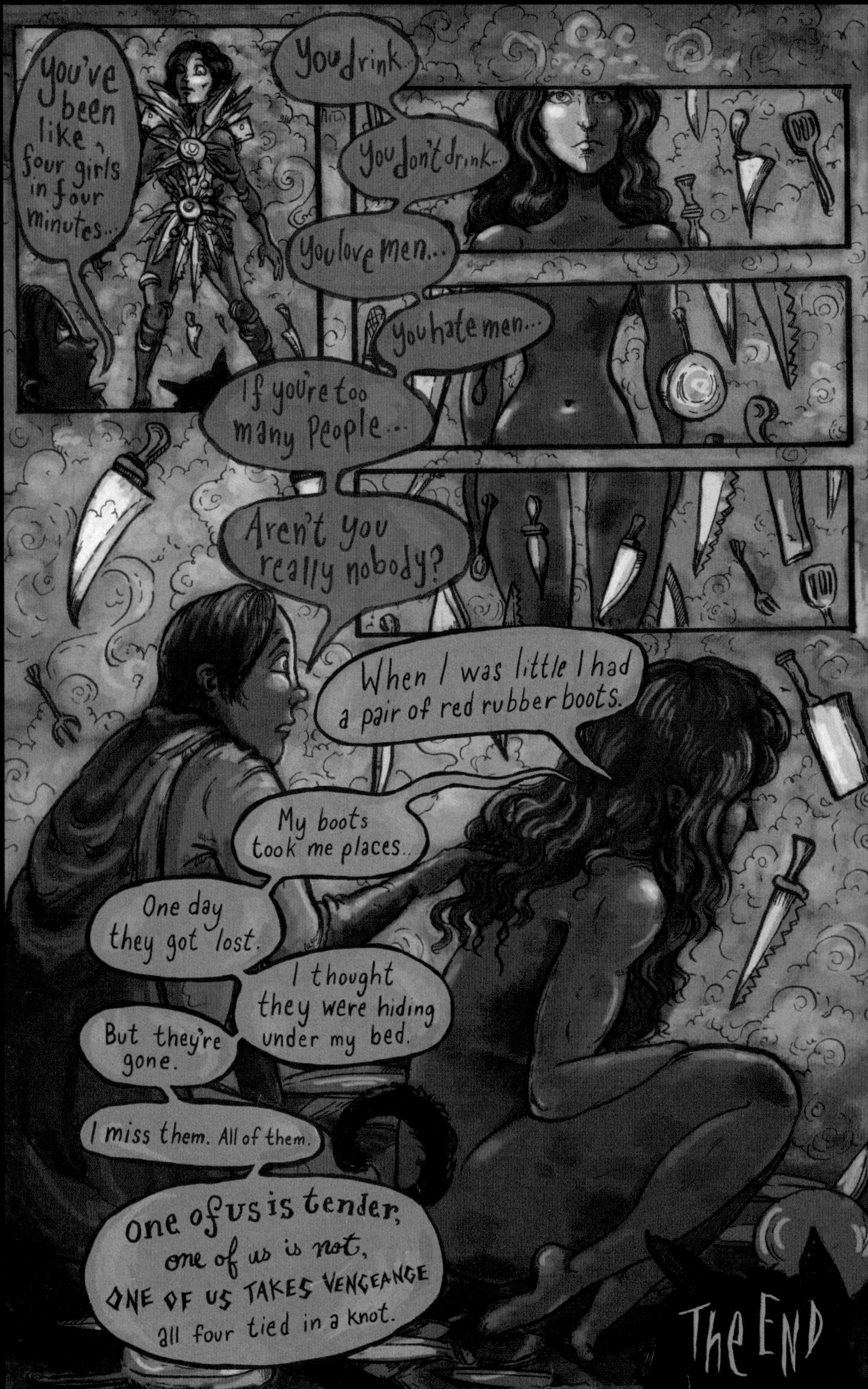
you've been like four girls in four minutes...
You drink...
You don't drink...
You love men...
You hate men...
If you're too many People...
Aren't you really nobody?
When I was little I had a pair of red rubber boots.
My boots took me places...
One day they got lost.
I thought they were hiding under my bed.
But they're gone.
I miss them. All of them.
One of us is tender, one of us is not, ONE OF US TAKES VENGEANCE all four tied in a knot.
The End

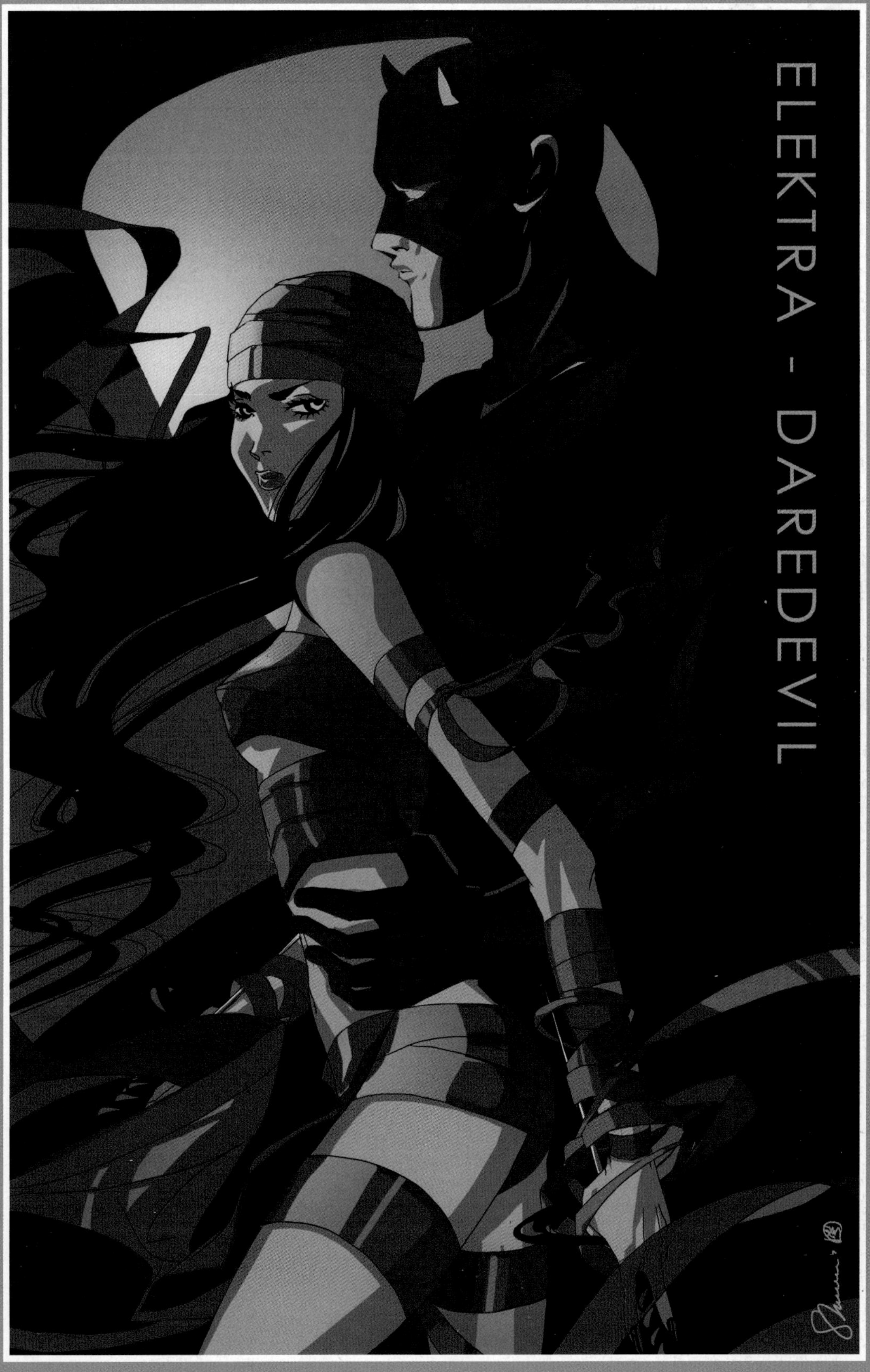
ELEKTRA - DAREDEVIL

ELEKTRA AND DAREDEVIL

By SHO MURASE

SPOTLIGHT

GLYNIS OLIVER

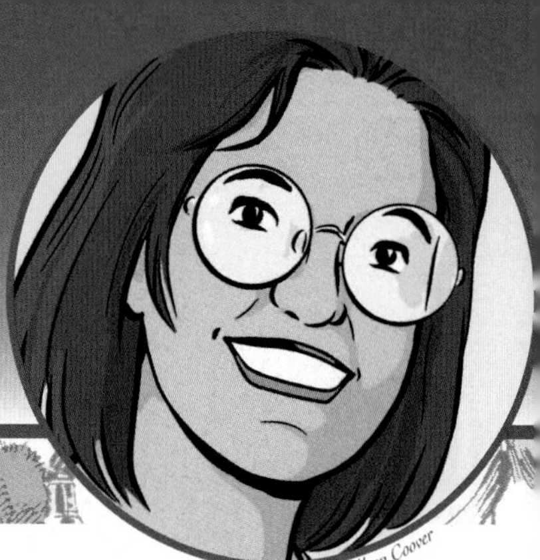

Illustration by Colleen Coover

In a bright career that has spanned almost three decades, Glynis Oliver spent most of those years as a colorist for Marvel. She has colored everything from *Power Pack* to *The Punisher*, including *X-Men* and the *Hulk*, two of her favorite series, and has been part of the rise of such longstanding characters as *Spider-Man* and *Fantastic Four*.

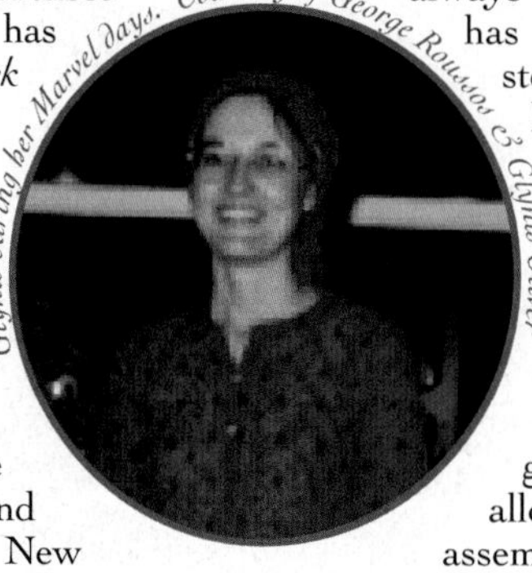

Glynis during her Marvel days. Courtesy of George Roussos & Glynis Oliver

Originally from England, Glynis lived for a time in Canada before finishing out her high school and college terms in the suburbs of New York. She earned degrees in Advertising Art and Design and before long entered the industry in the production department at DC Comics. Drawn to the comic world as a child by titles like *Little Lulu*, Glynis came to appreciate "the skill it takes to tell a story beautifully in a limited two-dimensional space." Inspired and eager to try her hand at coloring, she received the opportunity from Marvel to work on samples—specifically reprints of old Western tales—and Glynis' creativity with colors flourished.

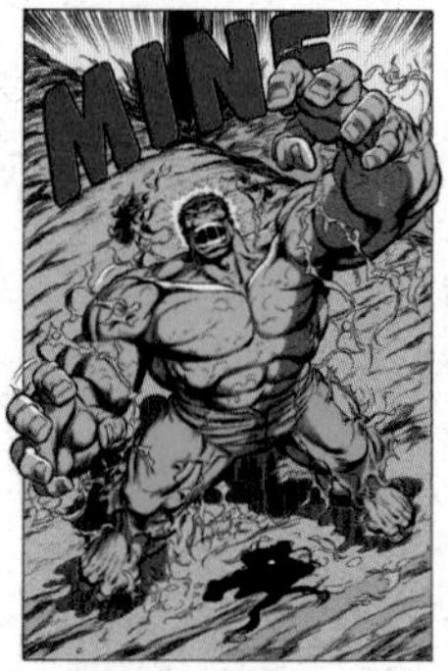

MINE

Splash from Hulk #372

Having impressed writer Roy Thomas, he brought Glynis into the fold of the Marvel Bullpen to work on his current *Avengers* series. This was the first of the bevy of Marvel characters that her brush would illuminate. In a time in the industry that was predominantly male—from writers to editors to the fans—Glynis had found a place for herself in the one discipline where women outnumbered the men. Working alongside department head Marie Severin, she learned the particulars on the job by actively studying the work of her mentor and fellow colorists. Each project was a new learning experience that honed her skills, and over the years her abilities have lent themselves to a range of titles.

Glynis' approach to the coloring process was always determined by the story. She has great admiration for the craft of storytelling and always considered how her palette would affect it. Of her method, Glynis says she "always began by reading the story first. I respected what the writer and artist had done before I got the pages to color... I felt this pre-reading was an important step because it gave me a sense of the story and I could get the feel of it." She worked to avoid allowing her procedure to become an assembly line and instead developed a setup that was creatively satisfying and best expressed the narrative. Glynis "would take note of the emotion of a scene and try to make the color choice reflect that."

Her departure from Marvel in 2000 gave Glynis an opportunity to set her sights on other interests, specifically dairy farming. What was initially a hobby became a profession. She now enjoys a new sort of creative environment and takes pride in the production of different types of cheeses'. Although she is no longer coloring the likes of her favorite X-Men, she continues to flourish in another venue. Fortunately for Marvel characters, Glynis has left a vibrant and indelible imprint on the entire Universe.

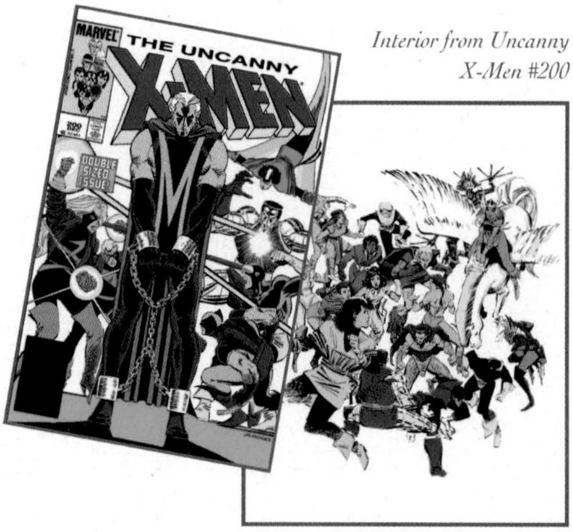

MARVEL
THE UNCANNY X-MEN
DOUBLE SIZED ISSUE!

Interior from Uncanny X-Men #200

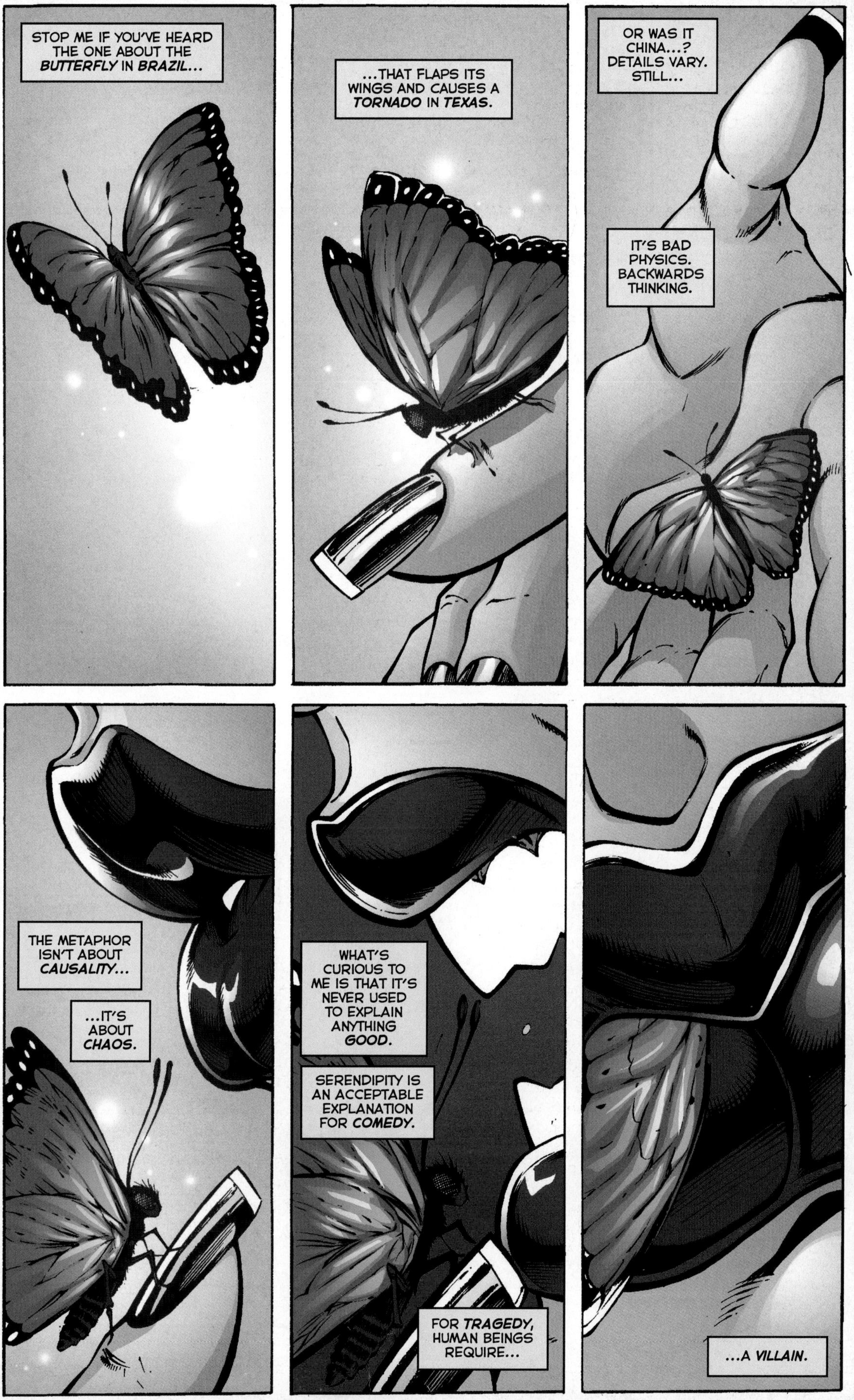
STOP ME IF YOU'VE HEARD THE ONE ABOUT THE *BUTTERFLY* IN *BRAZIL*...
...THAT FLAPS ITS WINGS AND CAUSES A *TORNADO* IN *TEXAS*.
OR WAS IT CHINA...? DETAILS VARY. STILL...
IT'S BAD PHYSICS. BACKWARDS THINKING.
THE METAPHOR ISN'T ABOUT *CAUSALITY*...
...IT'S ABOUT *CHAOS*.
WHAT'S CURIOUS TO ME IS THAT IT'S NEVER USED TO EXPLAIN ANYTHING *GOOD*.
SERENDIPITY IS AN ACCEPTABLE EXPLANATION FOR *COMEDY*.
FOR *TRAGEDY*, HUMAN BEINGS REQUIRE...
...A *VILLAIN*.

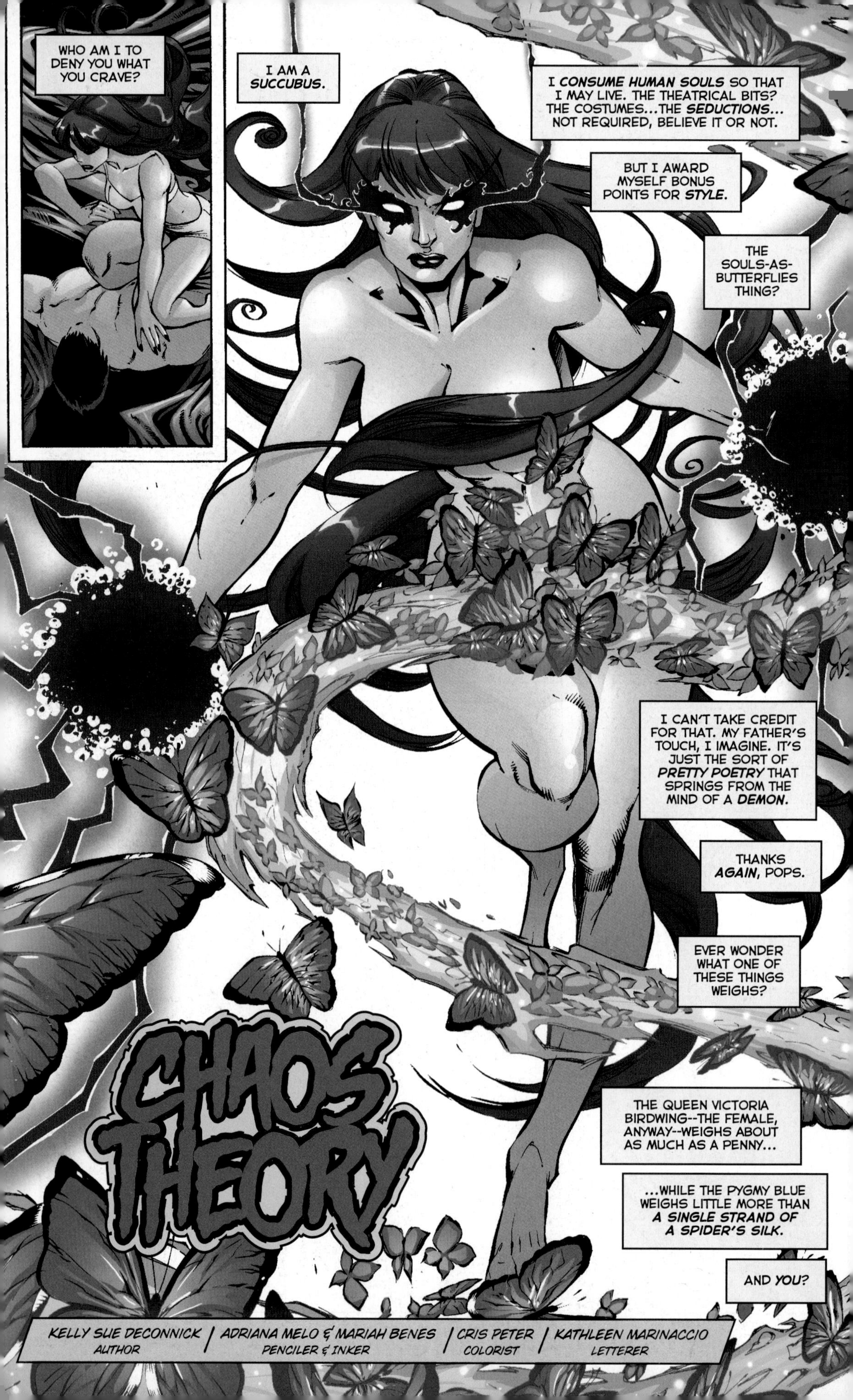
WHO AM I TO DENY YOU WHAT YOU CRAVE?
I AM A SUCCUBUS.
I CONSUME HUMAN SOULS SO THAT I MAY LIVE. THE THEATRICAL BITS? THE COSTUMES...THE SEDUCTIONS... NOT REQUIRED, BELIEVE IT OR NOT.
BUT I AWARD MYSELF BONUS POINTS FOR STYLE.
THE SOULS-AS-BUTTERFLIES THING?
I CAN'T TAKE CREDIT FOR THAT. MY FATHER'S TOUCH, I IMAGINE. IT'S JUST THE SORT OF PRETTY POETRY THAT SPRINGS FROM THE MIND OF A DEMON.
THANKS AGAIN, POPS.
EVER WONDER WHAT ONE OF THESE THINGS WEIGHS?
THE QUEEN VICTORIA BIRDWING--THE FEMALE, ANYWAY--WEIGHS ABOUT AS MUCH AS A PENNY...
...WHILE THE PYGMY BLUE WEIGHS LITTLE MORE THAN A SINGLE STRAND OF A SPIDER'S SILK.
AND YOU?
CHAOS THEORY
KELLY SUE DECONNICK AUTHOR
ADRIANA MELO & MARIAH BENES PENCILER & INKER
CRIS PETER COLORIST
KATHLEEN MARINACCIO LETTERER

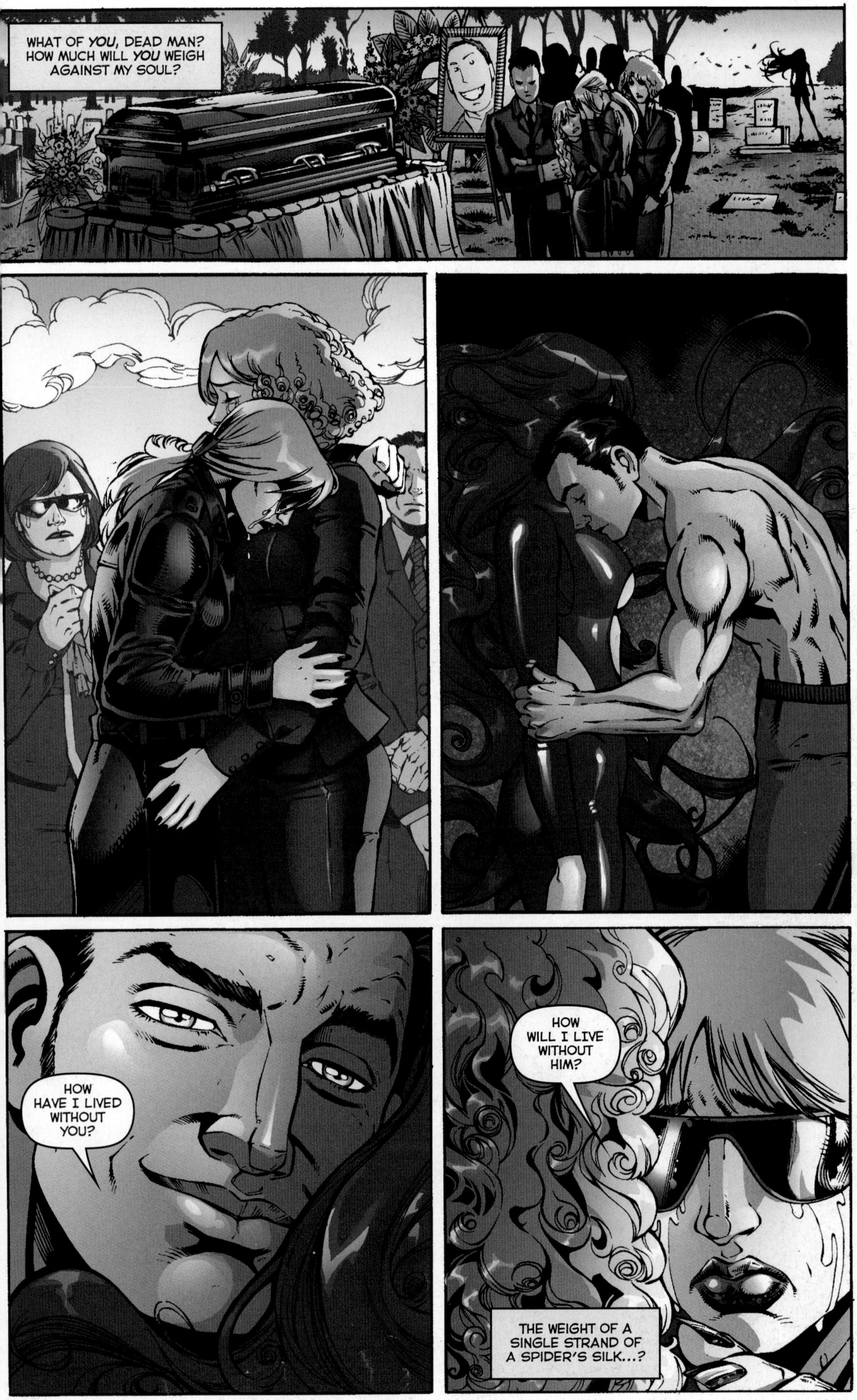
WHAT OF YOU, DEAD MAN? HOW MUCH WILL YOU WEIGH AGAINST MY SOUL?
HOW HAVE I LIVED WITHOUT YOU?
HOW WILL I LIVE WITHOUT HIM?
THE WEIGHT OF A SINGLE STRAND OF A SPIDER'S SILK...?

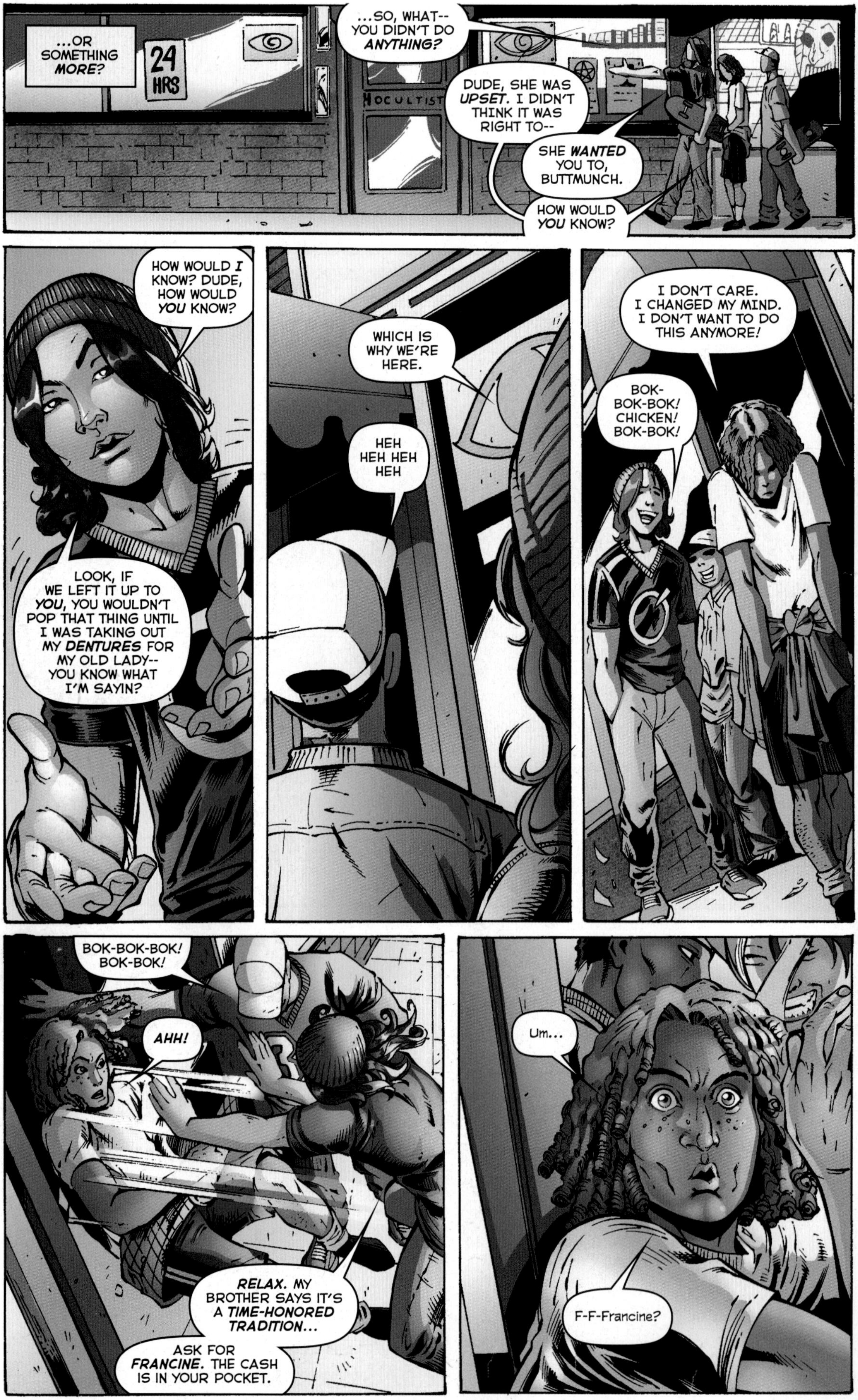

...OR SOMETHING MORE?
24 HRS
OCULTIST
...SO, WHAT-- YOU DIDN'T DO ANYTHING?
DUDE, SHE WAS UPSET. I DIDN'T THINK IT WAS RIGHT TO--
SHE WANTED YOU TO, BUTTMUNCH.
HOW WOULD YOU KNOW?
HOW WOULD I KNOW? DUDE, HOW WOULD YOU KNOW?
LOOK, IF WE LEFT IT UP TO YOU, YOU WOULDN'T POP THAT THING UNTIL I WAS TAKING OUT MY DENTURES FOR MY OLD LADY-- YOU KNOW WHAT I'M SAYIN?
WHICH IS WHY WE'RE HERE.
HEH HEH HEH HEH
I DON'T CARE. I CHANGED MY MIND. I DON'T WANT TO DO THIS ANYMORE!
BOK-BOK-BOK! CHICKEN! BOK-BOK!
BOK-BOK-BOK! BOK-BOK!
AHH!
RELAX. MY BROTHER SAYS IT'S A TIME-HONORED TRADITION...
ASK FOR FRANCINE. THE CASH IS IN YOUR POCKET.
Um...
F-F-Francine?

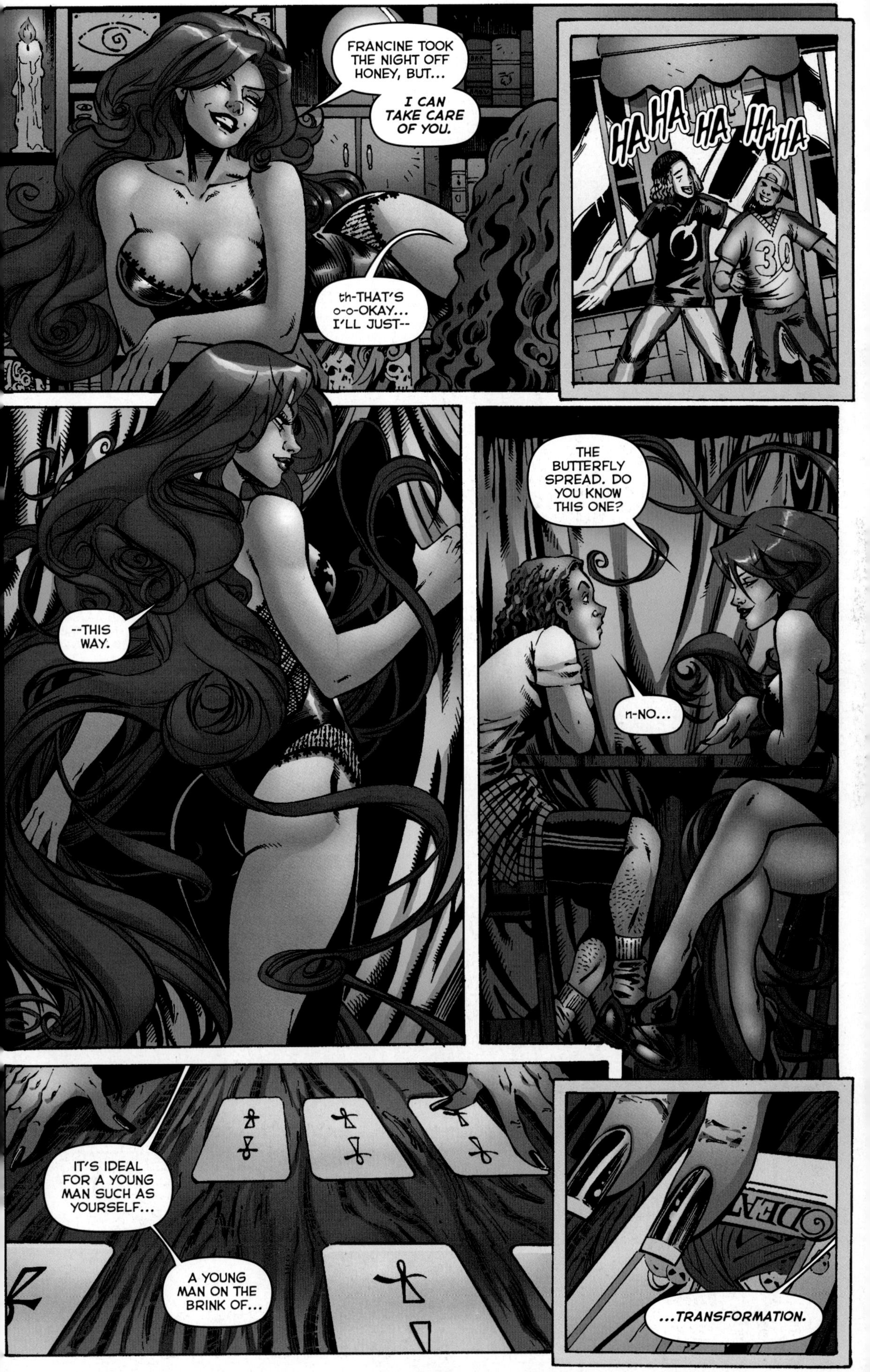
FRANCINE TOOK THE NIGHT OFF HONEY, BUT...
I CAN TAKE CARE OF YOU.
th-THAT'S o-o-OKAY... I'LL JUST--
HAHA HA HAHA
--THIS WAY.
THE BUTTERFLY SPREAD. DO YOU KNOW THIS ONE?
n-NO...
IT'S IDEAL FOR A YOUNG MAN SUCH AS YOURSELF...
A YOUNG MAN ON THE BRINK OF...
...TRANSFORMATION.

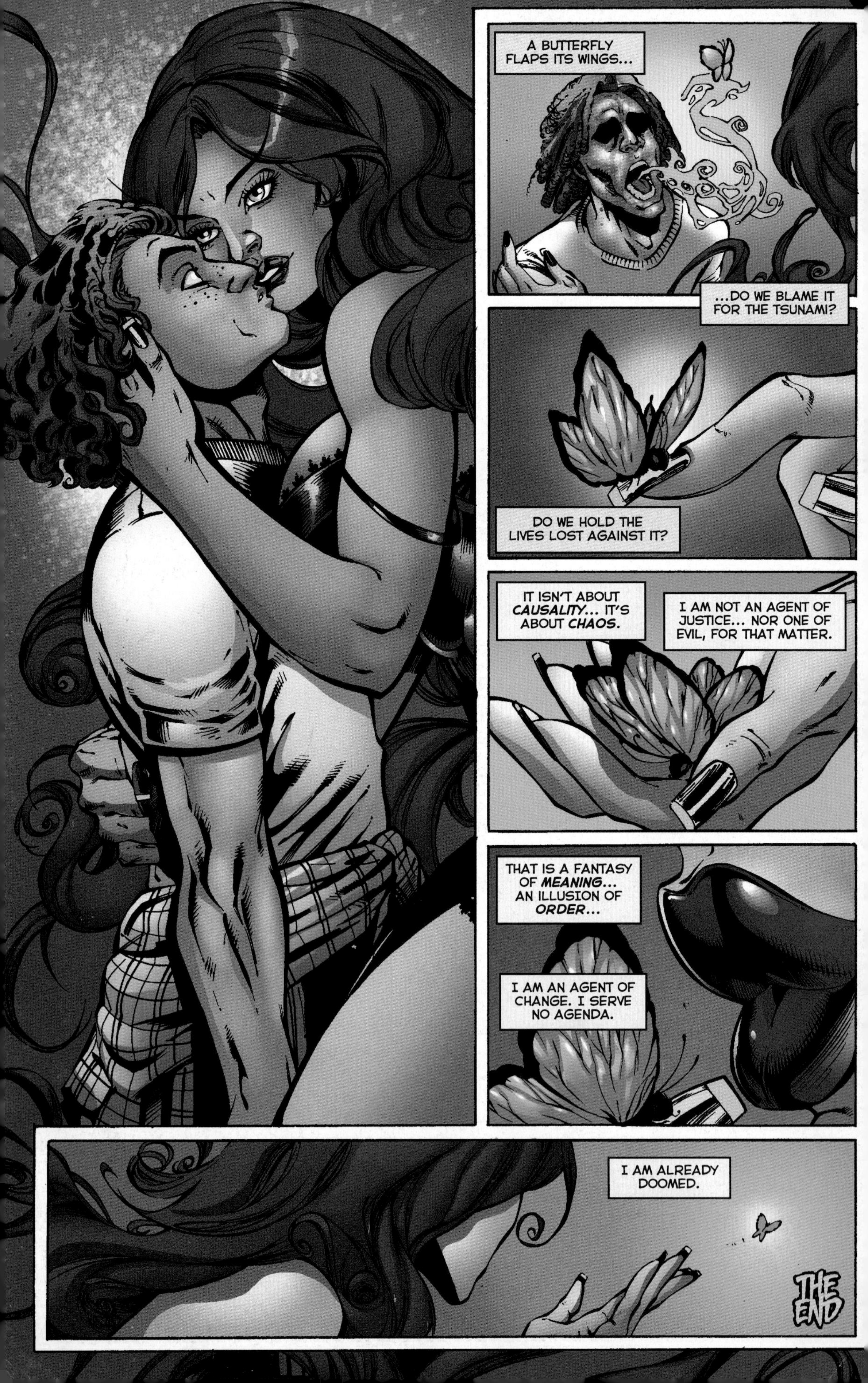
A BUTTERFLY FLAPS ITS WINGS...
...DO WE BLAME IT FOR THE TSUNAMI?
DO WE HOLD THE LIVES LOST AGAINST IT?
IT ISN'T ABOUT CAUSALITY... IT'S ABOUT CHAOS.
I AM NOT AN AGENT OF JUSTICE... NOR ONE OF EVIL, FOR THAT MATTER.
THAT IS A FANTASY OF MEANING... AN ILLUSION OF ORDER...
I AM AN AGENT OF CHANGE. I SERVE NO AGENDA.
I AM ALREADY DOOMED.
THE END

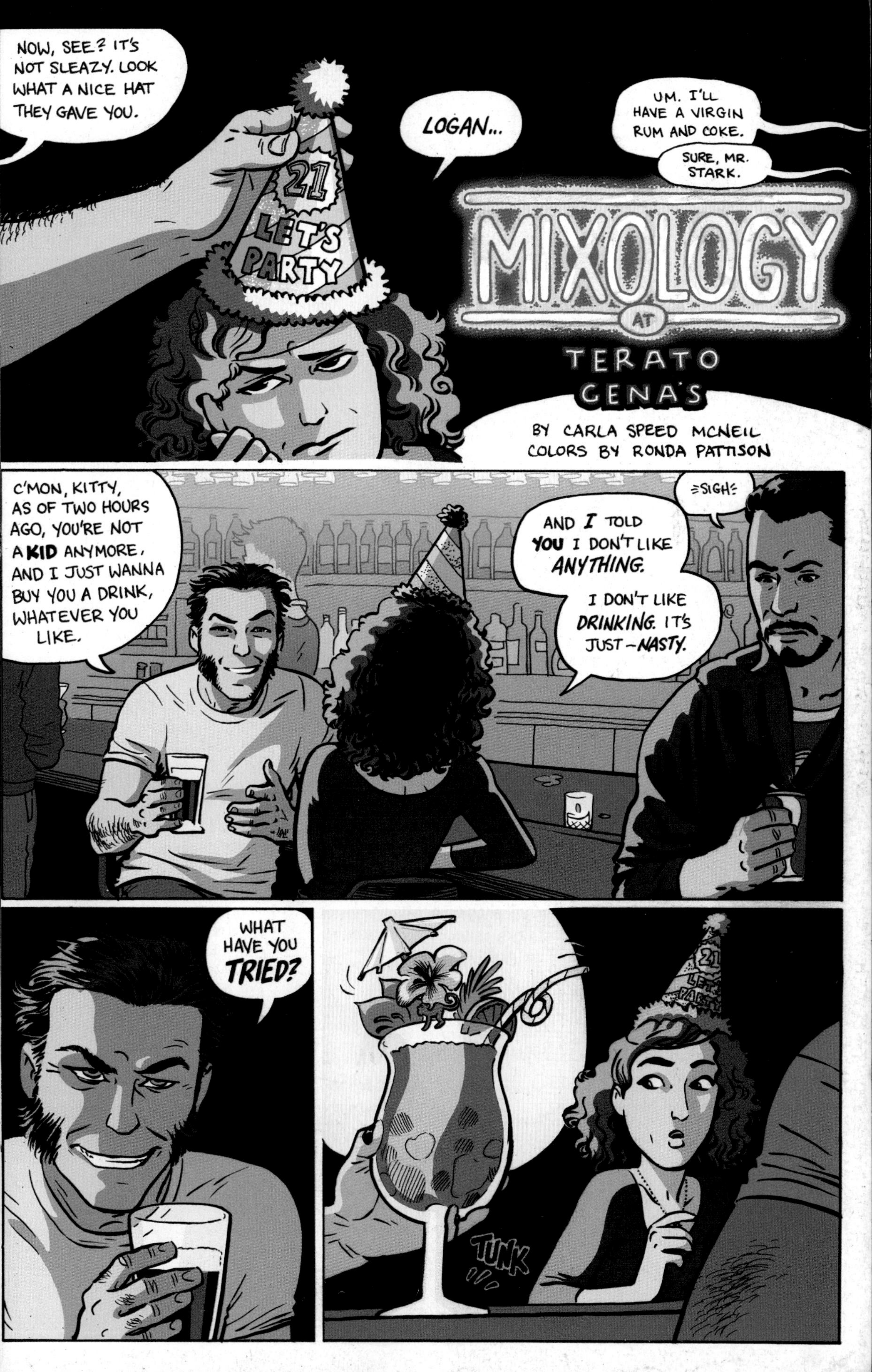
NOW, SEE? IT'S NOT SLEAZY. LOOK WHAT A NICE HAT THEY GAVE YOU.
21 LET'S PARTY
LOGAN...
UM. I'LL HAVE A VIRGIN RUM AND COKE.
SURE, MR. STARK.
MIXOLOGY
AT
TERATO GENA'S
BY CARLA SPEED MCNEIL
COLORS BY RONDA PATTISON
C'MON, KITTY, AS OF TWO HOURS AGO, YOU'RE NOT A KID ANYMORE, AND I JUST WANNA BUY YOU A DRINK, WHATEVER YOU LIKE.
=SIGH=
AND I TOLD YOU I DON'T LIKE ANYTHING.
I DON'T LIKE DRINKING. IT'S JUST--NASTY.
WHAT HAVE YOU TRIED?
21 LET'S PARTY
TUNK

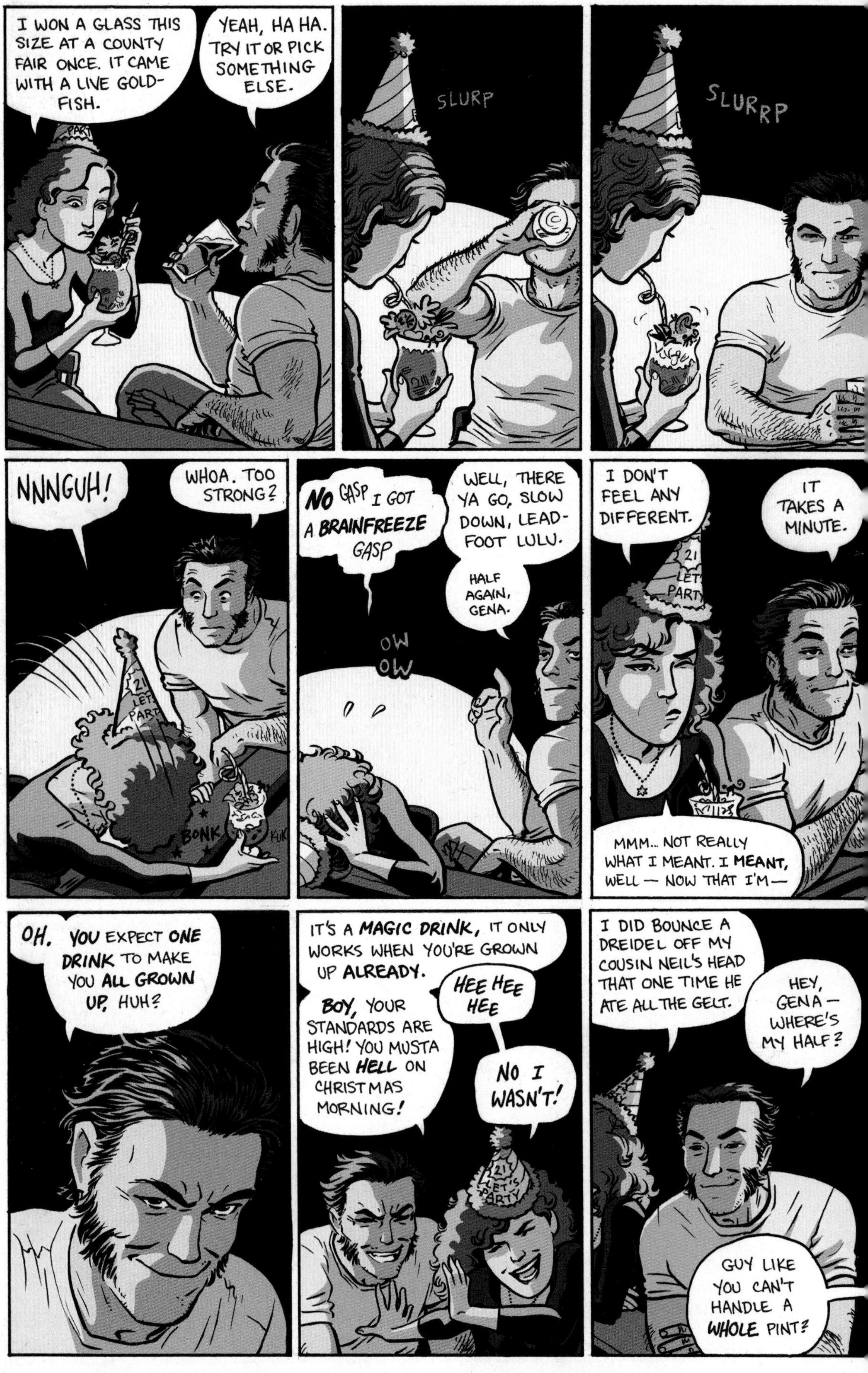
I WON A GLASS THIS SIZE AT A COUNTY FAIR ONCE. IT CAME WITH A LIVE GOLD-FISH.
YEAH, HA HA. TRY IT OR PICK SOMETHING ELSE.
SLURP
SLURRRP
NNNGUH!
WHOA. TOO STRONG?
BONK
NO GASP I GOT A BRAINFREEZE GASP
WELL, THERE YA GO, SLOW DOWN, LEAD-FOOT LULU.
HALF AGAIN, GENA.
OW OW
I DON'T FEEL ANY DIFFERENT.
IT TAKES A MINUTE.
MMM... NOT REALLY WHAT I MEANT. I MEANT, WELL — NOW THAT I'M—
OH. YOU EXPECT ONE DRINK TO MAKE YOU ALL GROWN UP, HUH?
IT'S A MAGIC DRINK, IT ONLY WORKS WHEN YOU'RE GROWN UP ALREADY.
BOY, YOUR STANDARDS ARE HIGH! YOU MUSTA BEEN HELL ON CHRISTMAS MORNING!
HEE HEE HEE
NO I WASN'T!
21 LET'S PARTY
I DID BOUNCE A DREIDEL OFF MY COUSIN NEIL'S HEAD THAT ONE TIME HE ATE ALL THE GELT.
HEY, GENA — WHERE'S MY HALF?
GUY LIKE YOU CAN'T HANDLE A WHOLE PINT?

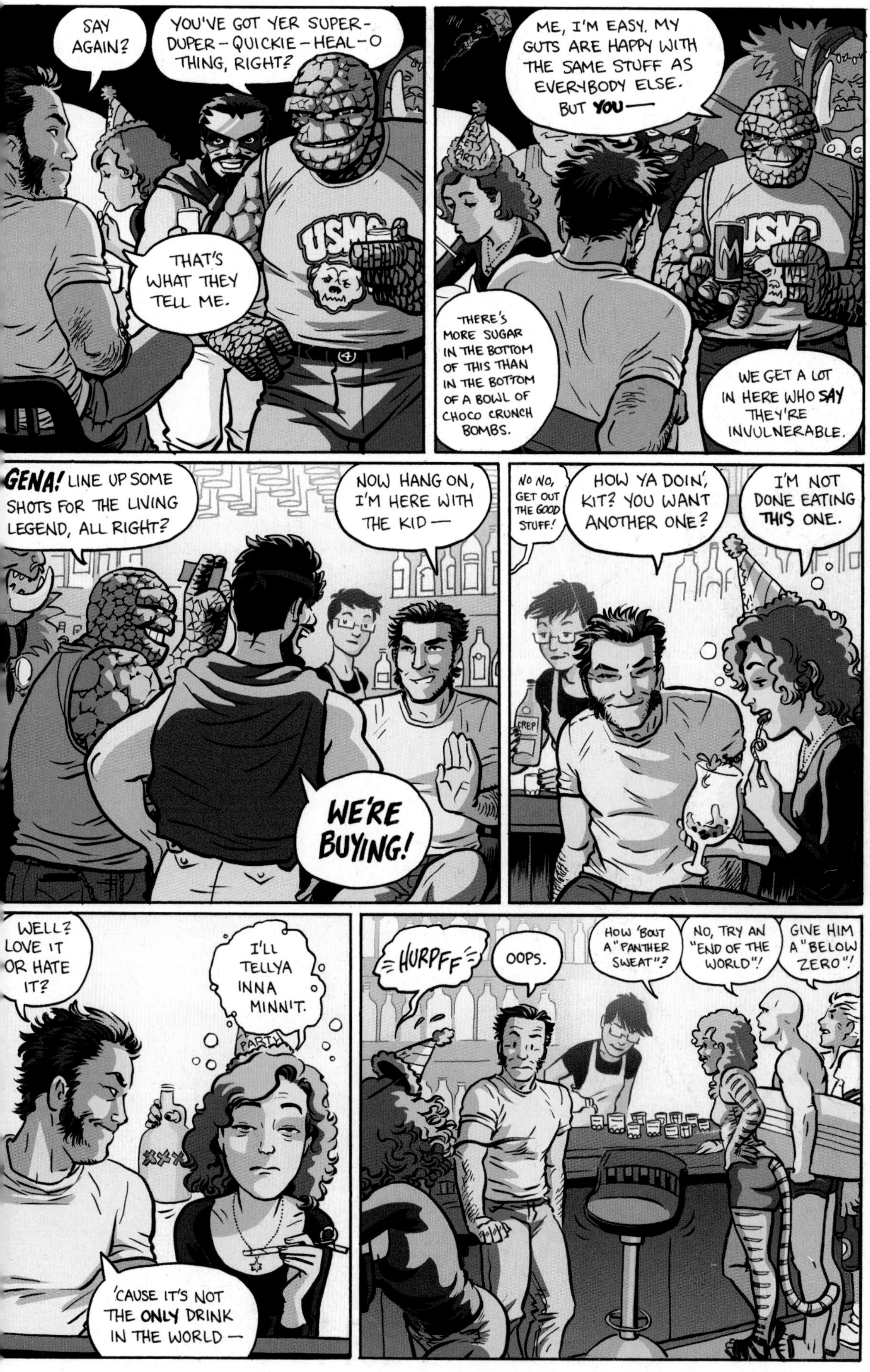
SAY AGAIN?
YOU'VE GOT YER SUPER-DUPER-QUICKIE-HEAL-O THING, RIGHT?
THAT'S WHAT THEY TELL ME.
ME, I'M EASY. MY GUTS ARE HAPPY WITH THE SAME STUFF AS EVERYBODY ELSE. BUT YOU—
LET'S PARTY!
THERE'S MORE SUGAR IN THE BOTTOM OF THIS THAN IN THE BOTTOM OF A BOWL OF CHOCO CRUNCH BOMBS.
WE GET A LOT IN HERE WHO SAY THEY'RE INVULNERABLE.
GENA! LINE UP SOME SHOTS FOR THE LIVING LEGEND, ALL RIGHT?
NOW HANG ON, I'M HERE WITH THE KID—
WE'RE BUYING!
NO NO, GET OUT THE GOOD STUFF!
HOW YA DOIN', KIT? YOU WANT ANOTHER ONE?
I'M NOT DONE EATING THIS ONE.
FREP
WELL? LOVE IT OR HATE IT?
I'LL TELLYA INNA MINNIT.
PARTY
'CAUSE IT'S NOT THE ONLY DRINK IN THE WORLD—
HURPFF
OOPS.
HOW 'BOUT A "PANTHER SWEAT"?
NO, TRY AN "END OF THE WORLD"!
GIVE HIM A "BELOW ZERO"!

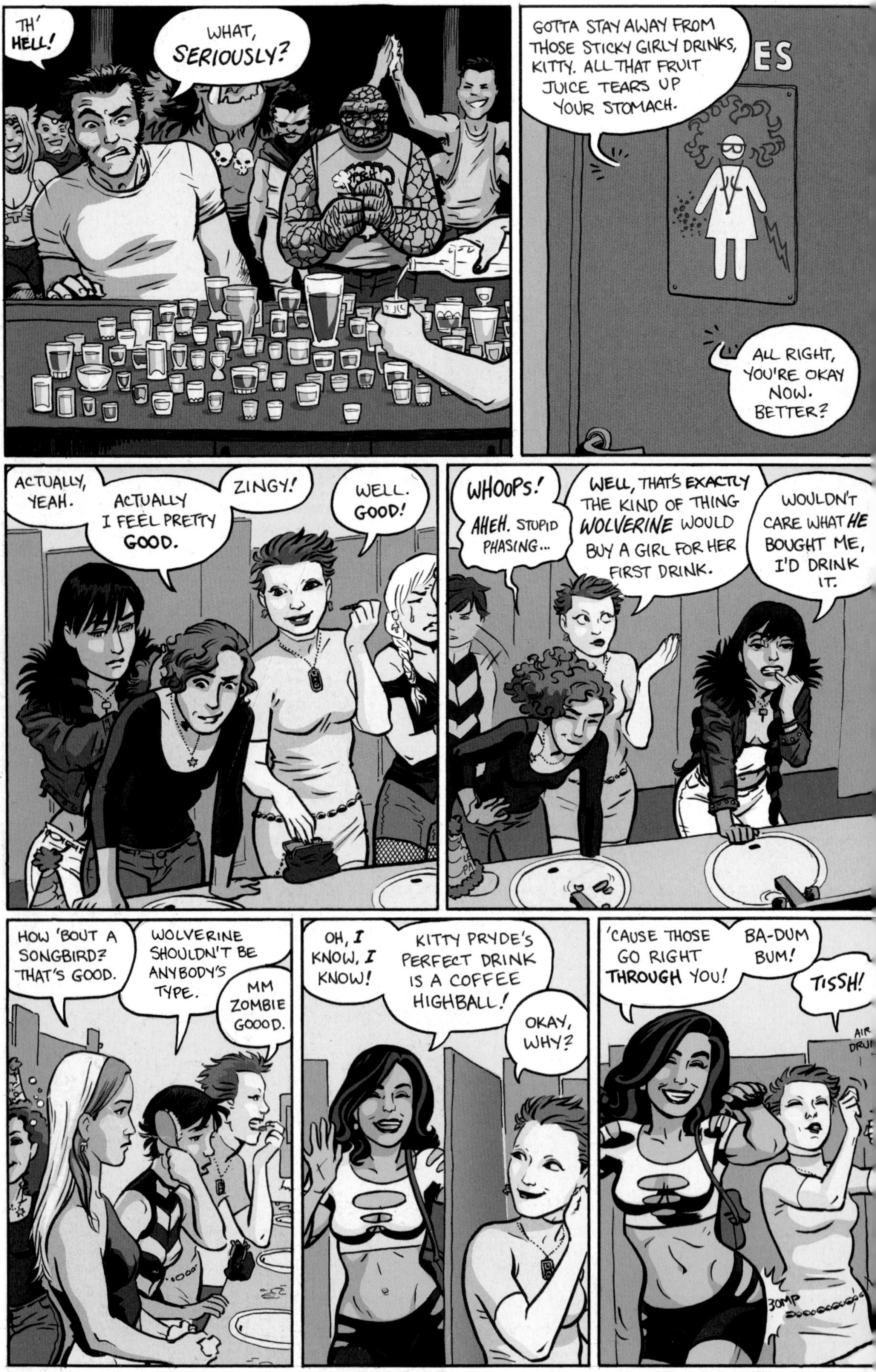

TH' HELL!
WHAT, SERIOUSLY?
GOTTA STAY AWAY FROM THOSE STICKY GIRLY DRINKS, KITTY. ALL THAT FRUIT JUICE TEARS UP YOUR STOMACH.
ALL RIGHT, YOU'RE OKAY NOW. BETTER?
ACTUALLY, YEAH.
ACTUALLY I FEEL PRETTY GOOD.
ZINGY!
WELL. GOOD!
WHOOPS!
AHEH. STUPID PHASING...
WELL, THAT'S EXACTLY THE KIND OF THING WOLVERINE WOULD BUY A GIRL FOR HER FIRST DRINK.
WOULDN'T CARE WHAT HE BOUGHT ME, I'D DRINK IT.
HOW 'BOUT A SONGBIRD? THAT'S GOOD.
WOLVERINE SHOULDN'T BE ANYBODY'S TYPE.
MM ZOMBIE GOOOD.
OH, I KNOW, I KNOW!
KITTY PRYDE'S PERFECT DRINK IS A COFFEE HIGHBALL!
OKAY, WHY?
'CAUSE THOSE GO RIGHT THROUGH YOU!
BA-DUM BUM!
TISSH!
BOMP

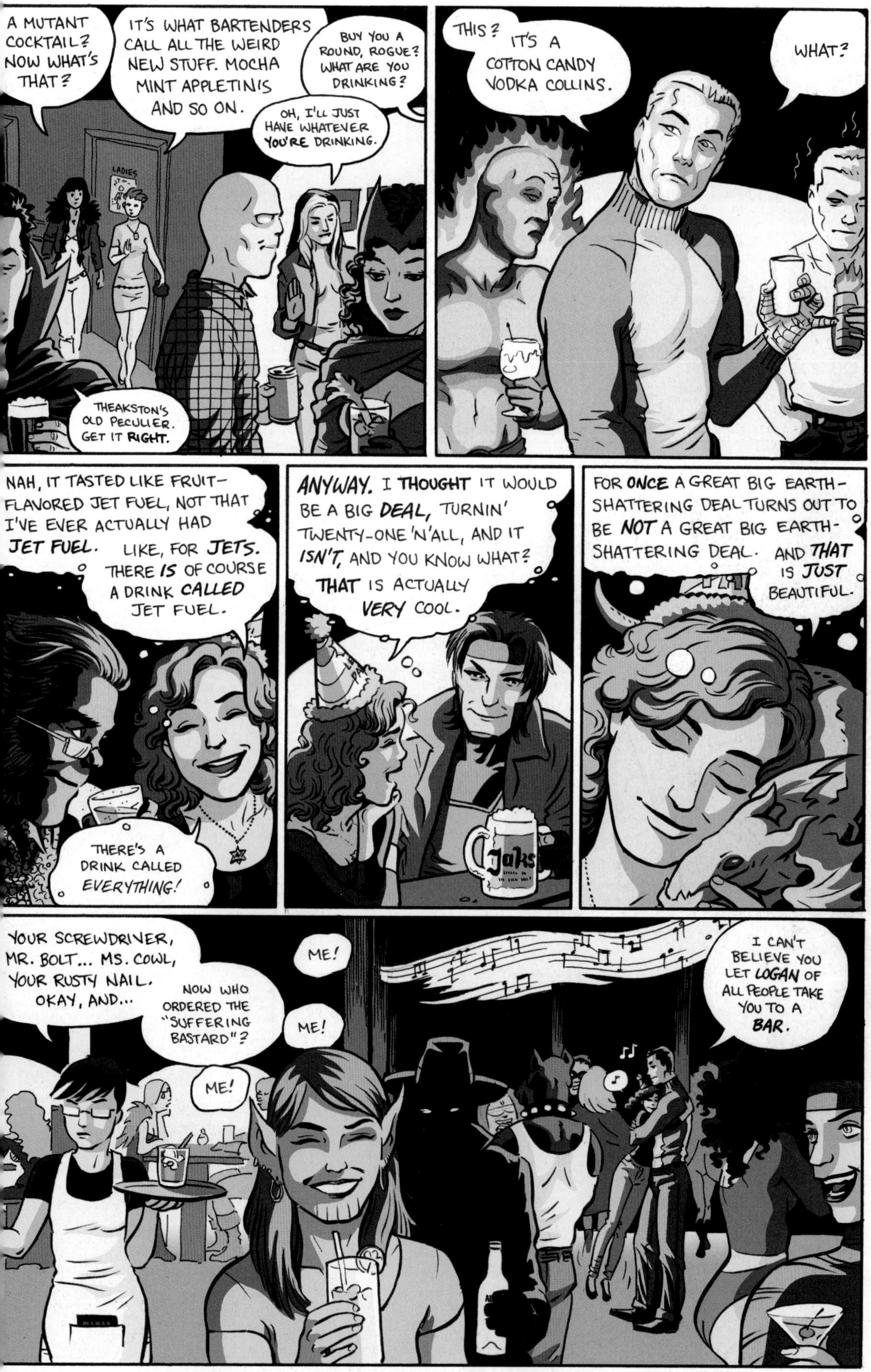
A MUTANT COCKTAIL? NOW WHAT'S THAT?
IT'S WHAT BARTENDERS CALL ALL THE WEIRD NEW STUFF. MOCHA MINT APPLETINIS AND SO ON.
BUY YOU A ROUND, ROGUE? WHAT ARE YOU DRINKING?
OH, I'LL JUST HAVE WHATEVER YOU'RE DRINKING.
LADIES
THEAKSTON'S OLD PECULIER. GET IT RIGHT.
THIS?
IT'S A COTTON CANDY VODKA COLLINS.
WHAT?
NAH, IT TASTED LIKE FRUIT-FLAVORED JET FUEL, NOT THAT I'VE EVER ACTUALLY HAD JET FUEL.
LIKE, FOR JETS. THERE IS OF COURSE A DRINK CALLED JET FUEL.
THERE'S A DRINK CALLED EVERYTHING!
ANYWAY. I THOUGHT IT WOULD BE A BIG DEAL, TURNIN' TWENTY-ONE 'N' ALL, AND IT ISN'T, AND YOU KNOW WHAT? THAT IS ACTUALLY VERY COOL.
Jaks
FOR ONCE A GREAT BIG EARTH-SHATTERING DEAL TURNS OUT TO BE NOT A GREAT BIG EARTH-SHATTERING DEAL. AND THAT IS JUST BEAUTIFUL.
YOUR SCREWDRIVER, MR. BOLT... MS. COWL, YOUR RUSTY NAIL. OKAY, AND...
NOW WHO ORDERED THE "SUFFERING BASTARD"?
ME!
ME!
ME!
I CAN'T BELIEVE YOU LET LOGAN OF ALL PEOPLE TAKE YOU TO A BAR.

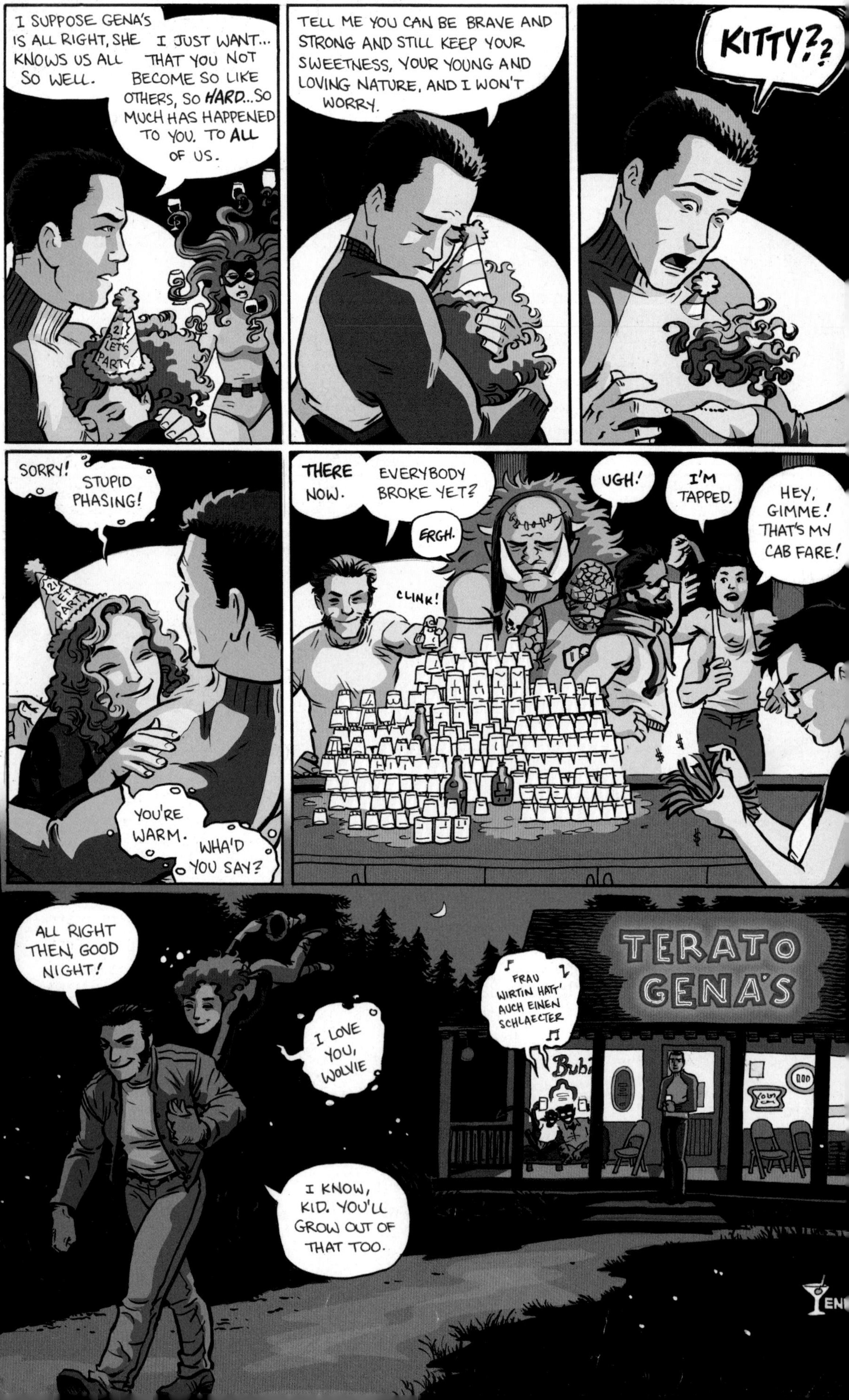
I SUPPOSE GENA'S IS ALL RIGHT, SHE KNOWS US ALL SO WELL.
I JUST WANT... THAT YOU NOT BECOME SO LIKE OTHERS, SO HARD...SO MUCH HAS HAPPENED TO YOU. TO ALL OF US.
21 LET'S PARTY
TELL ME YOU CAN BE BRAVE AND STRONG AND STILL KEEP YOUR SWEETNESS, YOUR YOUNG AND LOVING NATURE, AND I WON'T WORRY.
KITTY??
SORRY! STUPID PHASING!
YOU'RE WARM.
WHA'D YOU SAY?
THERE NOW.
EVERYBODY BROKE YET?
ERGH.
CLINK!
UGH!
I'M TAPPED.
HEY, GIMME! THAT'S MY CAB FARE!
ALL RIGHT THEN, GOOD NIGHT!
I LOVE YOU, WOLVIE
I KNOW, KID. YOU'LL GROW OUT OF THAT TOO.
TERATO GENA'S
FRAU WIRTIN HATT' AUCH EINEN SCHLAECTER

CREATOR BIOGRAPHIES

MARIAH BENES is a comics inker from Brazil. She has a prolific career, working on titles for Marvel (MS. MARVEL, X-MEN LEGACY, AMAZING SPIDER-MAN PRESENTS), DC (*Justice League of America*, *Teen Titans*, *52*, *Superman*) and Top Cow (*Witchblade*).

CHRISTINE BOYLAN has written comics and graphic novels for DC Comics (*Superman, Legion of Super-Heroes*), Tokyopop (*Star Trek: The Manga, Princess Ai*), Boom! Studios (*Zombie Tales, Cthulhu Tales*) and NBC/Universal (*Heroes*). A native New Yorker, Christine currently lives in Los Angeles where she writes for Electric Entertainment/TNT's critically acclaimed television series, *Leverage*.

ELIZABETH BREITWEISER has her roots in fine arts with a passion for color theory, and found her way to work for Marvel as a colorist in 2008. Since then she has lent her talents to titles such as CAPTAIN AMERICA: THEATER OF WAR, UNCANNY X-MEN, AGENTS OF ATLAS, THE INCREDIBLE HULK, and AMAZING SPIDER-MAN. Elizabeth leads a semi-reclusive lifestyle in Little Rock, AR with her comic artist husband, Mitch Breitweiser, and two crazy cats named Chumley and Ham.

JUNE BRIGMAN has twenty-five years experience as a comic artist. Probably best known as the co-creator and penciler of POWER PACK (with Louise Simonson) for Marvel, she's had a diverse career in comics, working at Marvel (X-MEN, SPIDER-MAN, BARBIE), DC Comics (*Supergirl*), and Dark Horse (*Star Wars: River of Chaos*). In addition to her comic work, she's provided art for National Geographic World Magazine (*Where in the World is Carmen Sandiego?*), as well as illustrating Star Wars novels and *Choose Your Own Adventure* books for Bantam Doubleday Dell. With her husband, Roy Richardson, she adapted and drew the Black Beauty graphic novel published by Puffin Books and illustrated *How to Draw Horses* for Capstone Press. Currently (and for the past 15 years), she is the artist for the nationally syndicated Brenda Starr comic strip. June is also a Professor of Sequential Art at the Atlanta campus of the Savannah College of Art and Design. When not sitting at the drawing board with a cat in her lap, she's sitting in the saddle riding her favorite horse, Lady Suede.

REBECCA BUCHMAN has been inking comics since 2007 for both Marvel and DC Comics (THUNDERBOLTS, AVENGERS: THE INITIATIVE, *Green Lantern Corps*) and lives in the Atlanta metropolitan area. She learned her craft by studying under Dexter Vines. When she's not inking, she can be found kayaking, skiing and motorcycling.

STEPHANIE BUSCEMA is a freelance illustrator and cartoonist based in Brooklyn, New York. She creates paintings with gouache, ink and cel-vinyl inspired by everything mid-century, vintage picture book illustration, early animation and horror/sci-fi films. Her paintings have appeared everywhere from gallery walls to picture book pages (such as the upcoming *Maybe I'll Sleep in the Bathtub Tonight: and Other Funny Bedtime Poems* from Sterling Books), and comic books such as WEB OF SPIDER-MAN, SPIDER-MAN FAMILY and AMAZING SPIDER-GIRL.

JO CHEN is an Eisner Award-nominated video game and comic book artist who has been working professionally since high school. Jo has produced comic book interiors and covers for most of the industry's biggest publishers — Capcom, Marvel, DC, Dark Horse, Top Cow and TokyoPop — and is best known for her covers for both Dark Horse's *Buffy the Vampire Slayer* Season 8 and Marvel's RUNAWAYS. She has also recently created the cover for Image's *Samarai's Blood* and Dark Horse's *Star Wars: Invasion*. Currently, she is working on package art for XBOX's *Fable III* game.

JUNE CHUNG graduated from the Rhode Island School of Design. She put her painting skills to good use, coloring such comics as MARVEL ZOMBIES, THOR, and numerous other titles. She lives in Las Vegas with her husband and a dog named Loki.

BARBARA CIARDO is an Italian colorist mainly active in the U.S. market. Her work can be seen in SHE-HULK and SECRET INVASION: FRONT LINE from Marvel Comics, and in the graphic novel *High School Musical: Lasting Impressions* from Disney. Most recently, she's best known for her work in DC's *Wednesday Comics* with artist Lee Bermejo.

AMANDA CONNER, an artist once best known for her long run on *Vampirella*, is now probably best known for reinvigorating *Power Girl* with her unmistakable blend of pop and super hero art. She's worked for almost every company in the business, from X-MEN: UNLIMITED to *Birds of Prey* to the creator-owned, Eisner-nominated *The Pro*. She also has the distinction of being the only woman to ever be featured in *Wizard Magazine's* Top Ten Artists.

NIKKI COOK is a cartoonist living in Brooklyn, New York. Her work has appeared in comics from such publishers as Vertigo, Image, and Boom! Studios, most notably *DMZ* and *Dog's Day End*. She has self-published for years, and was a founding member of Act-I-Vate, the webcomics collective. She is very tall and is descended from Norwegian prize fighters.

COLLEEN COOVER is a cartoonist living in Portland, Oregon. She is the creator of *Small Favors*, a romantic fantasy for adults, and artist of the all-ages *Banana Sunday*, written by her husband Paul Tobin. Their original graphic novel, *Gingerbread Girl*, is soon to be published by Top Shelf Press. She is a regular contributor to a variety of Marvel Comics, including X-MEN: FIRST CLASS, POWER PACK and PET AVENGERS.

MOLLY CRABAPPLE is an artist and the co-creator of the webcomic, *The Puppet Makers*, from DC Comics/Zuda. She is the founder of Dr. Sketchy's Anti-Art School, a globe-spanning chain of alt. drawing salons, and has spoken at the Museum of Modern Art and the Brooklyn Museum. She really likes absinthe, but she likes caffeine more. You can see her work at her self-titled website.

VALERIE D'ORAZIO is an author, blogger and the writer of Marvel's PUNISHER MAX: BUTTERFLY. She's currently at work on X-MEN ORIGINS: EMMA FROST, and has a story in the upcoming anthology, *Chicks In Capes,* from Moonstone Books, out late summer 2010. Valerie submitted her first Punisher pitch to Marvel when she was 13 years old.

KELLY SUE DECONNICK has written comics for Marvel (RESCUE, SIF, ENTER THE HEROIC AGE), IDW (30 *Days of Night: Eben and Stella* with Steve Niles),

and Image (the Eisner and Harvey Award-winning anthology, *Comic Book Tattoo* and *24Seven*), as well as the English adaptations of over 100 Japanese graphic novels for both Viz and Tokyopop (including the critically acclaimed *Sexy Voice and Robo, Black Cat, Fruits Basket, Blue Spring* and *Slam Dunk*). She lives in Portland and has at various times in her life been a professional actor, makeup artist, medical assistant, improv comedian, catwalk dresser and event clown. Yes, event clown.

ABBY DENSON is the Lulu Award-winning cartoonist and creator of the graphic novels *Tough Love: High School Confidential, Dolltopia,* and *The City Sweet Tooth,* a comic strip blog about NYC's desserts. She's scripted AMAZING SPIDER-MAN FAMILY, *Powerpuff Girls, Simpsons Comics* and too many other kids' comics to list here!

COLLEEN DORAN is an illustrator with hundreds of credits for clients including Marvel Comics (AMAZING SPIDER-MAN, X-FACTOR, CAPTAIN AMERICA), DC Comics (*Sandman, Wonder Woman, Teen Titans*), Lucasfilm, The Walt Disney Company, Reader's Digest, Scholastic, and many more. She is a frequent lecturer on graphic novels and was artist in residence at the Smithsonian Institute in Washington, DC where she lectured on Hokusai and ukiyo-e prints and their relation to pop culture and manga. Currently, she is working on two original graphic novels for Vertigo (*Stealth Tribes* and *Gone to Amerikay*), as well as one for publisher Houghton Mifflin with best-selling novelist Barry Lyga. Her graphic novel series with Image Comics, *A Distant Soil*, was listed among the 101 best graphic novels of all time, and has tens of thousands of readers as a webcomic.

MING DOYLE was born in Boston in the fall of 1984 to an Irish-American sailor and a Chinese-Canadian librarian. She has been working steadily in the comics industry since graduating from Cornell University in 2007 with a BFA in painting and drawing, sketching everything from supernatural schoolgirls and vengeful cowboys for Image to zombie super heroes and possessed cheerleaders for Boom! Studios.

KRISTYN FERRETTI provides design and branding services to worldwide corporate clients as an Art Director in NYC. In comics, she was the lead letterer for Tori Amos' Eisner and Harvey Award-winning *Comic Book Tattoo,* and has provided lettering and design for *Viking, 24Seven, The Cross Bronx, Grounded* and many others.

RAMONA FRADON studied art at Parsons School of Design and The Art Students' League in New York. Her first job was a war story for Timely in 1951; after various short features at DC Comics, she went on to pencil her first on-going gig, *Aquaman,* until 1960. In addition to creating the cast for and penciling *Metamorpho* at DC, she worked on numerous titles for both DC and Marvel, including FANTASTIC FOUR, THE CAT, *Metamorpho, House of Mystery, Plastic Man* and *Freedom Fighters,* to name a few. From 1980 through 1995, she was the regular illustrator on the Chicago Tribune Syndicated strip, *Brenda Starr.* In 2006, she received an Eisner Lifetime Achievement Award, and is currently illustrating an original graphic novel. She attends two or three conventions a year, and steadily accepts commissions.

ROBIN FURTH is the co-author of Marvel's award-winning DARK TOWER series, which grew out of her long-time work as Stephen King's research assistant. As well as continuing to do freelance work for the Master of Horror, she has adapted Sherrilyn Kenyon's *Lords of Avalon* into graphic novel form, is now working on the graphic novel adaptation of Stephen King and Peter Straub's novel, *The Talisman,* and has contributed to numerous comics anthologies, such as Marvel's LEGION OF MONSTERS. Her poetry has appeared in numerous magazines and journals both in the United States and Britain and she is presently finishing up a novel.

AGNES GARBOWSKA is a freelance illustrator who has a self-published book titled *You, Me, and Zombie.* She also has done work for the HERO Initiative contributing to the 100 HULK and WOLVERINE covers.

DEVIN GRAYSON is best known for her award-winning work on the Batman books, including *Batman: Gotham Knights,* a title she created, and *Nightwing.* She has also worked at Marvel on X-MEN:

EVOLUTION as well as penning BLACK WIDOW and GHOST RIDER miniseries for Marvel Knights. She recently she had an essay published in *She's Such a Geek: Women Write About Science, Technology, and Other Nerdy Stuff,* scripted an MMORPG, and written several articles about her experience with insulin-dependent diabetes and her Dogs4Diabetics-trained medical-alert dog, Cody.

STEPHANIE HANS is a digital painter, drawing influence from Art Noveau. She studied illustration at Ecole Superieure des Arts Decoratifs in Strasbourg, and, after graduating, published Galathea Volumes 1 and 2 for the French publisher Emmanuel Proust Editions. She went on to do cover work for many publishing houses, including young adult novels for Hachette. For Marvel, she's provided covers for PETER PARKER, DARK WOLVERINE, BLACK WIDOW, NAMORA and FIRESTAR. This October, you can find her back on interiors in *Heritages.* She loves her cover work and feels it's a great privilege to be the first communication with a reader.

LEA HERNANDEZ is a twenty-plus-years comics veteran who has published in traditional print and helped lead the charge to publish comics on the web. Her graphic novel series include *Texas Steampunk,* the tart pop satire, *Rumble Girls,* and the 90% true *Near-Life Experience.* Her comic, "Ribbons Undone" was part of the Eisner and Harvey Award-winning *Comic Book Tattoo* anthology. Lea is a single mom of two teenagers and lives in San Antonio, Texas. She's super-excited that after dozens of con sketches of Wolverine, she finally got paid to draw him. Bub.

FAITH ERIN HICKS has drawn thousands of comic pages over the past ten years, and has managed to get paid for some of them. She's written and drawn two graphic novels, *The War at Ellsmere* and *Zombies Calling,* both published by SLG Publishing and has drawn (but not written) a third graphic novel, *Brain Camp,* which will be out in fall 2010 from First Second Books. She's currently working on her fourth graphic novel, which she hopes will be out soon from First Second Books. She has lots of free comics and artwork on her self-titled website. She lives in Nova Scotia.

KATHRYN IMMONEN has written stories for both Marvel and DC Comics, but her favorite project so far is the PATSY WALKER: HELLCAT miniseries. She has made life difficult for the fan favorite RUNAWAYS, ruined high school for Pixie in the X-Men miniseries, PIXIE STRIKES BACK! with Sara Pichelli and continues her rampage with this June's HERALDS, with Tonci Zonjic. With Stuart Immonen, her creator-owned work includes *Moving Pictures*, from Top Shelf and *Never As Bad As You Think* from Boom! Studios. They are currently working on their next project, *Russian Olive to Red King*. She lives in Toronto with her very talented husband, her very tall son and their very bad dog.

LUCY KNISLEY is a writer and artist best known for the critically acclaimed graphic novel *French Milk* from Simon and Schuster. Her work can be seen in various comics anthologies, as well as in self-published collections like *Pretty Little Book* and *Radiator Days*, and the webcomic *Stop Paying Attention*.

MAIKO KUZUNISHI is a freelance graphic designer/illustrator and co-owner of Decoylab Design Studio, in Kansas City, Missouri. Her designs and logos can be seen on products from Marvel, Image, Coca-Cola, TNT, and AMC and she's done illustration work for Yen, an Australian fashion magazine, as well as Forum Snowboards. In addition to text design, she designs and sells clocks, some of which have been featured in magazines like *Cookie, Parents, Real Simple, Lucky* and *Nylon*.

MARJORIE M. LIU is an attorney and the *New York Times* bestselling author of the urban fantasy *Hunter Kiss* series, as well as the paranormal romance *Dirk & Steele* series. For Marvel, she writes DARK WOLVERINE (with Daniel Way), BLACK WIDOW, and the upcoming X-23. She lives in the American Midwest and Beijing, China.

KATHLEEN MARINACCIO is the Founder of Fishbrain, LLC and a professor at Otis College of Art and Design. Fishbrain is an award-winning design firm specializing in corporate identity, book design, packaging, promotions and event marketing. She lives in Los Angeles with her main squeeze, Dana Moreshead, and their two children, Franklyn and Hudson. Kathleen's comics career began in NYC in 1994, designing packaging and style guides for Marvel, before moving on to craft lettering and logos for Wildstorm, Image, Dark Horse, Top Cow, The HERO Initiative, Stan Lee, and a number of independent creators. She'd like to dedicate these pages, and every page she letters, to "the clowns who dragged me into the funny book business — Mike Thomas, Dana Moreshead and Paul Mounts."

CYNTHIA MARTIN was born in southern California and attended school there. At the age of 22 she was hired for her first professional assignment, penciling the monthly comic book, STAR WARS, for Marvel Comics. In the years since she's continued to work in animation and comics (SPIDER-MAN, *Wonder Woman, Blue Beetle* and the Boom! Studios anthology *Zombie Tales*), as well as children's publishing, working on a number of books in the last six years for scholastic publishers such as Eureka Press, Capstone Press, Stone Arch Books and ABDO Publications.

LAURA MARTIN is an Eisner, Harvey, and Wizard Fan Award-winning colorist known mostly for her work on ASTONISHING X-MEN, THE ULTIMATES, THOR, SECRET INVASION, STEPHEN KING'S THE STAND, *Planetary, The Authority, JLA, Serenity, Ruse*, and numerous other projects. She was given the chance to recolor Dave Stevens' *The Rocketeer* series in 2009. She is currently coloring SIEGE and ULTIMATE COMICS AVENGERS while continuing THE STAND.

CARLA SPEED McNEIL is writer and artist of the Eisner Award-winning, self-published and current webcomic *Finder*. She's been published by Oni (*Queen and Country*) and Vertigo (*Transmetropolitan*) and her work can be seen in the upcoming *Bad Houses* with Sara Ryan, also from Vertigo. Raised in Louisiana (and if the climate wasn't so horrific she'd go back there), she works too much, cooks too much and gets excited about teaching her kids weird science. She is a cavewoman with an iPad.

ADRIANA MELO is a penciler living in São Paulo, Brazil. She has been a comics penciler for almost ten years, working with Marvel Comics (IRON MAN, AMAZING SPIDER-MAN, FANTASTIC FOUR UNPLUGGED, SILVER SURFER, MS. MARVEL, EMMA

FROST), Dark Horse (*Star Wars Empire, RTX Red Rock*), Top Cow (*Witchblade*) and DC Comics (*Sinestro Corps: Parallax, Rose and Thorn*), among others. She's currently the on-going artist on DC's *Birds of Prey*.

SHO MURASE is an animation artist who was born in Japan but grew up in Spain. She has been working in animation and advertising in Europe with a client list that includes Nike, Virgin, Mattel, Evian, Sony and Electronics Arts. Her artwork has been exhibited in galleries and shows all around the world, most notably in Frankfurt's German Film Museum and the Louisiana Modern Art Museum in Denmark. In 2003, Image published her first graphic novel, *SEI*. She went on to create *ME2* and is the regular artist on the graphic novel adaptation, *Nancy Drew*, for Papercutz. Her work can also be seen in the upcoming *Star Wars Visions* from Abrams Books, and various fashion magazines.

ANN NOCENTI has a long history in comics, both as a writer and editor. When she was an editor at Marvel, she oversaw such titles as NEW MUTANTS and UNCANNY X-MEN. As a writer, she wrote for both Marvel (LONGSHOT, whom she co-created with Art Adams, SPECTACULAR SPIDER-MAN and WOLVERINE) and DC (*Batman, Kid Eternity*), but is probably best known for her groundbreaking run on DAREDEVIL, where she co-created Typoid Mary with John Romita Jr. Currently, she runs a school in Haiti where she teaches film, and is a screenwriter and filmmaker.

RONDA PATTISON is a Shuster and Eisner Award-nominated freelance colorist. While probably best known for her work on *Atomic Robo*, her efforts have also appeared in comics from such publishers as Marvel, DC, Dark Horse, Image, IDW, Red5 and more. She secretly plots to one day dominate the industry with a series of creator-owned titles and related tabletop role playing games.

CRISTIANE PETER has been a comics colorist for almost seven years, working with Marvel (SPITFIRE, DAZZLER), DC (*Superman/Batman, Blue Beetle*), Dark Horse, Image *(The Mice Templar)* and Boom! Studios (*Hexed, Hunter's Fortune*). She's currently hard at work on the remastered, colored edition of

the critically acclaimed CASANOVA, from Marvel's ICON imprint, and is the series' regular colorist.

SARA PICHELLI is an artist currently living in Rome, Italy. She worked in the local animation industry as a storyboard artist and character designer before taking a chance on the comic business. Her first gig was with an Italian publisher, and she went on to work as a layout assistant for David Messina on *Star Trek* for IDW. In April of 2008, she was one the winners of the Chesterquest international talent search and has since worked for Marvel Comics on such titles as NYX, RUNAWAYS and ETERNALS. Her most recent work can be found in X-MEN: PIXIE STIKES BACK and NAMORA. She draws digitally and on paper with pencils, pens and brushes. She's definitely restless and still doesn't know if that's a good thing.

EMMA RIOS is a writer and artist, best known for her magazine illustration work and self-published comics in Spain, before being introduced to the American market with *Hexed* from Boom! Studios. She then worked on RUNAWAYS, and just finished up the miniseries, STRANGE, as well as FIRESTAR, both for Marvel.

TRINA ROBBINS, award-winning herstorian and writer, has been writing graphic novels, comics and books for over thirty years. Her subjects have ranged from *Wonder Woman* to her own teenage superheroine, *GoGirl!*. She is considered the expert on the subject of early 20th century women cartoonists, and is responsible for rediscovering many brilliant but previously forgotten women, including Golden Age Fiction House cartoonist, Lily Renee, and the great Nell Brinkley. Her full-color book, *The Brinkley Girls: the Best of Nell Brinkley's Cartoons from 1913-1940*, was published by Fantagraphics in April 2009. She collects vintage clothing (medium) and shoes (size 6).

RACHELLE ROSENBERG has always had a unique love of making art come alive, from the pages of her childhood coloring book to the pages of mainstream comics. Though new to the industry, she's taken her BFA in illustration and a formal oil painting background to quickly become an in-demand force in the world of coloring. Her colors span the pages of NAMORA from Marvel, *Jersey Gods*, Tyrese Gibson's *Mayhem!*, *Hack/Slash*, *Barack the Barbarian* and Boom!Studios' *Cars* and *The Incredibles*.

LOUISE SIMONSON is an award-winning writer who has worked in comics publishing for thirty-five years, first as an editor for Warren and Marvel, then as a writer. For Marvel, she co-created and wrote POWER PACK (with June Brigman) and wrote X-FACTOR, THE NEW MUTANTS, and WEB OF SPIDER-MAN and co-created the characters Apocalypse and Cable. For DC, she wrote *Superman: Man of Steel* and created and wrote *Steel* as part of the "Death of Superman" storyline. With her husband, Walter Simonson, she co-wrote *World of Warcraft* for Wildstorm. She has also written twenty books for kids and adults. She is currently writing X-FACTOR FOREVER and working on a YA novel.

STAR ST. GERMAIN is a tornado disguised as a girl. Her lettering work has appeared in books like Marvels STRANGE TALES, and Tori Amos' Eisner and Harvey Award-winning *Comic Book Tattoo*, as well as in magazines like *Weird Tales* and *Other*. She co-hosts Destroy All Podcasts, a commentary on animated and cult cinema. In her spare time, she makes pretty noises with a cello and a large collection of toy instruments. She likes you a lot.

SANA TAKEDA is an artist from Japan who does everything from pencils to color. In the American market, she's best known for her work on MS. MARVEL and X-MEN: FAIRY TALES, as well as the creator-owned *Drain* from Image. Before becoming a comic artist, she did design work for video games.

JILL THOMPSON is a multiple Eisner Award-winning comic book creator. She has been drawing comics for well over half her life and is proud to have collaborated with many of this industry's great talents. She has garnered acclaim for her work on titles such as *Classics Illustrated*, *Wonder Woman*, *Sandman*, *Death: At Death's Door*, *The Little Endless Storybook* and *Beasts of Burden*, but she is probably best known for creating and illustrating *The Scary Godmother* series which not only have been adapted for the stage, but for television as well. In 2008,

Harper Collins released *Magic Trixie*, Jill's latest all-ages series. Jill loves being an ambassador of comics to libraries and schools across the country and often lectures and conducts workshops. One day she will have a large art studio where she can conduct workshops…well, she will if that Lotto ticket comes through. When she's not writing and illustrating comics, Jill enjoys painting landscapes and city scenes. She also enjoys creating all manner of things, cooking, sewing, knitting, gardening, studying languages, building things and riding her bike. She wishes she had learned how to ride a motorcycle when she had one…

EMMA VIECELI is a freelance artist and writer based in Cambridge in the UK. She's the artist for two of the acclaimed *Manga Shakespeare* graphic novels, and was featured in the Eisner Award-winning *Comic Book Tattoo* amongst other publications. She is currently working on two graphic novel series, one for Oni Press and one for Penguin Books, while continuing to work on her own independent series, *Dragon Heir*, printed through Sweatdrop Studios in the UK. It's a good thing she likes comics so much, as she doesn't seem to leave much time for anything else!

EMILY WARREN is an illustrator and colorist who lives in Los Angeles, California. In 2007 she graduated from the Illinois Institute of Art in Chicago with a Bachelor of Fine Arts in Media Arts & Animation. As a colorist, she has worked on BIG HERO 6, DARK REIGN: YOUNG AVENGERS, INCREDIBLE HERCULES, SECRET INVASION, X-BABIES and CLOAK AND DAGGER. She has also done cover art for BIG HERO 6, SHE HULK SENSATIONAL, *Grimm Fairy Tales* and *1001 Arabian Nights: The Adventures of Sinbad*.

G. WILLOW WILSON is the Eisner-nominated author of the ongoing series *Air* and the graphic novel *Cairo* (both with artist MK Perker). Her first nonfiction book (which contains no pictures whatsoever), *The Butterfly Mosque*, is due out in June 2010 from Grove/Atlantic.